Religion and the Origins of the
German Enlightenment

Rochester Studies in Philosophy
Senior Editor: Wade L. Robison
Rochester Institute of Technology
ISSN: 1529-188X

The Scottish Enlightenment: Essays in Reinterpretation
Edited by Paul Wood

Kant's Legacy: Essays in Honor of Lewis White Beck
Edited by Predrag Cicovacki

Plato's Erotic Thought: The Tree of the Unknown
Alfred Geier

Leibniz on Purely Extrinsic Denominations
Dennis Plaisted

Rationality and Happiness: From the Ancients to the Early Medievals
Edited by Jiyuan Yu and Jorge J. E. Gracia

History of Reasonableness: A Testimony and Authority in the Art of Thinking
Rick Kennedy

State of Nature or Eden?
Thomas Hobbes and His Contemporaries on the Natural
Condition of Human Beings
Helen Thornton

Fire in the Dark:
Essays on Pascal's Pensées and Provinciales
Charles Natoli

Destined for Evil?
The Twentieth-Century Responses
Edited by Predrag Cicovacki

David Hume and Eighteenth-Century America:
The Reception of Hume's Political Thought in America, 1740–1830
Mark G. Spencer

Nietzsche's Anthropic Circle:
Man, Science, and Myth
George J. Stack

Religion and the Origins of the German Enlightenment:
Faith and the Reform of Learning in the Thought of Christian Thomasius
Thomas Ahnert

Religion and the Origins of the German Enlightenment
Faith and the Reform of Learning in the Thought of Christian Thomasius

Thomas Ahnert

UNIVERSITY OF ROCHESTER PRESS

First published 2006

University of Rochester Press
668 Mt. Hope Avenue, Rochester, NY 14620, USA
www.urpress.com
and Boydell & Brewer Limited
PO Box 9, Woodbridge, Suffolk IP12 3DF, UK
www.boydellandbrewer.com

ISBN: 1-58046-204-9

Library of Congress Cataloging-in-Publication Data

Ahnert, Thomas.
  Religion and the origins of the German Enlightenment : faith and the
reform of learning in the thought of Christian Thomasius / Thomas
Ahnert.
    p. cm. – (Rochester studies in philosophy, ISSN 1529-188X ; 12)
  Includes bibliographical references and index.
  ISBN 1-58046-204-9 (hardcover : alk. paper)
  1. Thomasius, Christian, 1655-1728. I. Title. II. Series.
B2605.Z7A36 2006
261.5′1092–dc22
[B]

                          2005027917

A catalogue record for this title is available from the British Library.

This publication is printed on acid-free paper.
Printed in the United States of America.

CONTENTS

Acknowledgments   vi

Introduction: Christian Thomasius and the Early
German Enlightenment   1

PART I: FAITH

1   Religion, Law, and Politics: Historical Contexts   9

2   Religion and the Limits of Philosophy   27

3   The Prince and the Church: The Critique of
"Lutheran Papalism"   43

PART II: HISTORY

4   Ecclesiastical History and the Rise of Clerical Tyranny   59

5   The History of Roman Law   69

PART III: NATURE

6   Natural Law (I): The *Institutes of Divine Jurisprudence*   83

7   Natural Law (II): The Transformation of Christian
Thomasius's Natural Jurisprudence   94

8   The Interpretation of Nature   107

Conclusion: Reason and Faith in the Early German
Enlightenment   121

Notes   127

Bibliography   169

Index   185

ACKNOWLEDGMENTS

This book is the revised and shortened version of a doctoral dissertation that was accepted by the Faculty of History at Cambridge University in 1999. I should like to thank the British Academy for a three-year doctoral research scholarship. The Studienstiftung des Deutschen Volkes also provided generous financial support, for which I am grateful. I should also like to thank the Dr. Günther Findel-Stiftung for a research scholarship to work at the Herzog-August-Bibliothek in Wolfenbüttel, and the Max-Planck-Institut für Europäische Rechtsgeschichte in Frankfurt am Main for a scholarship that allowed me to spend four very productive months at the institute. I am especially grateful to my doctoral supervisor, Tim Hochstrasser, for his careful guidance and encouragement, and to my examiners, Istvan Hont and Richard Tuck, for their very helpful comments and suggestions. Tim Blanning, Mark Goldie, and Alain Wijffels provided welcome advice in the early stages of the dissertation project. I have also benefited greatly from discussions with Hans-Erich Bödeker, Horst Dreitzel, Frank Grunert, Knud Haakonssen, Ian Hunter, Susan Manning, Nicholas Phillipson, Sandra Pott, John Robertson, Peter Schröder, and Tony La Vopa, and I am particularly grateful to Ian Hunter and Sandra Pott for their generous and helpful advice on the revision of the manuscript. I should also like to thank Friedrich Vollhardt and an anonymous reader for comments on an earlier version of the manuscript. The final revisions were completed while I was a postdoctoral fellow at the Institute for Advanced Studies in the Humanities at the University of Edinburgh, and I am very grateful to Anthea Taylor and Donald Ferguson for their excellent administrative support. My greatest debt is to my parents and my wife. Any errors or inaccuracies are my own.

T. A.
Edinburgh
January 2006

INTRODUCTION

CHRISTIAN THOMASIUS AND THE EARLY GERMAN ENLIGHTENMENT

This book examines the intellectual importance of religion for the origins of the German Enlightenment around 1700. In particular, I shall focus on a central figure of early eighteenth-century intellectual history: the jurist and philosopher Christian Thomasius (1655–1728). Now known mainly for his criticism of witchcraft trials and judicial torture, Thomasius's reputation in German intellectual history is comparable to that of John Locke in England. He is considered to be one of the first and most influential representatives of the early Enlightenment in the German territories.[1] His status as such was well established by the late eighteenth century. In the course of the famous debate on the nature of "Enlightenment," to which Immanuel Kant contributed his well-known essay, the writer Friedrich Gedike described Thomasius as the founder of the Enlightenment in Germany, the philosopher to whom "we owe a large part of our intellectual and material happiness."[2] A few years later, Friedrich Schiller praised him for his fearless opposition to scholastic "pedantry."[3] In recent scholarship, Thomasius continues to be credited with weakening the authority of obsolete, "scholastic" learning and with contributing to the intellectual revival of German universities after a period of decline in the second half of the seventeenth century, following the destruction caused by the Thirty Years' War.[4]

As a religious thinker, he is usually presented as a classical theorist of the Enlightenment, who separated the question of religious truth from the pursuit of secular philosophy. He is not considered an atheist, but it is widely claimed that Thomasius's secular philosophical positions were in some sense "independent" from his religious beliefs. Werner Schneiders, for example, wrote that although Thomasius's philosophy was for a short time in the 1690s strongly influenced by religious mysticism, this was no more than a passing phase. It reflected a religious and psychological crisis, from which Thomasius recovered around 1700, making it possible for him to return to a rationalist and secular philosophy.[5] In a recent important work,

Ian Hunter has argued that Thomasius's aim was to "detranscendentalize" political philosophy, that is, to separate it from the pursuit of true faith by relegating religious belief to a private, spiritual relationship with God, which did not interfere with philosophy's monopoly in worldly affairs.[6] And Frank Grunert has recently argued that Thomasius's appeals to scripture in his philosophical works were rhetorical and prudential, rather than signs of a meaningful connection between his religion and his philosophy.[7]

Research has therefore concentrated on Thomasius's secular moral and political ideas, rather than his religious thought.[8] The emphasis of this book, however, will be on Thomasius's religious beliefs, because these are also important in understanding his significance for the intellectual history of the early German Enlightenment, more important, perhaps, than has been thought before. There are two main reasons for directing particular attention to Thomasius's religion. One is that his contemporaries often considered his writings to be controversial, not so much because they were a-religious, but because they were heterodox. Thomasius often appeared dangerously close to a form of religious "enthusiasm," which was associated with politically and theologically subversive millenarian sects. This in itself makes Thomasius's religious views worth attention.

But Thomasius's supposedly "secular" thought also has deeper roots in these controversial religious beliefs and his seemingly idiosyncratic arguments about the nature of Christian faith than has previously been suggested. As we shall see, faith and philosophy in Thomasius's thought are more closely intertwined than his well-established reputation as a champion of a secular Enlightenment suggests. This raises important questions about the nature of the early Enlightenment in the German territories.

In recent years, the notion of the Enlightenment as the story of the "rise of modern paganism" and the transition to a modern secular society has been questioned. A number of scholars have shown the extent to which religious concerns formed an integral part of enlightened thought.[9] David Sorkin, for example, has argued that there was a "middle way" between a secular Enlightenment and a traditional theology that was hostile to enlightened thought. This was the "theological" or "religious Enlightenment," which aimed to use "modern" rational thought to reform theology and to bring it closer to the essence of religious faith. Its representatives attempted to reconcile reason and revelation and "to promote a version of the *Aufklärung* that also promoted the cause of the church—a middle way that enabled them to use Enlightenment ideas to fortify the institution they held dear."[10] Thomasius's thought, however, was not an example of a "religious Enlightenment" of this kind. His religious views were often closer to the anti-intellectualist enthusiasm that has been described as the "anti-self" of the Enlightenment than to the moderate, rational theology associated with the "religious Enlightenment."[11] His notions of religious faith were similar to the beliefs of the extreme sects on the fringes of German Protestantism, which emphasized the importance of sincerity and the believer's heart over the authority of institutions, formulaic professions of faith, and subtle doctrinal argument. And yet, these "enthusiastic" views, which Thomasius adopted and never quite abandoned, are closely related to his secular thought on history, moral philosophy, and the interpretation of natural phenomena.

The first section of this book, "Faith," examines the complex development of Thomasius's religious beliefs, from the late 1680s to the first decade of the eighteenth century, a period in which Thomasius was involved in a series of controversies with two groupings within the Lutheran church: orthodox, traditionalist Lutherans and the so-called "Pietists," a loosely defined, quasi-Puritan group of religious reformers, which had emerged in the late 1680s in Leipzig. The issues over which Thomasius and his opponents disagreed concerned central matters of Christian religion, in particular the proper foundation of religious faith. Thomasius defended a religion "of the heart," which did not require any deep knowledge of theological doctrine, while his opponents believed that feeling without understanding was not sufficient to guide believers toward salvation. The disagreement over the nature of faith also reflected different notions of human nature and the powers of its constituent parts. In particular, Thomasius appeared to be downplaying the importance of the intellect as the guide of human actions, and to be emphasizing the role of the passions instead, an argument his orthodox opponents considered part of his dangerous "enthusiastic" religiosity.

This bitter debate over the nature of faith played a central role in discussions of the proper relationship between the prince and his church. This was a particularly difficult question in the territories of the Calvinist elector of Brandenburg, who faced a very hostile Lutheran population and estates, but insisted on performing the same role in his territory's Lutheran church as a Lutheran prince would have done, against the Lutherans' will. The Lutherans' definition of true faith and heresy was essential to justifying their opposition, but Thomasius argued that this definition had become an instrument with which the Lutheran clergy in Brandenburg exercised political power under the pretext of Christian religion. They distorted faith in such a way that it supported their "priestcraft," to use a contemporary English expression, or "papalism," to apply Thomasius's equivalent term.[12] "Papalism" in Thomasius's terminology was not restricted to Roman Catholicism, but described the use of religious pretexts by any clerical caste for secular and self-interested ends. True religion did not lend itself to these corrupt purposes, and Thomasius argued that a reform of faith would also remove the unlawful influence of priests on secular political and legal affairs.

This "papalism" had taken root gradually from the very earliest centuries of Christianity onward, and the history of the church provided evidence of this corruption. Although the decline of Christianity and the growth of the "papist" church had been a common subject of Protestant historiography since the Reformation, Thomasius questioned the standard chronology, in which the era of the early Christian emperors appeared as a sort of golden age of Christianity and of church-state relations, which had only gradually declined, until it reached its nadir in the investiture contest of the Middle Ages. Instead, Thomasius followed a line of mystically inclined, spiritualist historiographers, who dated the corruption of the church to a much earlier period than orthodox writers, an argument that had important implications for the definition of true faith itself, as it overturned the theological authority of early Christian authors and councils, on which orthodox Lutherans often relied. The Roman law of Justinian's *Corpus Iuris Civilis*, which continued to be used extensively in the Holy Roman Empire of the early Enlightenment, furnished additional evidence of the depraved state of the church under the early Christian emperors, since many of its laws allowed the clergy to influence legal matters, matters which properly belonged to the jurisdiction of the prince and of secular jurists.

Thomasius's theory of natural law also shared central concerns with his conception of religious belief, in particular with its underlying anthropology. Thomasius's notion of a "religion of the heart" rather than the "head" minimized the importance of the intellect in human nature, in a way that implied that morality also did not depend on the education of the intellect, but on the pre-intellectual guidance of the "heart." As we shall see, the result was a remarkable transformation of Thomasius's natural jurisprudence between 1688, the date of the publication of his first treatise on natural law, and 1705, when his second work on this subject appeared.[13] He began to regard the passions as the essential springs of moral action, rather than a disruptive force that clouded moral judgment, as he had argued in his earlier work, in 1688. He also redefined the relationship between the moral and the natural world, moving from a strict Pufendorfian separation of moral and physical entities to a belief that moral phenomena were, in some sense, part of the natural world, and moral philosophy, in essence, was no more than the study of certain natural properties of "man." For this, Thomasius drew on a hermeticist natural philosophy, which has often been considered a marginal curiosity in his thought but in fact was closely related to his moral and religious ideas.

The analysis of this wide range of Thomasius's interests is important, and not only because it has never been done before. It also makes it possible to identify a consistent *Leitmotiv* in his thought, one that is about the reform of religion as much as about secular philosophy. Previously, the nature and intellectual coherence of Thomasius's "enlightened" reform program has proved difficult to identify. In a recent work, for example, Martin Gierl concluded that Thomasius's thought was "enlightened" not so much because of the particular ideas he put forward, but because of his contribution to the creation of a public sphere of free, noncoercive debate.[14] Thomasius opposed the dogmatic style of scholarly controversy that was typical of his orthodox opponents, and put forward a new model of conducting scholarly debates. The aim of this was not the pursuit of absolute truth but the harmonious management of disagreements. It reflected a commitment to a dialogical communicative ideal rather than the judgment and condemnation of opponents; it was also, Gierl argues, the main reason for the affinity between Thomasius and the Pietists. Like Thomasius, the Pietists were highly critical of the disputational practices in Protestant theological faculties and wanted to replace them with a new style of learned discourse and debate. It was this shared communicative model, not the intellectual content of their respective arguments, that produced the alliance between Thomasius and the Pietists. The tensions between Thomasius and the Pietists from the later 1690s onward reflected the fact that Pietists were abandoning this communicative model and were turning to forms of controversy that were increasingly similar to traditional orthodox Lutheran polemic theology (*Kontroverstheologie*).

Gierl's argument emphasizes the formal and procedural aspects of theological and learned controversy, but the content of Thomasius's ideas seems more important in explaining both his relationship to his opponents and his place in the early Enlightenment than Gierl's interpretation suggests. Thomasius's views on the nature of religious belief, in particular, were central to orthodox Lutheran and Pietist criticisms of his thought, and are therefore crucial to explaining Thomasius's disagreements with these two ecclesiastical factions. These views are also important to explaining his "enlightened" program of intellectual reform. Faith and philosophy were distinct in Thomasius's thought, but at the same time dependent on each other. The reform of one required the reform of the other. They both formed part of his criticism of orthodox Lutheran "scholasticism," a phenomenon that, according to Thomasius's definition, encompassed bookish pedantry as well as religious hypocrisy, and to which he opposed "wisdom" (*sapientia*), standing for religious as well as philosophical truth. Thomasius's program of "enlightened" intellectual reform cannot be understood without his "enthusiastic" religious beliefs. This book examines the often complex relationship between the two.

PART I

FAITH

CHAPTER ONE

RELIGION, LAW, AND POLITICS: HISTORICAL CONTEXTS

CHRISTIAN THOMASIUS (1655–1728)

Christian Thomasius was born on New Year's Day in 1655,[1] the son of the Leipzig professor of rhetoric and moral philosophy, Jacob Thomasius (1622–84), and his wife Maria, daughter of the archdeacon of the Leipzig Nicolai Church and professor of theology, Jeremias Weber. Jacob Thomasius was also headmaster of the *Nicolaischule* between 1653 and 1676, and later, until his death in 1684, of the *Thomasschule*. In 1663, he was the *praeses* of the young Gottfried Wilhelm Leibniz's bachelor's thesis.[2] Although Jacob Thomasius's fame was later eclipsed by that of his more prolific son, he enjoyed a high scholarly reputation until well into the first decades of the eighteenth century, especially as an authority on the history of philosophy. Even in 1745 he is referred to as a "famous philosopher and polyhistorian" in Zedler's *Universal-Lexikon*.[3]

Jacob Thomasius's son Christian entered the philosophical faculty of the University of Leipzig at the age of fourteen in 1669 and received his first academic degree, the bachelor of arts, as early as November 1669. In January 1672, he acquired the master of philosophy degree, but he remained at the philosophical faculty for another two years before entering the faculty of law. Thomasius later claimed that his decision in favor of law rather than theology had been influenced by reading Samuel Pufendorf's main work on natural jurisprudence, *De Jure Naturae et Gentium*, first published in 1672. In 1675, Thomasius held his first disputation, *De iniusto Pontii Pilatii iudicio* (*On the Unjust Judgment of Pontius Pilate*), at the legal faculty of the University of Leipzig.[4] After a year and a half he moved from Lutheran Leipzig to the Calvinist University of Frankfurt an der Oder, where he was taught by Samuel Stryk (1640–1710), later his colleague at the University of Halle, and Friedrich Rhetius (1633–1707). It appears that his father encouraged him to move to Frankfurt, where Thomasius could deepen his knowledge of the natural law theories of Grotius and Pufendorf. There he also seems to have become acquainted with a number of Calvinists and Roman Catholics. This experience, he later wrote, brought him to realize that everywhere, "among all nations, societies and religions," both good-hearted and malicious people were to be found, but that the latter were always in the majority, among Lutherans no less than among Calvinists and Roman Catholics.[5] It is probable that his later interest in a nonsectarian conception of Christian faith owes something to his sojourn in Frankfurt. Following his disputation *pro licentia*, which qualified him to teach, he lectured in Frankfurt an der Oder, mainly on natural jurisprudence, until he advanced to the doctorate in law in 1679.

It is often assumed that Thomasius visited the Low Countries and attended university there, after completing his legal studies in Frankfurt, but there appears to be no evidence for such a sojourn, and it probably never took place.[6] Thomasius returned to Leipzig, where he married Anna Christina Heyland[7] and began to practice as a lawyer, but he soon took up teaching as a private lecturer, out of dissatisfaction, as he later wrote, with the life of an advocate.[8] His choice of subjects and style seems to have startled the university's professors, though it is likely that Thomasius, in retrospect, exaggerated the effect of his lectures in order to dramatize his dispute with the university, which formed the background to his departure to Brandenburg in 1690.

As early as 1685, his disputation *De Crimine Bigamiae* (*On the Crime of Bigamy*)[9] appears to have put him in opposition to Valentin Alberti, a professor of theology at the university and eminent opponent of Samuel Pufendorf.[10] In his disputation, Thomasius adopted a position on natural law close to Pufendorf's, with whom Thomasius by now was corresponding regularly.[11] In a letter to Thomasius, written soon after *On the Crime of Bigamy* had been published, Pufendorf warned him that he would now have to expect Alberti's hostility. On 31 October 1687, Thomasius made a public announcement, in writing, of a lecture to be held in German, an unusual event at a time when Latin was the language of university lectures, but probably not the "horrible and . . . unprecedented crime" as which, Thomasius later claimed, the university regarded it.[12] In the same year, Thomasius published a piece on natural law, which later became book 1 of his first complete natural jurisprudential treatise, the *Institutiones Jurisprudentiae Divinae* (*Institutes of Divine Jurisprudence*).[13] In this work, Thomasius put forward an extensive critique of Alberti's *Compendium Juris Naturae Orthodoxae Theologiae Conformatum* (*Compendium of Natural Law, Conforming to Orthodox Theology*), in which Alberti had tried to repudiate the *De Jure Naturae et Gentium* of Pufendorf.[14]

Thomasius's sarcastic attitude toward the established university teachers, many of whom, like Johann Benedict Carpzov (1639–99), had been friends of Thomasius's father,[15] eventually caused grave offence. From January 1688 onward, Thomasius published a monthly journal, the *Monatsgespräche* (*Monthly Conversations*), a mixture of book reviews and articles. This often commented satirically on members of the university who, although they were not referred to in the journal under their own names, were easily recognized as the victims of Thomasius's barbs. In 1688, Thomasius dedicated the January edition of the *Monatsgespräche* to Barbon and Tartuffe, Moliere's pedantic pedagogue and hypocrite, a thinly disguised reference to his adversaries at the university.[16] Even Pufendorf urged Thomasius to restrain his mordant style.[17] Finally, Thomasius's opponents lodged a complaint at the electoral court in Dresden, while the philosophical faculty of the University of Leipzig appealed to the Upper Consistory (*Oberkonsistorium*), the body of theologians and lawyers entrusted with guarding doctrinal orthodoxy in the Lutheran church. In January 1689, Thomasius was admonished by the Upper Consistory, with the approval of the Saxon Elector John George III, and threatened with a ban on lecturing if he continued his attacks.[18]

Thomasius ignored the injunction and continued to write against what he termed the pedantic, scholastic orthodoxy represented by the university and its theological faculty in particular. He dedicated the January 1689 edition of the *Monatsgespräche* to the elector, either to flatter him or to embarrass the censors, and issued complaints about Alberti and the philosophical faculty. These were settled by arbitration in March 1689, but soon after this, Thomasius accused one of the professors of theology of slander. The theological faculty reacted with a counteraccusation before the *Oberkonsistorium*, which decided in favor of the faculty.

At the same time, Thomasius was also embroiled in a controversy with the Danish court preacher Hector Gottfried Masius, who, in a treatise, *Interesse principum circa religionem evangelicam* (*The Interest of Princes Concerning Protestant Religion*), of 1687,[19] had sought to prove that Lutheranism was alone among the three main Christian confessions in recognizing the subjects' duties of obedience toward their prince.[20] The work was directed against Calvinist "Monarchomachs"[21] and must probably be seen against the background of the Revocation of the Edict of Nantes in France in 1685, of which Masius's argument, it appears, is, to some extent, a justification. Masius argued that Calvinists were politically unreliable and potentially seditious. It may be no accident that Masius had been the chaplain of the Danish ambassador in Paris, before becoming court preacher in Copenhagen.[22] The Calvinist theologian Johann Christoph Becmann responded by arguing that Calvinists as subjects were as loyal as Lutherans, and there were examples of rebellious Lutherans, too.[23] Thomasius took a different course and denied Masius's claim that *maiestas* was derived immediately from God, while rejecting the Monarchomach theory that *maiestas* was produced immediately by the people. The Danish court complained to the court in Dresden about Thomasius's attacks on Masius, with the result that Thomasius was ordered to submit his works to a censor before publication and was forbidden to write against Masius.

Thomasius's continual provocation of the university in Leipzig and the electoral court of Saxony was balanced by astute efforts to cultivate the favor of the Calvinist elector of Brandenburg. For some time before his departure from Leipzig in March 1690, Thomasius seems to have contemplated moving to a university in the territories of the elector of Brandenburg. As early as December 1688, Pufendorf wrote to him, suggesting that Rhetius in Frankfurt an der Oder would be happy for Thomasius to return there when a position became vacant.[24] The Calvinist University of Duisburg, which was also situated in one of the widely scattered territories of the elector of Brandenburg, was another possibility. Thomasius, however, seems to have been particularly interested in Halle. At the time, Halle could boast only of an academy for noblemen, founded in 1680. No university existed there, but it was known that the elector was considering founding one.[25]

As Leibniz noted in a letter, it was suspected that Thomasius had attacked Masius's anti-Calvinist tract "pour flatter le cour de Berlin."[26] In 1689, Thomasius also published a defense of the marriage between the Lutheran Prince Maurice William of Sachsen-Zeitz and a Calvinist, the widow of Duke Charles William of Mecklenburg-Güstrow and sister of the elector of Brandenburg, Frederick III.[27] The marriage was opposed by the court in Dresden but supported by Berlin, so that Thomasius's intervention could be expected to work in his favor in Brandenburg.[28]

In Saxony, the conflict between Thomasius and the orthodox Lutherans was finally brought to a head by his support for the Pietist religious revival movement, which had its roots in the so-called *Collegia Philobiblica* in Leipzig. The *collegia* owed their existence to two students at the University of Leipzig, August Hermann Francke (1663–1727) and Paul Anton (1661–1730). Francke in particular was to become one of the most influential figures in German religious culture of the eighteenth century. He was born in Lübeck in 1663, studied at Erfurt, and came to Leipzig in 1684, where he acquired his master's degree in January 1685 and received his *Habilitation* in July of the same year with a philological dissertation on a subject in Hebrew grammar.[29]

In his autobiography, which characteristically ends with an account of his spiritual rebirth in 1687, Francke wrote that he and Anton had noted the neglect of the two *fundamental Sprachen* of theology, Greek and Hebrew, at the theological faculty in Leipzig. Their *collegia*, exegetical meetings, which were held on Sundays between four and six, and at which passages from scripture were analyzed philologically, were intended to remedy this deficiency. At the university, lectures on dogma and homiletics seem to have preponderated, in part, as Heinrich Leube has observed, because the poverty of many theology students forced them to concentrate on these central subjects in order to complete their degree as quickly as possible.[30] The introduction of these exegetical meetings was at first welcomed by the faculty, and Valentin Alberti, the professor of theology, even undertook to direct the meetings and hold them in his own home.[31]

Problems arose when Francke decided to turn the philological classes of the *collegia* into theological meetings with a practical religious interest: "It is not enough," he declared, "to be a scriptural critic, but one must become more pious by reading and examining scripture."[32] He appears to have come to this conclusion during a period of absence from Leipzig between 1687 and 1689, during which period he spent some time at the home of the Lüneburg superintendent, Sandhagen.[33] It was in Lüneburg that Francke experienced what he later described as his spiritual rebirth. For several years before coming to Lüneburg, Francke had been tortured by doubts about his faith, but one evening in prayer "at the turn of a hand all my doubts vanished, I was assured in my heart of God's grace in Jesus Christ."[34] From Lüneburg, Francke went to Dresden, where he met Philipp Jakob Spener, whose advice reinforced Francke's new frame of mind. Spener, at whose house Francke spent the months of January and February 1689, appears to have encouraged Francke to turn the Leipzig *collegia* into meetings for the practical inculcation of piety. When Francke returned to Leipzig, he began to put this advice into action.

The Leipzig theological faculty, however, objected because Francke's meetings were no longer purely philological exercises. They now concerned theological questions they believed Francke was not competent to discuss because he had no theological degree.[35] That the theological faculty's main concern was Francke's lack of formal qualifications is clear from the case of Francke's colleague Paul Anton. When Anton, at Spener's urging, acquired a degree at the faculty of theology, the university withdrew its case against him. Francke, however, persistently refused to study for a degree in theology, presumably because he rejected the notion that only the clergy was authorized to interpret scripture.

At the same time, Francke opposed the theological faculty on the question of the training of theology students, criticizing the excessive emphasis on philosophy in theological debate, a point made already by Spener and central to Thomasius's critique of university learning.[36] Francke later claimed that he had only wanted to remove the abuse of philosophy, not philosophy itself, from theological training. The result, however, was that students began to desert the lectures on philosophy, which were considered a necessary preparation for theological study. A student named Johann Christian Lange sold his philosophy books, while another burnt his notes on a philosophy lecture by the Leipzig theologian Valentin Alberti.[37]

Nevertheless, the university was not implacably hostile toward the Pietists. An inquiry by the university, held at the request of the elector in Dresden, did not lead to a condemnation of Francke, who successfully defended himself against all accusations of heterodoxy. On 4 November the report was handed over to the elector and the affair seemed to be over. The electoral court itself had links to "Pietist" theologians, including Clemens Thieme, who was appointed to the position of *Reiseprediger* by the elector. Also, the theological faculty was not uniformly opposed to the Pietists. The son of Johann Olearius, a professor of theology, had become a Pietist. His daughter married Paul Anton, who had first instituted the *collegia* together with Francke. Johann Benedict Carpzov once even allowed Francke to preach in his stead.[38]

The strained relationship between theological faculty members and Pietists, however, ruptured soon afterwards. Francke had been allowed to examine the documents relating to the inquiry into the Pietist conventicles by the theological faculty. When he did, he brought along Thomasius, who advised Francke to copy the documents of the inquiry, which were published later.[39] Thomasius was, by then, already embroiled in the controversy with the theological faculty and the electoral court and discredited in the eyes of both. The faculty had already lodged its complaint against him, and his criticism of Masius had damaged his position at the court in Dresden.[40]

Both Francke and Thomasius now published sharp criticisms of the theological faculty and its inquiry into the Pietist movement. Francke wrote an *Apologia oder Defensions-Schrifft*, Thomasius the *Rechtliches Bedencken über die Leipzigschen Universitätsakta*. Francke claimed that the theological faculty prohibited the *collegia* but allowed the desecration of the Sabbath in the public houses. The language of Thomasius's work was similarly confrontational. In addition, he criticized the orthodox clergy's sermons in his lectures *De praejudiciis* (*On Prejudices*).[41] The faculty reacted with a complaint to the electoral court, pointing out Francke's connection with Thomasius, whose satirical comments on the state of learning at the University of Leipzig had already become notorious. This time the electoral court, at the request of the professors of the Leipzig theological faculty, banned the Pietist conventicles on 10 March 1690. On 23 March, a university edict also forbade all "conventicles . . . and congregations in which sacred scripture has commonly been explained both to literate and to illiterate people [the conventicles had attracted a number of nonstudents] according to private whim and without the authority of superiors."[42]

The result was an almost complete disappearance of Pietist conventicles, whose leaders departed from Saxony. Deprived of all official support in Saxony, they found a protector in the Calvinist elector of Brandenburg, whose territories provided a haven for all those who had been prominent in the Leipzig Pietist movement. Francke became the pastor of the congregation in Glaucha near Halle in the duchy of Magdeburg; Johann Caspar Schade, one of the most active Leipzig Pietists, accepted a position at the *Nicolaikirche* in Berlin. Spener, who had not been involved in the Pietist disturbances in Leipzig and was often critical toward them, became pastor at the *Nicolaikirche* at the same time, mainly because his criticism of the Saxon elector's extravagance and lack of earnest piety had alienated him from the Saxon court.[43]

Thomasius had lost the support of his remaining patrons at the Dresden court. In March 1690 the university was ordered to summon Thomasius and inform him that he was forbidden to teach, publish, and conduct disputations. If he disobeyed, he was to be punished with a fine of 200 *Reichsthaler*. Soon after this ban on his teaching was announced, Thomasius moved across the border to the territories of the elector of Brandenburg, where his moderate stance on the doctrinal differences between Lutherans and Calvinists made him particularly welcome to the elector. The duke of Sachsen-Zeitz and Pufendorf paved the way to a favorable reception at the electoral court.[44] The duke of Sachsen-Zeitz, whose marriage Thomasius had defended, wrote to his brother-in-law, the elector, praising Thomasius's "moderation" in religious matters, an aspect that would have been especially welcome to the Calvinist electors of Brandenburg, who were continually confronted by the hostility of their Lutheran estates. Thomasius himself, in a letter to the elector on 22 March 1690, drew attention to his belief in the need for mutual toleration among Lutherans and Calvinists, a belief that, he claimed, had been the reason for his expulsion from Saxony.[45] Within less than a month, Thomasius was appointed a councillor of the elector and permitted to lecture on philosophy and law at the academy for noblemen (*Ritterakademie*) in Halle. In his first disputation in Halle, which he dedicated to Elector Frederick III, Thomasius praised the electoral edicts against *Kanzelpolemik* (pulpit polemics), the defamation of another confession in a sermon.[46]

Once appointed, Thomasius urged the foundation of a university in Halle. In March 1691, he put a proposal to the government of the duchy of Magdeburg, which was one of the territories of the elector of Brandenburg. The duchy presented the proposal to the elector, who eventually agreed to it. In the autumn of 1692, the first professors were appointed, and less than two years later, in July 1694, the university was opened. In the following years, Thomasius continued to publish widely and was involved in a series of literary disputes. He wrote a number of treatises and disputations on the definition of heresy and the rights of the magistrate over the church: the *De Jure Principis circa Adiaphora* (1695), the *Das Recht evangelischer Fürsten in theologischen Streitigkeiten* (1696), the *De Jure Principis circa Haereticos* (1697) and the *Problema Juridicum: An Haeresis sit Crimen?* (1697). All of these were directed against his orthodox Lutheran critics, such as Johann Benedict Carpzov in Leipzig, Albrecht Christian Roth, Johann Stoltzen, Gustav Mörl, and the theologian Joachim Fecht in Rostock. These critics often equated Thomasius's position with that of the Pietists and described both Thomasius and the Pietists as religious enthusiasts who neglected the importance of doctrine to Christian faith. From 1696 onward, however, a rift had developed between Thomasius and August Hermann Francke, until then his friend and personal confessor, which turned into an open controversy over Francke's project to found an orphanage and school in Halle, the famous *Paedagogium*.

In November 1695, Francke had taken nine orphans into his care and placed them under the supervision of a theology student, Georg Neubauer.[47] At first the children had been lodged with friends of Francke, but as their number had increased to over a hundred by the spring of 1698 and Francke, moreover, had succeeded in collecting somewhere between 18,000 and 19,000 *Thaler* in donations, he decided to have a central *Paedagogium* built to house and teach them in.[48] Throughout the following year, Francke lobbied the court in Berlin to obtain the elector's support for his project. He already enjoyed influential patronage from several pro-Pietist members of the Lutheran bureaucratic and military nobility,[49] including the *Geheime Rat* von Schweinitz, the *Hofrat* Willmann, the *Generalleutnant* Dubislav Gneomar von Natzmer, the *Freiherr* von Canstein (who procured a low-interest loan of 7,000 *Thaler* for Francke's orphanage in spring 1698)[50] and the minister for church affairs, Paul von Fuchs. In late August 1698, Fuchs invited Francke to present his project at the court in Berlin. Francke spent two weeks in Berlin making contacts, a period in which he met several times with von Fuchs and the *Kammerpräsident* of the *Kurmark*, Samuel von Chwalkowski, who cultivated the society of Pietists such as Francke, Socinians, and Jews.[51]

At court, Francke appears to have met with a very favorable reception, and he succeeded in securing the support of the Calvinist court preacher Jablonski and the Calvinist court nobility. Even the elector himself declared that "the man had to be supported by all means."[52] On 9 September 1698, Chwalkowski informed Francke that almost all his requests for the *Paedagogium* had been granted. These were mainly economic privileges, such as an exemption from excise duties and permission to run a pharmacy and a printing press, and pursue other trades usually subject to guild restrictions. Francke had also been promoted from his chair in oriental languages at the philosophical faculty to the more prestigious chair in theology. On 19 September, the orphanage was declared an *annexum* of the University of Halle and subject directly to the jurisdiction of the elector without mediation by the courts of the duchy of Magdeburg. Generous donations by the elector, his wife, and members of the court soon followed.[53]

The purpose of the *Paedagogium* was to instill a practical piety in its students. Francke defined three aims of a good education: an adolescent should be led to true piety, be taught the necessary sciences and learn good manners, "wherein lies the foundation of their temporal and their eternal well-being."[54] The means to inculcating piety into the pupils of the orphanage was a minute regulation of the pupils' daily life.

Thomasius, however, doubted that Francke's proposals would generate true piety in his pupils. The cause of evil in human nature, Thomasius wrote, did not lie in education and upbringing, but in the inherent corruption of human nature since original sin and the Fall from Grace. Francke's measures, Thomasius suspected, would change external conduct, but this would only amount to a superficial and hypocritical piety, which was far more dangerous to social life than the obvious impiety of those who could not conceal their depravity. Francke's *Paedagogium*, Thomasius claimed, could at most help to suppress the vices connected to lust, but was likely to encourage avarice and ambition in their place.

By that time, Thomasius had also alienated the other Pietist theologians at the University of Halle, who joined in Francke's criticisms. As we shall see, Thomasius's religious views steadily became more extreme from the mid-1690s onward and moved closer to the ideas of the millenarian, "enthusiastic" sects on the fringes of German Protestantism. The Halle theological faculty, in spite of its criticism of traditionalist Lutheranism, was anxious to uphold a reputation for doctrinal orthodoxy and to distance itself from the more extreme forms of Protestant sectarianism.[55] They accused Thomasius of examining questions he was not competent to discuss and of encouraging skeptical attitudes toward the authority of scripture. Thomasius was compelled to retreat in 1703 and promised not to touch on theological questions in his lectures and writings again. Thomasius's succession to Samuel Stryk's position as director of the university in 1710 strengthened his position *vis-à-vis* the university's theologians, but the tensions between him and the Halle theologians never disappeared entirely, lasting until his death on 30 September 1728.[56]

RELIGION AND THE LEGAL-POLITICAL ORDER OF THE HOLY ROMAN EMPIRE AFTER THE THIRTY YEARS' WAR

Religion continued to play a significant role in the intellectual life, politics, and legal order of the *Reich* in the half-century after the end of the Thirty Years' War. The war itself had been fought to a great extent, though not exclusively, over religious issues, and although confessional loyalties had not corresponded invariably to political alignments, in general, religious and political interests were inseparable. The revolt of the Bohemian estates with which the war began had been a defense of Protestantism as much as of the estates' traditional rights against the Austrian Hapsburgs, and the emperor's attempts at counter-reformation in the empire during the war were seen as an example of tyranny, which violated the religious as well as the political freedoms of the imperial estates.

The purpose of the Westphalian peace treaties of 1648 was to provide a stable legal framework for the relationship between the different confessions of the empire and to remedy the defects of the 1555 Peace of Augsburg. Calvinists, for example, were now included in the religious peace and for the first time had their legal status guaranteed by imperial law. Because of the fluctuating confessional allegiances of different territories over the previous decades, the year 1624 was selected as a *Normaljahr*, a base year for settling the rights of the three confessions.[57] This abolished the prince's *ius reformandi*, the right to impose his own confession on his territory's church, so that the confessional situation of 1624 was fixed: if a prince changed confession from now on, he could not compel his territory's established church to follow suit.

Toleration was now extended to all three main confessions of the *Reich*, those of Roman Catholics, Lutherans, and Calvinists, though its degree could vary from territory to territory. The established church of a territory, as determined by the *Normaljahr*, had the right to the *exercitium religionis publicum* in churches with spires and bells. Those with rights in the territory dating before 1624 enjoyed the right to the *exercitium religionis privatum* in chapels without bells. The remainder could only practice the *exercitium religionis domesticum* with prayers in the family home and the right to visit churches of their own confession in a neighboring principality. But although toleration was sometimes limited, it was guaranteed by imperial law and there was no longer a compulsion to adopt the confession of the territory's established church. The former *ius emigrandi*, the "right" to leave a territory rather than having to convert to the beliefs of the established church, thus became superfluous.

The Peace of Westphalia therefore did bring about a basic religious freedom for the members of the three main confessions in the *Reich*, but the treaty did not introduce general religious toleration. Its purpose was to regulate the status of Catholics, Lutherans, and Calvinists within the framework of a complex system of legal rules and guarantees. It made no provision for religious sects other than the three main confessions, and the decision whether or not to tolerate the members of a Philadelphic society, for example, was left to the discretion of the territorial prince, the *Landesherr*.

Another problem was the fact that in several cases the confession of the *Landesherr* differed from that of his territory's established church. This was the case in the Palatinate from 1685, for example, when a Catholic line succeeded to the electorate, or in Württemberg in the early eighteenth century, when the duke converted to Catholicism but could not impose his beliefs on his territory's established church because its confession had been guaranteed by the Peace of Westphalia. In Brandenburg, the Calvinist electors faced an often hostile Lutheran established church. When the electors had converted to Calvinism in 1613, they had abstained from exercising their *ius reformandi*. Their self-restraint was due to the particular variety of Lutheranism in Brandenburg, which was extremely hostile to Calvinism and even considered itself closer to Roman Catholicism than to the other main Protestant church. The Lutheran reformation carried out by Elector Joachim II in Brandenburg in the 1540s had been a very cautious modification of Catholicism, a so-called *via media*, which left many of Catholicism's ritual practices intact: chasubles, auricular confession, epitaphs in churches, and even exorcism in baptism were retained in the Lutheran church in Brandenburg. When Elector Johann Sigismund converted to Calvinism in 1613, his aim was to complete the reformation of Christianity in his territories and remove these remnants of "papist superstition,"[58] but his attempt to do so met with the determined resistance of the overwhelmingly Lutheran population. When, for example, Johann Sigismund in 1615 tried to strip the Berlin Cathedral, his court church, of all images, crucifixes, and side-altars, this led to anti-Calvinist riots, during which the elector's staunchly Lutheran wife took the side of the protesters. The mob stormed the houses of the Calvinist court preachers Sachse and Füssel, vandalizing and looting the contents. Füssel and Sachse barely escaped, the former with no more than the clothes he was wearing at the time, so that for Good Friday services later that week Füssel appeared in the pulpit in his underwear, stockings, a borrowed gown, and a green vest.[59]

The antagonism between the electors and the Lutheran population continued throughout the seventeenth century. During their occupation of the Mark Brandenburg in the Thirty Years' War, for example, the Swedes were able to exploit this hostility of the Lutheran population toward their elector very effectively.[60] In the 1660s, Great Elector Frederick William's efforts to ban exorcism in baptism brought him into conflict with his Lutheran subjects, particularly in Berlin.[61] An attempt by the Great Elector to reconcile Lutherans and Calvinists at a series of religious talks in Berlin in 1661–62, the *Berliner Religionsgespräche*, failed.[62] Although the electors, throughout, claimed the same rights over their territory's Lutheran church as a Lutheran prince enjoyed, their attempts to exercise this right by appointing clergymen or members of consistories were regularly foiled by their Lutheran subjects. Thus the prince's own confession in Brandenburg was a dissenting sect, based on the electoral court and isolated in a sea of hostile Lutheran opinion. Under the terms of the Westphalian peace treaties, the only clergymen the elector could appoint were court preachers, and, unsurprisingly, the number of electoral courts multiplied, with many members of the electoral family having their own courts, often in administrative centers, where the Calvinist members of the electoral bureaucracy required a preacher to conduct services.[63]

It has been argued that the elector's conversion to Calvinism in 1613 was largely guided by considerations of *raison d'état*, to gain the support of the Calvinist United Provinces in the dispute over the succession in Jülich-Cleve.[64] But as Bodo Nischan has shown, there is little evidence for this interpretation. Instead it seems clear that the elector's motive in converting was a desire to reform religious life and purge his territorial church of its "left-over papal dung."[65] The aim to cleanse the church of superstition and superficial, formulaic faith continued to be a constant theme later in the seventeenth century, too. The intellectual context of this concern for sincere piety was the rise of devotional Christianity throughout Europe in the seventeenth century, which in Germany manifested itself in the Pietist reform movement.

Pietism and the Rise of Devotional Christianity[66]

The rise of devotional religiosity was one of the most prominent developments in seventeenth-century intellectual life. Across Europe, several religious movements emerged with broadly similar concerns: to replace superficial and formulaic religious practice with a true, "living," or "spiritual" Christianity, based on charity. In Germany this took the form of Pietism,[67] while in England there was Puritanism. Spain produced a comparable phenomenon in Quietism, as did France, Austria, and Italy in Jansenism. In Holland, a number of religious groupings with similar aims were to be found. Despite the undoubted differences between these movements, a number of scholars have argued convincingly for the comparability of these developments in different parts of Europe and in all three of the major Christian confessions, Lutheranism, Calvinism, and Roman Catholicism.[68]

The similarities of these different groupings' interests are shown by the extent to which writings from one country were translated and read in others and sometimes even crossed confessional boundaries. Works by English Puritans, for example, were widely disseminated in Germany, beginning with the writings of William Perkins, the main English import until about 1630.[69] In 1628, Lewis Bayly's *Practice of Piety* was printed in a German edition by König in Basel. Three years later, Joseph Hall's *Arte of Divine Meditation* was published as the second part of the German edition of the *Practice of Piety*. In this form, the *Practice* became the most successful piece of English devotional literature in the German territories.[70] The other most popular devotional books stemming from English Puritanism were the *Güldenes Kleinod der Kinder Gottes*, a Protestant version of a Jesuit work on spiritual exercises, by an English merchant called Thompson, writing under the name of Emmanuel Sonthom, and David Dyke's *Nosce te ipsum*.[71]

English religious literature appeared first in the Calvinist territories of Germany, to which these books were introduced via Switzerland, Geneva and Basel in particular. The earliest centers for the production of translations of English devotional works were the Calvinist printing presses of Basel, Hanau, Herborn, and Oppenheim.[72] From about 1630 onward, these books began to gain ground in the Lutheran territories of the *Reich*. In 1631, a Lutheran version of the *Practice of Piety*, modified in accordance with Lutheran doctrine, was printed by Stern in Lüneburg. A dogmatically censored and expanded Lutheran version of Thompson's *Güldenes Kleinod* followed a year later.[73]

The influx of English devotional literature reinforced an already existing indigenous strand of writing with recognizably similar concerns. The *Vier* [later *Sechs*] *Bücher vom Wahren Christentum* by Johann Arndt (1555–1621), who is often described as the forefather of German Pietism, is probably the most famous and influential example: it saw ninety-five editions in German alone between its first publication in 1605 and 1740, quite apart from the twenty-eight editions in other languages, from Latin to Icelandic. The total number of copies printed in German has been estimated at 100,000.[74] Later German examples in this genre are works by figures like Jakob Böhme (1575–1624); the author of the utopian *Christianopolis,* Johann Valentin Andreae (1586–1654); Christian Hoburg (1607–75); and Joachim Betkius (1601–63). The person considered to be the immediate founder of Pietism, however, is the theologian Philipp Jakob Spener (1635–1705), from whose *Pia desideria* (*Pious Desires*) the Pietists derived their name.

Philipp Jakob Spener grew up in an environment in which this type of devotional literature was firmly established. He was born in Rappoltsweiler in Württemberg on 13 January 1635,[75] at a time when the fortunes of the Protestant League in the Thirty Years' War were at a particularly low ebb, after the Protestants' champion Gustav Adolf of Sweden had died in the battle of Lützen in November 1632. The Habsburgs had defeated an inferior Protestant army at Nördlingen in November 1634, and the Peace of Prague (1635) seemed to mark the triumph of Habsburg power in the *Reich* south of the Main, until France, after suppressing the Huguenots within its own boundaries, came to the help of Protestants in Germany to counter the threat of Habsburg power.[76]

Protestants interpreted their misfortunes and the misery of war generally as signs of divine anger at the spread of irreligion and hypocrisy, a belief that stimulated an interest in religious revival and works of religious devotion. Johann Schmidt, the *Kirchenpräsident* of Strasbourg, to which the Württemberg court had fled from the fighting, permitted and probably even encouraged the printing of Bayly's and Sonthom's books in Strasbourg, soon after they had appeared in Lüneburg.[77] The themes of religious sincerity and practical Christianity were prominent in the sermons Schmidt gave in the Strasbourg Munster.[78] Schmidt was also Spener's teacher in theology from 1651, when the latter began studying in Strasbourg.[79] Spener was also instructed by Johann Conrad Dannhauer, who provided Spener with the Lutheran doctrinal framework to which Spener seems to have adhered throughout his life.

In 1666, Spener was offered and persuaded to accept the position of *Senior*, the highest-ranking clergyman, in the Lutheran church in Frankfurt am Main. From there he advanced in 1686 to the position of court preacher to the Saxon elector in Dresden. This was one of the most prestigious clerical appointments for a Lutheran in Germany, as the elector headed the Protestant estates, the *Corpus Evangelicorum*, in the imperial diet. Spener was also given a seat on the *Oberkonsistorium*, the body regulating ecclesiastical affairs, and was appointed confessor to the elector. Within a few years, however, Spener's admonitions to the elector to drink less and moderate his choleric temper had soured relations between them,[80] and in 1691 Spener left Saxony to accept the position of provost (*Propst*) at the *Nicolaikirche* in Berlin, where he remained until his death in 1705.

During his time in Frankfurt, Spener had introduced the *Collegia Pietatis*, private meetings at which a passage from a devotional work was read and then discussed. The express purpose of the meeting was to further practical piety, not to debate points of doctrine. Spener described the *collegium* as an *ecclesiola in ecclesia*, a private gathering within the public, institutional church. The function of the public *ecclesia* was only to act as messenger of God's word and to prevent its adulteration; but faith, Spener wrote, required more than hearing God's word and accepting its truth. It required a reform of the heart, reflected in the believer's conduct, not just a reform of his or her doctrinal opinions. The *collegia* were intended to gather the truly pious, who strove to turn their Christian faith into a practical holiness of life. The problem of the existing Lutheran doctrine of salvation *sola fide*, Spener wrote in the *Pia desideria* of 1675, was its apparent implication that salvation required no more than holding the opinion that Christ's death on the cross atoned for humanity's sinfulness. It was not realized that sincere faith also led to a transformation of the entire nature of the believer, a spiritual rebirth, which restrained the believer from committing further sins.

Unlike Luther, who had been preoccupied with original sin and the resulting damnation of humanity in the afterlife,[81] Spener's attention was focused more strongly on humans' particular sins, which flowed from the corruption of human nature by the Fall from Grace and which turned the verbal profession of Christian faith into an act of hypocrisy,[82] a fault from which none of the three estates in society and the church, the magistracy, the clergy, and the laity, was exempt. The *Obrigkeit* neglected its duties toward religion.[83] The clerical estate sought its own interest instead of serving Christ. Clergymen understood Christian doctrine and assented to it but "were far removed from the heavenly light and the life of faith,"[84] because their supposed faith had not brought about a reform of their nature and day-to-day conduct. Their failings were particularly damaging, because they were the spiritual teachers of the other two estates, and thus were responsible for the poor state of Christianity in these estates.[85]

The good works Spener expected of a Christian were, strictly speaking, irrelevant to salvation. To believe otherwise was papist, but what Spener argued was that if Christian faith was adopted sincerely, this would necessarily be reflected in the believer's conduct. Although good works did not save a person from damnation, anyone who did not act righteously could not be a sincere Christian.

Spener's *collegia* were not intended to prepare the secession of the truly pious from the general congregation, which only attended the normal services, and the formation of an *ecclesiola extra ecclesiam*, like that of the contemporary Labadists.[86] Spener believed the doctrine of the institutional, established church was true, and the church was not required to be a community of the truly pious, but only to communicate God's word to all members of the congregation. Spener did not advocate excommunicating those who did not adopt Christian faith sincerely, but his aim was to strengthen the practice of piety and holiness of conduct without undermining the framework of the institutional church.

There have been many attempts to define the importance of Spener and his *Pia desideria* for Pietism. Martin Schmidt selected the idea of spiritual rebirth as Spener's distinctive contribution to Lutheran theology and the main characteristic of Pietist theology. Johannes Wallmann took Spener's concepts of the *ecclesiola in ecclesia* and the *collegium pietatis* to be the defining features of Pietism. At the very least, however, it can be said that these ideas represented no very radical departure from the many religious reform programs before Spener's *Pia desideria*. In addition, Spener's ideas do not differentiate him sharply from so-called orthodox Lutherans, who were often very receptive to efforts at inculcating greater religious sincerity. Several of the most orthodox Lutheran divines welcomed the reform program of the *Pia desideria*.[87] The orthodox theologians of eight Lutheran universities expressed their approval of Spener's proposals.[88] Both "Pietism" and "orthodox Lutheranism" are often too rigid as categories to characterize particular positions[89] and some definitions of Pietism may include non-Pietists, while others exclude persons and groups described as Pietist.

The differences between "separatist" Pietists, who aimed to secede from the established church, and Spener, for example, often seem more marked than between Spener and certain non-Pietists. Samuel Pufendorf (1632–94), a theorist better known for his works on natural law, criticized religious hypocrisy and insincerity in terms that were similar to Spener's, insisting that faith without holiness of life was a "dead Tree without Fruit."[90] "For the Profession of the Covenant in Christ requires another sort of Life and Manners than those of Heathens, and of them who follow the Inclination of the Flesh, or of the Corruption which proceeds from Original Sin."[91] The "holiness of life" in post-lapsarian nature could never be as complete as before the Fall from Grace, since the depraved motions of human nature were ineradicable and would already merit man's eternal damnation by God,[92] and even the regenerate did not have the power utterly to extinguish all evil inclinations of human nature, which follow from the Fall from Grace, "tho' this is what they ought continually with all Diligence to endeavour."[93] Humans, however, Pufendorf writes, enjoy at least the liberty of preventing their inherent sinfulness from issuing into outward action.[94] If they do this and grieve for their sinfulness, the "Satisfaction of the Saviour" Jesus Christ means that the imperfections of post-lapsarian human nature are "as it were overlook'd, as are also the Faults committed without our Choice, and the evil Motions proceeding from the original Pollution."[95] Although Pufendorf welcomed Pietists' emphasis on the holiness of life, he was at the same time critical of them in other respects.[96]

The work of Veit Ludwig von Seckendorff (1626–92)[97] reflects a similar preoccupation with sincere, active piety, although, like Pufendorf, he has never been described as a Pietist. An advisor to the duke Maurice of Sachsen-Naumburg Zeitz from 1665 and briefly the chancellor of the University of Halle, he was in close contact with Spener, and in his *Christen-Stat* set out to demonstrate that Christian faith necessitated the practical holiness of life.[98] Only atheists, he maintained, could act immorally, because they denied the existence of punishments by God in the afterlife. No difference existed between atheists and hypocrites. Hypocrites could be insincere only because they feared no God. They adopted the mask of religion only because atheists were considered unreliable and suffered many disadvantages in society.[99]

At the same time, Pietism itself was far from homogeneous. The Pietist movement, as it developed in Leipzig from the 1680s, often pursued aims incompatible with Spener's. Spener had persuaded the Pietist Paul Anton to acquire a theological degree before conducting *Collegia Pietatis*, while Anton's colleague Francke consistently refused to do so.[100] And while one of Francke's followers, Joachim Feller, was the first to accept the title of

"Pietists" to describe the new movement, Spener said that Feller had acted unwisely, because the term Pietists "seems to indicate a sect," separate from the orthodox Lutheran church.[101] When the term "Pietists" appeared for the first time, during Spener's period in Frankfurt am Main, he discouraged its use. His reform program had been designed precisely to help end sectarianism in the Christian church by emphasizing holiness of life as the proper foundation of Christianity and suggesting the irrelevance of many of the doctrinal disputes dividing the various Christian confessions.[102]

In contrast to Spener, Pietists like Johann Caspar Schade at the *Nicolaikirche* in Berlin or August Hermann Francke in Glaucha sought to enforce the sanctity of life among the members of their congregation with measures of ecclesiastical discipline and to transform the earthly *ecclesia visibilis* into a community of the truly pious. Nevertheless, even Francke's doctrinal views were orthodox. His rigid ecclesiastical discipline was not intended to segregate his congregation from an impious Lutheran church, but to purify the church by excluding the impious from it. Francke, too, denied that he had founded a "sect."[103] One motive for denying sectarian tendencies, no doubt, was the fact that many Pietists became salaried ministers of the Lutheran church in Brandenburg and Magdeburg and were allowed to hold services and preach, privileges they would not have enjoyed as religious dissenters.

The orthodox Lutherans agreed with the Pietists in believing that sincere Christianity required practical piety as well as the profession of the correct doctrines. The orthodox Lutheran polemicist Valentin Löscher's motto, for example, was *Doctrina et Pietas*.[104] However, the reformatory zeal of Pietists like Francke in Glaucha and Schade in Berlin seemed to show a contempt for existing doctrine and ritual, which had been established by consensus in the Lutheran church. Both Francke and Schade appealed to their consciences to justify their opposition, but this recourse to "conscience" seemed to many Lutherans little more than an enthusiastical excuse to bypass established doctrine and ritual. The Pietists, orthodox Lutherans maintained, believed in regeneration without the belief in particular doctrines, opening the way to dangerous enthusiastical claims to direct inspiration by God. In response to the Pietists' accusations of insincerity and formalism, orthodox Lutherans emphasized that although regeneration was part of faith, doctrine was not worthless without regeneration. As Löscher wrote:

> A person in whom the correct beliefs do not bear spiritual fruits, can be said, despite his knowledge, to be spiritually dead because of his sinfulness, and faithful only in a narrowly literal sense. But the orthodoxy he does hold is not in itself dead or merely literal, but is only imprisoned in spiritual death.[105]

Pietists, by contrast, stressed that without spiritual rebirth the understanding of Christian doctrine was superficial and ineffective.[106] This could, however, be taken to imply that regeneration was not only prior to, but also independent of, doctrine. In orthodox Lutherans' eyes, this opinion came dangerously close to *Schwärmerey*, that is, enthusiasts' reduction of faith to divine illumination and the rejection of all doctrine. Valentin Löscher formulated the difference as one between an orthodox position that "fides, quae justificat, practica est" and a Pietist that "fides, *quatenus* justificat, practica est [my italics]": that is, the orthodox believed that justificatory faith was expressed in holiness of life, but the Pietists maintained that it was only the holiness of life that made faith justificatory.[107] There are numerous orthodox Lutheran works depicting the Pietists as a new form of Anabaptist Fanaticism and sedition, particularly from the time of the rupture between the Leipzig theological faculty and the Leipzig Pietists in the late 1680s. In 1690, the orthodox Lutheran theologian Ehregott Daniel Colberg dedicated two large volumes to refuting the "fanatical spirits" in his *Platonisch-Hermetisches Christenthum*.[108] In spring of the same year, three Pietist pastors in Hamburg were blamed for what were considered enthusiast movements in the city.[109] A year later, the Halle archdeacon Albrecht Christian Roth published a critique of Pietism, the *Imago Pietismi*, in which he listed the faults of Pietist religiosity, among which were unauthorized religious teaching, an overemphasis on love rather than doctrine, perfectionism, and chiliastic tendencies.[110] In 1699, a Danzig pastor named Bücher argued that the Pietists were Fanatics and Satan's most effective instrument in spreading atheism.[111]

Thomasius's interest in the Pietist movement is often described as a passing phase and the reflection of a temporary religious and psychological "crisis," which began in the early 1690s and ended around 1700. As chapter 2 will show, however, the role of religion in the general development of Thomasius's thought was more significant and his relationship to Pietism more complex than the idea of a "religious crisis" suggests.

Chapter Two

Religion and the Limits of Philosophy

In the course of the 1690s and early 1700s, Thomasius acquired the reputation of being a religious "enthusiast," someone who set aside the formulaic creeds of the institutional churches in favor of an anti-intellectualist "faith of the heart" of the individual. His beliefs were in many ways similar to those of religious mystics and the many millenarian religious sects, which were excluded from the three established churches, Lutheran, Catholic, and Calvinist, within the Holy Roman Empire.[1] This side of Thomasius's thought has so far received little attention in the secondary literature, especially as it has seemed difficult to reconcile with his reputation as an enlightened thinker. But there are important reasons for paying attention to Thomasius's religious beliefs, one of which is that his contemporaries often regarded him as a controversial figure because of his religious heterodoxy. Another is that the connections between Thomasius's "enthusiastic" religious beliefs and his "enlightened" philosophical program of reforming "scholasticism" are closer than they might at first appear to be. For, although faith and philosophy were conceptually distinct, Thomasius also believed that they were dependent on each other, in particular, because religious faith was easily corrupted by the overestimation of the powers of the human intellect in religious matters. Although he was never opposed to philosophy as such, Thomasius criticized his opponents for exaggerating the extent to which it could be of any use in matters of faith. This skepticism about the usefulness of philosophical reasoning and the powers of the human intellect in religion was a long-standing preoccupation in Lutheran thought, dating back at least to the reintroduction of metaphysics into Protestant theological curricula at the end of the sixteenth century, if not to Luther himself.[2]

The present chapter[3] examines this relationship between faith and philosophy, and its complex development in Thomasius's thought between the late 1680s and the early 1700s. This development can be roughly divided into three phases. The first of these, in the late 1680s and early 1690s, is characterized by a voluntarist theology, which emphasized God's omnipotence and the inscrutability of his will; the second, beginning in the early to mid-1690s, reflected a shift to a more extreme position, which his contemporaries suspected of religious "enthusiasm"; the third, from around 1703, is marked by an attempt to avoid some of the enthusiastic implications of his earlier thought, though Thomasius's religious beliefs remained very heterodox and therefore continued to attract criticism from more conservative contemporaries. At the end of this development, Thomasius emerged not only with a particular view of religious faith but also with a notion of human nature and a particular conception of the importance of religious faith for secular thought.

THOMASIUS'S THEOLOGICAL VOLUNTARISM AND THE REVIVAL OF PIETY AROUND 1690

Around the time of his expulsion from Leipzig in 1690, Thomasius's thought on the relationship between faith and rational philosophy was an example of classical theological voluntarism, which assumed that divine nature and the decisions of the divine will were unknown to humans. Although God had revealed certain truths to humanity in scripture, these were of a different order from the truths of philosophy, which were founded on natural reason. This meant that philosophy could not be used for the explication of truths of faith. And yet, Thomasius wrote, this was exactly what the "scholastics," a broadly defined group, which included his orthodox Lutheran opponents, had done. They had used philosophy like the ancient pagans and had "attempted to deduce the mysteries of faith from philosophy, and made philosophy the measure of theology, contrary to the precept of the apostle, who admonished the Colossians not to allow themselves to be deceived by philosophy and vain fallacy."[4] Philosophy, however, had to be taken in a narrower sense than it had been by the classical pagan philosophers, who had described it far too broadly as "the knowledge of the affairs of Gods and humans."[5] 'The "characteristics of that ancient philosophy, which acted as the queen" of all sciences,[6] should not be confused with "philosophy today, to which the honest glory of serving is reserved."[7]

The mixture of philosophical reason and scriptural revelation corrupted not only the theoretical understanding of Christian faith but also its practice, because it led to an emphasis on excessively subtle argumentation rather than the practical charity worthy of a Christian believer, when "careless people mixed gentile philosophy with Christianity, light with darkness."[8] Thomasius's criticism was very similar to that put forward by contemporary

"Pietist" religious reformers such as Philipp Jakob Spener,[9] whose aim was the moral and spiritual regeneration of the Christian church, which, he believed, had degenerated into a hypocritical formalism. Sermons were preached without true devotion, and there was little of the practical, active piety that Christianity demanded of its adherents, since religion had been corrupted by the introduction of "much that is extraneous, useless and smacks more of worldly wisdom,"[10] that is, philosophical argument. Spener believed this was a strategy of Satan to divide Christians into conflicting theological sects, which disagreed over doctrinal subtleties and ignored the practical charity Christ expected from his followers.[11]

Thomasius praised Spener's intention of restoring Christian sanctity and piety[12] and like him criticized those who "put forward most arguments from human writings, and very few from the word of God, [those] who inculcated philosophical doctrines instead of theological ones, and laboriously twisted any controversy to suit any passage, in order that they could satisfy only their desire to quarrel, calumniate and argue."[13] Only when theologians ceased to mix scripture and the symbolic books of the early church with human writings, would the differences over the interpretation of scripture, which separated different sects from each other, disappear. In every essential question of faith, scripture and the symbolic books of early Christianity were self-evident and easy to understand.[14] They did not have to be glossed by theologians for their meaning to be clear.

Thomasius's skepticism about the usefulness of reason questioned the validity of established orthodox Lutheran theological debate. Orthodox Lutheran theorists such as the Leipzig theologian Valentin Alberti were prepared to grant a more extensive role to philosophical argument in the explication of revealed truth. Even though the human intellect was weak, and weakened further by original sin, it was assumed that human reason was similar in kind to the divine intellect and could form at least some conclusions on divine matters.[15] Indeed, such beliefs sustained philosophical and theological teaching in the curricula of orthodox Lutheran universities like that of Leipzig.

Thomasius' views thus were considered provocative by orthodox Lutherans and viewed sympathetically by leading Pietists. From the mid-1690s, however, Thomasius moved toward a position that appeared even more radical to many of his contemporaries and eventually also drew the criticism of a number of prominent Pietist theologians, such as August Hermann Francke.

THOMASIUS'S RELIGIOUS "ENTHUSIASM"

In the early to mid-1690s, Thomasius redefined the relationship between faith and philosophy in a way that earned him the reputation of being a religious "enthusiast." Broadly, the change in his thought can be described as a change from a theological to an anthropological voluntarism. Although he continued to emphasize the limitations of the human intellect in understanding matters of faith, he also began to emphasize the importance of the human will rather than the intellect in human nature. Of particular significance was the question of the freedom of the human will. In his early works, such as the *Institutes of Divine Jurisprudence* of 1688, Thomasius had followed Pufendorf and argued that the essence of the human will was the freedom to choose between any of the available courses of action. This, however, raised difficult questions about human agency. If the will was capable of acting entirely freely and indifferently toward any course of action, what was the reason for its choice of one action over another? On the other hand, if something external to the will determined its decision, how could it be described as free?

Several other philosophers, including Hobbes and Leibniz, had developed their own solutions to this classical problem,[16] and in 1723, Christian Wolff was expelled from his post at the University of Halle for holding the view that every decision of the will was determined by a sufficient reason, a view that seemed to deny the freedom of the will, which was essential to moral imputability; it is alleged that Frederick William I of Prussia was persuaded to banish Wolff when he was informed that Wolff's doctrine made it impossible to punish deserters from his army, because they could not be held responsible for their crime.[17] Thomasius's conclusion in the early 1690s was that the essence of the will could not be an ability to choose, as he had believed before, but was a form of love (*amor*), which he defined as a desire or passion for a particular end, a radically different concept from his earlier, Pufendorfian notion of an indifferent will. Reason did not have the power to guide this will-as-desire, but was only the instrument for satisfying its passion or desires by helping to achieve the ends this will defined. As David Hume would later put it, reason was the slave of the passions and ought to be nothing else.[18]

There were several varieties of *amor* within human nature; these were, in essence, different wills, competing with each other for the control of human actions. Each of these wills was directed to a different end, but it was impossible for humans to choose freely between these different wills. They were, so to speak, hard-wired in human nature, although their proportions differed from one person to the next. Thomasius combined his new notion of the human will as a form of *amor* with an Augustinian conception of faith as the love for God, which was opposed to the love for the world by the godless.[19] Thomasius was probably familiar with Augustine's writings, but the immediate source for his ideas seems to have been French, particularly Jansenist, religious and moral philosophical texts, and the works of mystical theologians, which he had been studying since the late 1680s.[20] One of the most important pieces in which he put forward his new view of faith and his revised anthropology was an introductory essay in 1694 to a work by the French mystic Pierre Poiret (1646–1719). He also strongly praised the mystic and ecclesiastical historian Gottfried Arnold, as well as many other similar figures, such as the theologian Christian Hoburg, the author of numerous spiritualist works.[21]

Thomasius identified four basic types of *amor*, each of which stood for the desire for a particular end. Three of these were corrupt and oriented exclusively toward worldly goods: avarice, which was directed toward material wealth; ambition, which was directed toward external honor; and lust, which was directed toward all forms of physical pleasure. The fourth, "reasonable love" (*amor rationalis*), was identical to the Christian faith. It represented the longing for God and, in the state of innocence, had been powerful enough to control the three corrupt desires, but it had been weakened by original sin and was now too feeble to prevent humanity from falling into depravity.

This capacity for faith in the sense of *amor rationalis* and the three corrupt forms of *amor* was rooted in human nature, which Thomasius said consisted of three parts. The first was the material body. The second was the soul (*anima*), which was the seat of the three corrupt passions. The third was the spirit (*spiritus*), on which the love of God was based.[22] The crucial difference between soul and spirit was that the former was part of created nature, while the latter was a supranatural, divine spark, which did not perish in death, but returned to God.

Thomasius thought that although the spirit had lost its control over the passions in the *anima* through original sin, this control could be reestablished, after a lengthy process of regeneration, which could only be completed with the supranatural intervention of divine grace. Natural reason, located in the *anima*, could begin this process of regeneration by allowing us to recognize the particular misery of the human condition and to understand our inability to change our condition. Humans were in one of three conditions: bestiality, humanity, or Christianity (a distinction that is reminiscent of Pascal's three orders, those of the flesh, the mind, and charity).[23] In the first they were not even conscious of their corruption, but natural reason could raise them to the stage of humanity, in which they recognized the misery of their condition, although they had not yet found a remedy. The highest stage, that of Christianity, was achieved with the help of faith, after a long process of regeneration, culminating in the gift of divine grace. Thomasius illustrated the limited, but nevertheless real, utility of natural reason with the image of a candle, which a man used to find his way in a dark cellar. Eventually this man reached a heavy, barred door, through which, faintly, daylight shone. Once this person had been admitted through this door by the doorkeeper, that is, Christ, the candle could be cast away.[24] Natural reason was superseded by the superior truth of divine grace.

An important implication of Thomasius's new anthropology and view of faith was to render doctrines superfluous to religious belief, and it was this that exposed him to the charge of enthusiasm. Orthodox theorists objected that Thomasius's view of regeneration presented conversion to the true faith as the result of a direct communication between the individual and God, which was only made possible by the presence of a spark of the divine essence in human nature. As a result, the clear distinction between God and creation was removed and the two were conflated in a way that could be suspected of "Spinozism." By positing a divine, and therefore uncreated, particle of divine essence in each human, it was argued, Thomasius turned created beings into a part of God himself. Thomasius's argument was seen as a typically enthusiastical interpretation of the world as an emanation of God's essence, rather than as his creation. Valentin Löscher, one of the most eminent orthodox Lutheran theologians, claimed that the belief "that there is a divine particle in every creature" reflected the enthusiasts' identification of the world and God.[25] In Greifswald, the orthodox theologian Justus Wesselus Rumpaeus noted that, like Thomasius, "all Fanatics who have ever existed defended the opinion that *God created this universe and whatever is in it out of himself or out of his essence.*"[26]

By emphasizing divine inspiration, Thomasius thus appeared to dispense with the role of Christ and doctrine as necessary mediators between God and humankind. If regeneration was brought about by direct interaction between God and the individual believer, there was no need for his Son, and no need for revealed scripture to direct humans toward the salvificatory faith. Orthodox Lutherans rejected Thomasius's anthropology, insisting that human nature had no divine third part, no *spiritus*, needed to provide humans with the "illumination" that gave them direct contact with God. Believers, the orthodox held, were enlightened by understanding and accepting the doctrinal truths revealed in scripture, not by God directly. Thomasius's belief in the *Christus internus* as the divine spark within, the orthodox Wittenberg theologian Wernsdorfer believed, made the revealed word redundant. "Therefore the word, Christ, the spirit, the seed, the light, the Gospel, according to the Fanatics, are all one and the same."[27]

Thomasius believed, however, that doctrine was ineffectual for achieving faith. Faith depended on the redirection of the will from the corrupt love of the world to the pure love of God. Doctrines were opinions adopted by the intellect, but Thomasius's new anthropology downplayed the importance of the intellect in relation to the will-as-desire. This will, not the intellect, was the driving force of human nature; the intellect was merely an instrument in fulfilling the desires determined by the will, not its guide.[28] Belief in the intellect as the essential and most important part of human nature was the "common error of pagan philosophy"[29] and typical of his "scholastic" orthodox Lutheran opponents, who, like the pagan philosophers, had not recognized that the "will is the more eminent part of man, whether in the state of innocence, in that of sin or after regeneration, for love is the function of the will, not the intellect."[30]

From about 1693 onward, Thomasius had also begun to doubt that there could be such a thing as a single true Christian doctrine at all. In his earlier writings, he had still assumed the existence of a body of Christian doctrine, which was simple, evident, and based on scriptural revelation, and whose meaning would become clear once philosophy had been banned from theological debate. From the mid-1690s, however, Thomasius denied even the existence of this simple doctrine. The reason was that the subject of doctrines was God and the divine mysteries, which were incomprehensible to human understanding. Thomasius now concluded that no doctrinal opinions could be an accurate representation of God's attributes or of mysteries such as the Holy Trinity. For, even if these doctrines were based on divine revelation, revelation had been presented and adapted to a weak and limited human understanding by the Creator. Doctrinal opinions were only metaphors, which were derived from things familiar to humans and which represented their divine objects "improperly and imperfectly."[31] No metaphor was ever exclusively true. Metaphors could be false, because they could be misleading, but it was also possible for several different metaphors to be used to signify the same mystery of faith. "Orthodoxy" in the proper sense of the word, an exclusively true belief, thus did not exist, because there were several ways to conceive of the divine mysteries, which ultimately were beyond human comprehension. The love and veneration of God, which was the essence of faith, could be expressed in many different opinions or doctrines, all of which were equally valid, if they were professed with a sincere heart. The purpose of scripture was not to provide humans with doctrines, but to be a sort of manual of regeneration, which informed humans of the origins and nature of their corruption and the nature of its remedies.

Orthodox Lutherans considered Thomasius's arguments to be typical of millenarian, enthusiastic sects such as the Quakers or the Philadelphic societies, who rejected the formulaic faith of established churches in favor of a "living" or "spiritual" faith of the heart. Although the orthodox generally agreed that doctrine was not alone sufficient for faith, "faith," however sincere, that was not guided by true doctrine was blind. An important distinction made by the orthodox in this context was that between *fides quae creditur* and *fides qua creditur*. *Fides quae creditur* ("faith that is believed") came from the doctrines based on scripture. *Fides qua creditur* ("faith with which a belief is held") represented the trust in God and the sincerity with which a person believed in these doctrines. Sincere faith, the orthodox argued, required both. As Gustav Philipp Mörl wrote, "true faith was never found without love toward God, nor love toward God without true faith."[32] However, enthusiasts like Thomasius, the orthodox claimed, reduced faith to a pure *fides qua creditur*, a trust or love that was not guided by doctrinal beliefs. "We should beware," Mörl warned, "how the Devil could try to subvert our faith by spreading this dogma."[33] According to Joachim Fecht, "our reverence must not be stupid [*brutus*], such that we revere God and Christ but are ignorant of who he is, whom we revere, or how we should revere him or why; instead it must be with the mind and the understanding."[34] And in the words of Albrecht Christian Roth, a preacher at the Leipzig *Nicolaikirche* and adversary of Thomasius throughout the 1690s, faith required first knowledge (*notitia*) of its message, then assent by the intellect (*assensus*). The recognition of scriptural truth then led to trust in God (*fiducia*).[35]

Justification and salvation required *fides quae creditur*. The virtuous conduct and love for God that Thomasius expected to be brought about by regeneration were by themselves insufficient. In particular, the orthodox insisted that regeneration in Thomasius's sense did not eradicate the guilt of original sin. A person who had undergone regeneration might lead a perfectly blameless life, but even then he or she would be damned in the afterlife, if the stain of original sin remained, inherited from the protoplasts. Nobody could expunge this by his or her own efforts without the help of Christ, whose death on the cross had offered humankind the remission of its sins. Without Christ's intercession with the Father, eternal death was inevitable, but Christ would only intercede on behalf of those who believed in him. However piously and uprightly a person lived in this life, nobody could escape eternal damnation without Christ's *meritum*, his atonement for original sin: "God makes a person just (but he makes him just, who believes in Christ)."[36] As Roth put it, Thomasius failed to keep apart *fides justificans* (the faith that justifies before God) and *fides regenerans* (the faith that leads to regeneration) and simply conflated the two.[37] The belief that justification required only regeneration rather than the knowledge of Christ's sacrifice, the orthodox believed, was in effect a return to the papist belief in the efficacy of good works.

In addition, Thomasius's opinion on doctrine and the written word could not be reconciled with the orthodox Lutherans' basic conceptions of the church, religious faith, and salvation. The institutional church, the *ecclesia visibilis*, in orthodox theology was defined by its consensus on a body of doctrine derived from scripture. Orthodox Lutheran theory distinguished between the church triumphant after the Last Judgment and the church militant in the *saeculum*, the world before that time. The church militant consisted of the *ecclesia invisibilis* and the *ecclesia visibilis*. The former was the invisible and universal church of all Christians, the latter the sum of all human congregations, which contained the members of the invisible church as well as those who were formal members of a Christian congregation without being true Christians, such as hypocrites, sinners, and those still struggling to attain Christian faith. In exceptional cases there might be Christians outside the visible church, but normally Christian faith was presented to a person through the visible church, and God's providence took care that nobody would be denied the opportunity of accepting the gift of salvation before the Last Judgment.[38]

Membership in the visible church thus did not guarantee salvation. Nevertheless, it fulfilled an important role in guiding its members toward eternal life, because it taught the saving doctrine of the Gospel to them. Whether they adopted this doctrine or not was something the visible church could not determine, but it had to ensure that the doctrine of the Gospel was presented correctly and went unchallenged in public, though every member of the congregation was free to differ from the church's opinion in private. The visible church was not meant to be identical with the invisible community of the saints, but it had to be undisturbed in its task of teaching the foundations of Christian faith. As Johann Benedict Carpzov, a Leipzig professor of theology and opponent of Thomasius in the 1690s, wrote, in the human church it was requisite that "a sentence [was] passed, in which the errors [were] condemned and silence [was] imposed on their authors or protagonists, and which [was] brought to the notice of everyone by promulgating it in public."[39] This, he continued, differed from the private opinion of individual believers.[40] The purpose of such a sentence by the church was threefold: to separate true from false doctrine, end disputes among theologians, and restore peace in the church. The peace might not be perfect, because it permitted sinners, hypocrites, and imperfect Christians to rub shoulders with the true Christians in the visible church, but it was a state of peace appropriate to the *ecclesia militans*.[41]

Thomasius's reduction of faith to love and of doctrines to metaphors made it impossible for the church to distinguish true doctrines from false. The result, orthodox Lutherans claimed, would be "indifferentism," the belief that salvation was possible with any set of religious beliefs.[42] Wernsdorfer in a Wittenberg dissertation included Thomasius in a long list of "indifferentists" and "Fanatics."[43] In Rostock, the orthodox theologian Joachim Fecht criticized Thomasius's "indifferentism" in doctrinal questions;[44] this, far from reflecting tolerance in questions of doctrine, was a sign of Thomasius's characteristically enthusiastic hostility toward *any* doctrinal conception of Christian faith.

THE RESPONSE OF THE HALLE THEOLOGIANS

It was not only orthodox Lutherans, however, who considered Thomasius's change of mind to be a case of religious enthusiasm. Even Pietists were keen to distance themselves from Thomasius's recent, more extreme views. However critical Pietists were of traditional Lutheranism, they did not agree with Thomasius's complete "enthusiastic" abandonment of orthodox doctrine as a standard of true faith.

This is brought out particularly clearly by the disputes that developed from Johann Friedrich Mayer's critique of Pietism, the *Report of a Swedish Theologian on the Pietists* in 1706,[45] in which he accused the Halle theological faculty of "enthusiasm." Within a year, both the Halle theological faculty and August Hermann Francke had published replies in which they claimed their own teachings to be impeccably orthodox. The Halle theologians protested against the very term "Pietists," saying that their opponents should consider "the unspeakable harm that has been done with the word 'Pietists'" and avoid it.[46] It was, moreover, unjust defamation to describe theologians such as Spener or Francke as "the most terrible enthusiasts and seducers," as their opponents did.[47]

Mayer had accused the theologians in Halle of locating faith "not in the intellect, but exclusively in the human will,"[48] because they did not consider scripture to be God's word,[49] denied the existence of heresy,[50] and believed that salvation was possible without Christ's death on the cross, on the basis only of the individual's holiness of life, which was achieved in regeneration.[51] They thus came full circle and returned to a papist belief in the sufficiency of good works in attaining salvation.[52] Whether they admitted it or not, they were enthusiasts.

All of these accusations, the Halle theologians protested, were unfounded, because they believed faith to be *fides quae creditur*, though it had to be adopted sincerely in order to bring about the regeneration of the will.[53] Orthodox Lutheran doctrine, they wrote, conformed to scripture, Christ was the necessary mediator between God and humans, and good works did not contribute to salvation. One important reservation the Halle theologians did express was that the orthodox emphasis on justification through faith alone was excessive and instilled a false sense of security in believers. By saying that good works were not necessary for salvation, orthodox theologians led their congregations to believe that faith was not even necessarily accompanied by good works. Good works, the Halle theologians insisted, were not meritorious or efficacious with respect to salvation, but once a person had been truly converted, he or she inevitably performed good works, because faith effected the regeneration of the believer's nature.[54] Insisting on good works, therefore, did not mean that they were held necessary to contribute to salvation. It meant that a person who professed to be Christian but did not perform good works could not be sincere. The excessive insistence on justification through faith alone and the neglect of good works thus encouraged a superficial and superstitious faith, by which the members of a congregation hoped to achieve eternal life even though their corrupt nature had not been transformed by faith.[55] There was no reason, however, why an insistence on good works should not be compatible with the Lutheran belief in justification by faith alone, not works. As Paul Anton, one of the leading figures of the Leipzig Pietist movement and later of the movement in Halle, wrote, "living faith is not without the effort to perform good works, but faith justifies man before God without the assistance of our works."[56]

In his critique, Mayer often referred to Thomasius, who, he wrote, "had defended the cause of many main enthusiasts against the orthodox."[57] Also, together with his students Enno Brenneysen and Jakob Friedrich Ludovici, Thomasius had written in defense of indifferentism,[58] ridiculed doctrinal orthodoxy, and asserted that pagans could be saved without believing in Christ.[59] He had rejected the *fides quae creditur* altogether and maintained that saving grace was a matter of the will, not the intellect.[60] In effect, Mayer equated Thomasius's position with that of the Halle theological faculty.

The Halle theologians' response was to distance themselves from Thomasius by protesting that he and his students were jurists, over whom the Halle theological faculty exercised no influence. Although the works of some of the jurists that had offended the orthodox (such as Johann Samuel Stryck's *De Jure Sabbathi*) had been printed at the Halle orphanage's press, the Halle theological faculty was not responsible for them. The orphanage press was also the university press and censorship was a matter for the faculty whose member published the work, not the director of the orphanage, that is, August Hermann Francke.[61] In its defense, the faculty could point to the fact that Breithaupt, one of the professors of theology in Halle, had criticized Thomasius's writings on heresy in 1697. Breithaupt had argued that there could be criteria of true and false in questions of doctrine, contrary to Thomasius's opinion. While the divine mysteries themselves might be incomprehensible, they had to be distinguished from the meaning of words used to describe them in scripture, which could be understood and which conveyed an imperfect but nevertheless "positive and truthful knowledge [of them] . . . insofar as the Holy Ghost intends to produce it in us, according to humans' capacity to understand them."[62] Thomasius had clearly become the cause of deep irritation to the Halle theological faculty. In 1700, Francke and Breithaupt had written a letter to Thomasius, in which they criticized him for encroaching on theological matters in his law lectures and putting forward his own interpretations of scripture in public, which only trained theologians were permitted to do. It was also claimed that he mocked theologians and led his students astray, encouraging them to stay away from church, avoid confession, and scorn the truths of salvificatory faith.[63]

THE REJECTION OF ENTHUSIASM

Although Thomasius never succumbed to his critics, the charge of enthusiasm was sufficiently serious for him to clarify his notion of religion a second time from the early 1700s onward. In a second piece, published in 1708, on Poiret's *De Eruditione*, Thomasius explained that he had distanced himself from the view he had held in 1693, namely, that regeneration was brought about by the divine illumination of the spirit, which then was able to discipline the natural *anima* and suppress its corrupt desires. In 1708, Thomasius observed that this conception of regeneration was prone to lead to enthusiasm, as it was criticized and described by Locke in his *Essay concerning Human Understanding*.[64] "Gradually," Thomasius wrote in 1708, "I was convinced by various observations that this path was highly dangerous and led to enthusiasm,"[65] the appeal to personal religious experiences as foundation of faith.

From around 1700, therefore, Thomasius tried to find a middle way between traditional orthodoxy, which he continued to oppose, and enthusiasm. This middle way, however, differed from the moderate and rational "religious Enlightenment" described by David Sorkin, which combined a confident philosophical rationalism with the acceptance of scriptural revelation.[66] Thomasius's compromise between orthodox superstition and fanatical enthusiasm was not based on a particularly optimistic view of the powers of natural reason. He retained his belief in the primacy of the human will over the intellect, which meant that reason followed, rather than guided, the impulses of the will. As long as the will was not reformed, therefore, reason would remain the instrument of its corrupt desire. It was not in itself and never could be a self-sufficient standard of truth and virtue.

One reason why his earlier view seemed so close to enthusiasm was that the regeneration by divine grace Thomasius wrote of in his 1694 piece was a supranatural event. Regeneration restored the rule by the divine spirit in humans over the corrupt nature of the soul. It was a miraculous occurrence, in that it took place outside of the natural order, and there could be no "natural method of moving from the state of foolishness to that of wisdom, but all improvement would be supranatural and by miracle."[67] Because regeneration thus took place by miracle, not in a way that was accessible to the natural powers of understanding, it had to remain mysterious to anyone but the person who had experienced it. This opened the door to enthusiasts' claims to personal inspiration by God, claims that were unverifiable by others, as Locke had noted: "Every Conceit that thoroughly warms our Fancies must pass for an Inspiration, if there be nothing but the strength of our Perswasion."[68]

Thomasius continued to argue that faith was brought about by regeneration and that regeneration was a gift of divine grace. The difference, however, between this form of regeneration and his earlier "enthusiastic" beliefs was that Thomasius now considered regeneration to be a natural rather than a supranatural process. This change required first of all a modification of his anthropology, in particular the rejection of his previous belief in a tripartite human essence (material body, soul, and spirit) in which the divine spirit could be illuminated and strengthened by God to suppress the corrupt nature of the soul (*anima*). His earlier distinction between the natural *anima* and the divine *spiritus*, he said, had been the foundation of the other errors in his earlier, quasi-enthusiastic view.[69] This was an important concession to his orthodox critics. Roth, only a few years before, had described the notion of the tripartite nature of man as one of the principal errors in Thomasius's thought,[70] as had the orthodox theologians Valentin Löscher[71] and Justus Rumpaeus.[72] Thomasius now no longer located rational love in a separate, divine spirit that was opposed to the corrupt passions of the created soul. Human nature was bipartite, consisting of a material body and a spiritual, created soul (*anima*). *Amor rationalis* was the product of a balance between the three passions in this *anima*, which were not bad in themselves, but only if they were present in excess: "I no longer teach that man is composed of a good and an evil spirit, nor that rational love is a fourth passion, properly distinct from lust, avarice, and ambition, but that it [rational love] is a tempered mixture of these three."[73]

Although Thomasius had now abandoned the belief in supranatural divine illumination as the foundation of faith, he still considered regeneration to be a gift of divine grace, which was not necessarily mediated by scripture but came from God directly. Doctrine was still irrelevant to his notion of faith, and he continued to be described as an enthusiast by the orthodox. Regeneration followed prayers, meditation, and contrition: "Pray to God . . . that he direct your actions with his grace and providence, that you may attain the desired end by achieving felicity."[74] If there was a formula for imploring God for wisdom and temporal felicity, it lay in the Lord's Prayer,[75] though formulae themselves were never enough:[76] "before God, the scrutinizer of hearts, sighs effect more than prolixity."[77] For, in the last resort, wisdom was a "habit of divine virtue and the most subtle spirit," which was attracted by the "magnet of prayer, so to speak," and through which "foolishness in us is suffocated and bound."[78] As for scripture, it was still to be regarded as a sort of manual for regeneration, not as a source of doctrinal truth. It drew attention to the corrupt nature of humans, its causes in the will, and its remedy, divine grace. "The student of wisdom will find no better book that leads to a true understanding of nature and oneself than scripture."[79] Unlike the classical and mainly pagan philosophical texts, scripture did not assume that reason was the dominant part of human nature, and it was from this rather than from pagan authors that one was to look for "the basic principles about GOD, his works and creatures, the condition, essence and powers of humans, divine will, human felicity, and the means of acquiring it."[80] Although he had modified his earlier views to avoid enthusiasm, Thomasius's ideas therefore remained very heterodox, and were considered as such by his contemporaries. On many occasions he was cited together with radical theologians such as Conrad Dippel (the author of the *Papismus Protestantium Vapulans*), the ecclesiastical historian Gottfried Arnold, or even the French mystic Antoinette Bourignon.[81]

FAITH, PHILOSOPHY, AND WISDOM

It is important to realize that Thomasius's heterodox and "enthusiastic" religious beliefs were not opposed to his philosophical concerns but, on the contrary, were closely related to them. They were relevant in particular to his views on the need for a broader reform of learning and for removing the corruption caused by "scholasticism." In his *Cautelae circa Praecognita Jurisprudentiae* of 1710, for example, it is noticeable how faith is constantly linked to *sapientia* (wisdom), in a broad sense, while false faith is identified with foolishness (*stultitia*). For although Thomasius believed that philosophy and faith were conceptually distinct and, indeed, had to be kept distinct, he also argued that the corruption of either religion or philosophy inevitably affected the other. Correcting the orthodox views on religious faith, therefore, was also a necessary step toward the improvement of philosophy and secular learning in general.

Thomasius's deep concern with the close relation between faith and philosophy is already evident in his writings of the late 1680s and early 1690s. There he argued that the misguided application of philosophical arguments to theological controversies had led to sectarian disputes and the decline of charity. This damaging use of philosophical reasoning reflected misconceptions about the nature of both philosophy and theology, and was a sign that philosophers and theologians were overestimating the powers of natural reason, on which philosophy was based, and were also failing to understand that theology was based purely on scriptural revelation, without the addition of human argument. In essence, Thomasius's point was that we should be content with what God had revealed and resist the temptation to subject the divine to the scrutiny of human reason, which, while it was essential to understanding the temporal world, was an inadequate resource for exploring the divine.

As Thomasius's notion of faith and his anthropology changed from the mid-1690s onward, so did his notion of the relationship between philosophy and faith. Thomasius continued to emphasize the inscrutability of God, but he now also began to stress the importance of the will rather than the understanding in explaining human nature. The essence of the will, he now said, was not free choice but love, that is, a desire or passion that impelled humans toward certain actions, in pursuit of a particular end, be it wealth, honor, physical pleasure (the three ends of corrupt human nature), or the divine (the end of regenerate human nature). The understanding was the instrument of this will-as-desire, not its guide.

Thomasius also combined with this view of human nature a more common notion of the practical purposes of both philosophy and religion, without which all learning, whether theological or philosophical, was mere empty pedantry.[82] Clearly, this was similar to the religious concerns of contemporary theologians like Spener, that religion should not be limited to theoretical knowledge of the truths of faith but should be reflected in the believer's conduct. But it also drew on a much longer tradition of critiques of learned pedantry, which went back at least to early sixteenth-century satires by humanists such as Sebastian Brant on bookish learning.[83] The emphasis on the practical effect of learning meant that the will became the main focus of Thomasius's philosophy and religious thought. Informing the understanding was futile, because the end to which the will directed human actions was prior to the processes of the understanding. As Thomasius wrote in 1710, "foolish thoughts cannot be thrown out, as long as the will drives the understanding toward foolish thoughts."[84]

"Scholastic" orthodox Lutheranism, Thomasius believed, both reflected and reinforced a failure to understand these central truths about human nature. The "scholastics" assumed that the purpose of religion was to inform the *understanding* with the correct opinions about God, the nature of justification, the merit of Christ's death on the cross, and so on. In other words, they assumed that doctrinal truth would be the key to salvation. Thomasius not only claimed that a single correct opinion on questions of faith was not possible because ultimately divine matters were incomprehensible and could be represented only in metaphors. He also wrote that those doctrinal opinions were irrelevant to achieving faith, because they were powerless to lead to the redirection of the will from its corrupt love for worldly goods to the pure yearning for the true good, that is, God. In that respect, pride in even the subtlest knowledge was foolishness, because knowledge in itself was useless without the transformation of the will. It was a common error, Thomasius wrote, to believe that "subtle knowledge of the good is enough and . . . leads to human felicity."[85] In a footnote, he added that "[t]his final foolishness is therefore the greatest of all, because it is almost incurable, and it is founded in the universal doctrine of the schools that the felicity of man depends on the intellect. On this basis we have said elsewhere that the learned fools are greater than all others."[86]

Thomasius argued that the orthodox emphasis on doctrine rather than the state of the believer's will was deliberate and not an inadvertent mistake. It was part of an attempt to use religion as a pretext for the pursuit of secular power. In particular, it allowed the clergy to present theological doctrine as an essential part of Christian faith, while they claimed at the same time to be ultimate arbiters in all doctrinal questions. Thomasius argued that this allowed the orthodox Lutheran church to become a system justifying clerical political power, which was very similar to that exercised by the papal church over Roman Catholics. One of the aims of this critique of Lutheran "papalism" by Thomasius was political. It was intended to question the orthodox Lutherans' view of the proper relationship between the secular prince and his church, and to argue that the prince should enjoy far more extensive rights of intervention in the affairs of his territory's church than the orthodox Lutheran church was prepared to concede.

CHAPTER THREE

THE PRINCE AND THE CHURCH: THE CRITIQUE OF "LUTHERAN PAPALISM"

As early as the end of the 1680s, Thomasius had blamed the corruption of faith on the self-interest of clergymen, who tried to turn religion into a pretext for pursuing their own ends. Their contrived philosophical glosses on theological questions allowed them to distort revelation and to establish their "primacy within the church and [their] control of secular power,"[1] by pretending that their particular interpretation of scripture was based on superior expertise and represented the only true faith. Rival opinions were labeled heretical, although, Thomasius argued, it was precisely the "scholastics'" introduction of philosophy into religious debate that produced schisms and heresies, which eventually damaged the most important Christian virtue of all, charity. The critique of this orthodox Lutheran "priestcraft"[2] or "papalism" remained a central part of Thomasius's thought in the following years, and it became even more prominent when his theological views changed around 1693 and Thomasius no longer believed there was any need for doctrine in Christian religion at all.

An important aim of Thomasius's criticism was to strengthen the powers of the secular ruler over his territory's church, in particular, the powers of the Calvinist prince of Brandenburg to intervene in the affairs of his territory's Lutheran congregations. Thomasius's defense of the ruler's rights is often described as secular, absolutist, and statist. It is seen as part of the emergence in the Holy Roman Empire after the 1648 Peace of Westphalia of a deconfessionalized system of sovereign territorial states. The religious plurality and toleration introduced by the peace, it is argued, meant that political power could no longer assume confessional homogeneity in a particular territory and thus could not rest on a religious basis.[3]

The Peace of Westphalia, however, did not separate law and politics from confessional questions in principle, but produced only a multi-confessional settlement. It extended official toleration to one confession that had not enjoyed it previously under imperial law, because it had not been included in the Peace of Augsburg of 1555, that is, Calvinism. The 1648 Peace also abolished the prince's *ius reformandi*, the right to impose his confession on his territory's population, and allowed each of the three main confessions, Roman Catholic, Lutheran, and Calvinist, at least a limited measure of religious toleration and worship in the empire. The peace, however, did not apply to any further religious communities, and it remained legitimate for a prince to ban worship by other dissenting sects and to expel them from his lands. The 1648 settlement was intended only to define and protect the legal status of a limited number of specific confessions in the Empire, not to establish a general principle that religious beliefs could not be the subject of legal and political regulation.[4]

In addition, the 1648 Peace did not see the emergence of sovereign statehood within the empire, because territorial sovereignty continued to be restricted by the framework of imperial law and the imperial courts. The Holy Roman Empire remained a flawed but functioning system of legal arbitration and conflict resolution, until the invasion of the French revolutionary armies in the 1790s led to major territorial redistributions, which eventually brought about the demise of the empire in 1806. Until that time, the empire remained an association of nearly four hundred semi-autonomous territories, most of which were content with less than full sovereignty, because the legal framework of the empire, which restricted their independence, also guaranteed their existence against the ambitions of more powerful territorial states.[5]

Thomasius did not question this legal relationship between territorial princes and the emperor. The terms in which he justified the prince's rights against the clergy were not based purely on secular principles of government, although these did play some role in his argument. The prince's duty of preserving civil peace, in particular, was important. These ideas, however, are not sufficient to explain Thomasius's view of the powers he believed the prince should have over ecclesiastical affairs and his criticism of clerical interference in worldly government.[6] For this, Thomasius drew on a conception of the secular ruler as a godly prince who aimed to reduce or even remove superstitious beliefs and rituals within his territory's church.

RELIGIOUS DOCTRINE AND "LUTHERAN PAPALISM"

In contrast to his earlier writings, in which he had still distinguished true from false doctrinal orthodoxy, Thomasius from around 1693 onward criticized *any* emphasis on doctrinal orthodoxy as an example of clerical self-interest or "Lutheran papalism." The term "orthodox" (*rechtgläubig*) had still possessed positive connotations in a treatise he published in 1689,[7] but by the mid-1690s it had acquired a heavily ironical and negative undertone. He now conceived of the Christian church as a spiritual community, united by its members' charity toward each other and their love of God. Differences in doctrines and rituals did not distinguish true faith from false, but only particular sectarian communities from each other. Although he had stressed the need for charity and sincerity among Christians as early as the late 1680s, he had still assumed then that faith required the adoption of particular doctrinal beliefs, which were evident from scripture, unless it was polluted by philosophy. From about 1693, however, Thomasius went further and argued that not even scripture contained a self-evident doctrinal basis for Christian faith. No such thing as "orthodoxy" existed, but the belief in it was deliberately encouraged by the clergy to justify its authority over the laity. In two disputations on heresy, for example, the *An Haeresis sit Crimen* and the *De Jure Principis circa Haereticos*, both published in 1697, Thomasius criticized the orthodox Lutherans for their conception of heresy as the deviation from a certain set of doctrines. Orthodoxy was never the true faith, but only the opinion of the sect which happened to be dominant at a particular time. The clergy of the orthodox faction "wants to hold sway over consciences and has a secular arm willing to serve its intention, that is, either the prince or the greater part of the people. That is, they have the intention and the means to dominate."[8] "Orthodoxy" was a pretext to stigmatize dissenters as heretics who could then be persecuted.

For example, the excommunication of those who dissented from orthodox doctrine was not a legitimate measure of ecclesiastical discipline but an instrument of clerical domination: "the clerics have turned ecclesiastical discipline into a secular punishment. . . . ecclesiastical discipline is a matter of coercion, for it is imposed, so to speak, by the verdict of the consistory and is often executed by the worldly power, if they [the excommunicated] are not tolerated in the congregation."[9] Excommunication, as it was practiced, was contrary to the nature of the church. While human societies based on an agreement (*pactum*) could exclude any of their members who did not adhere to the society's rules, Christian congregations were different, because they were not founded for the sake of the self-interest of their members but for a higher purpose, their salvation. They were comparable to marriage, which, similarly, should not be dissolved lightly. In the very early Christian church, when faith was still pure, a person who did not act as a Christian should was shunned, but never excluded from communion and the church.[10]

Doctrine could be an instrument of clerical deceit only because the structure of the church government gave the clergy the power to define which doctrines were to be considered true. The administration of the church's affairs in orthodox Lutheran theory was founded on the so-called *Dreiständelehre*, according to which the church consisted of the same three estates that also constituted secular society, that is, the clergy, the secular magistrate, and the remainder of the laity. The categories of the three estates already had been used by Luther, but only to describe human society in general, not as a principle on which to found the regulation of ecclesiastical affairs. One of the first to incorporate the *Dreiständelehre* into a theory of church government was the jurist Theodor Reinking in his Giessen doctoral dissertation of 1616,[11] and in 1695, Thomasius's adversary in Leipzig, Johann Benedict Carpzov, also drew heavily on the *Dreiständelehre* in his defense of traditional Lutheran church government.

According to this theory, each of the three estates fulfilled a particular function in the administration of the church, "according to the respective capacity of each estate."[12] The purpose of this distribution of functions was to maintain *ordo*, order, in the human church's regulation of its affairs, but this *ordo* was disturbed and the teaching of Christian faith suffered if any of these estates exceeded the limits of their proper role in church government and encroached on the rights of the other estates. When, for example, the clergy assumed more than its legitimate authority, the church lapsed into Papo-Caesarism, of which the papal church was the classical example, though Thomasius argued that orthodox Lutheranism suffered from the same problem.[13] When the magistrate usurped the rights of the other two estates, the government of the church degenerated into Caesaro-Papism, while church government by the laity alone was described as Fanaticism or Enthusiasm and associated with the complete rejection of all established doctrines and rituals, as well as civil unrest and sedition. The historical example orthodox Lutherans referred to frequently was the Anabaptists of the 1520s and 1530s,[14] while late seventeenth-century Pietists and millenarian sects were considered the Anabaptists' modern equivalent.

In a well-ordered church, as orthodox Lutherans understood it, the clerical estate acted as a repository of doctrinal truth, which was the standard of Christian faith. As Carpzov explained, referring to a passage from the Old Testament, Malachi 2:7, the "priest's lips shall preserve the doctrine, in order that the law be sought from his mouth, for he is a messenger of the Lord."[15] Although this passage was from the Old Testament, its formulation showed that it expressed a general rule, which was applicable to Christianity, too.[16] The "priest's lips" signified that the priest's duty consisted not only in preparing sacrifices but, even more importantly, "in explaining and preaching God's words."[17] The priest was "like a kind of ark in which the saving doctrine received in the word rests pure and unblemished like the most precious treasure."[18] This function did not confer a particular power of interpretation on the priesthood. Any Christian was competent to determine scriptural truth, but it was the particular duty of the priesthood to pronounce this evident scriptural truth when asked to do so in doctrinal controversies, so that the infallibility of the clergy's statements was inherent in scripture, not produced by its clerical interpreters.

Though the clergy pronounced on scriptural truth, they could not turn their opinion into a binding decree without the concurrence of the magistrate. His power, the *potestas externa* over the church, extended "to the degree that he [the magistrate] assembles the ministers to resolve controversies, entrusts them with taking a decision, examines, decrees, executes and also prescribes the procedure."[19] The laity had the right to approve the decisions taken by the clergy and the magistrate. In the case of the appointment of ministers, for example, this could mean that a candidate for a position was rejected by the congregation. "And, to put it briefly," the jurist Theodor Reinking summarized the distribution of functions in the example of the appointment of ministers, "the ecclesiastical estate must advise on the proper person; the people must give its approval, and the magistrate must take the decision."[20] Every measure by the church had to be an act of the entire church, the product of the concurrence of all three estates.[21]

This orthodox Lutheran *Dreiständelehre* imposed two main restrictions on the prince's power over the Lutheran church within his territory. First, it limited participation in ecclesiastical affairs to those princes who were also members of the Lutheran church. Although these princes regulated the *externa* by virtue of their role as magistrate, they first had to be a member of the Lutheran church. For if the prince believed in false doctrines, he could not be involved in a process whose purpose was the determination of doctrinal truth. Thus a prince like the Calvinist elector of Brandenburg, for example, could not be admitted to a role in Lutheran church government. His exclusion from church government, however, Lutherans argued, did not imply political disobedience on their part, since the administration of the church's affairs was no part of the prince's *secular* duties, which were separate from his *religious* functions as a Lutheran, and denying him a role in church government therefore did not encroach on his secular power. The prince thus sustained two separate and independent *personae*, one secular and one religious. No prince, whether he was Lutheran, Calvinist, or of any other religion, had any reason to interfere in ecclesiastical matters *qua* secular prince. He only did so as a *Lutheran* prince, and this was why the Calvinist elector should not insist on intervening in the affairs of his Lutheran church if he did not share their doctrinal beliefs. Civil peace did not require him to decide on the appointment of ministers or any other question in which the Lutheran ruler was involved, and so he should respect his Lutheran subjects' conscience and not intrude on the matters central to their faith.

Thomasius criticized this orthodox Lutheran argument as no more than a pretext. By arguing that there was no such thing as a "true" orthodox doctrine, he suggested that there was no real religious reason why the Calvinist prince should not appoint Lutheran ministers, for example. The Calvinist prince's doctrinal beliefs were just one set of opinions, a set that was not necessarily any more or less true than that of another religious sect. At first, Thomasius's indifference to doctrinal truth might appear to imply that the prince could impose his doctrines on the Lutheran church, since there was no single set of true doctrinal beliefs. This, of course, was what the Lutherans feared. Thomasius, however, was not suggesting that the prince could *impose* his doctrinal beliefs on the Lutheran church but that the Lutherans had no reason to fear he would do so. As there was no such thing as doctrinal truth, the Calvinist prince had no reason to want to compel his Lutheran subjects to adopt his beliefs, and therefore it was safe to allow him to perform the same functions as a Lutheran prince in the government of his church's affairs.

The second limitation on the prince's power was that, even if he was Lutheran, the *Dreiständelehre* did not allow him any influence over the so-called internal matters (*interna*) of the church, that is, its doctrinal beliefs and rituals, without the authority of the clergy. Thomasius had argued that there was no need for either the prince or the church to prescribe certain doctrinal beliefs, since all doctrines were no more than metaphors. Rituals were, however, different from doctrinal beliefs, and Thomasius was concerned to show that the prince did have the power to change or even abolish certain ritual practices.

The Godly Prince and the Reform of Ritual

The reformation of ritual practices was a major issue of contention between the Calvinist prince of Brandenburg and the Lutheran church in his territories. When the elector turned to Calvinism in 1613, his aim was to purge the Protestant church in his lands of vestiges of "superstitious" and "papalist" ceremonies. The first Reformation in Brandenburg had been a particularly cautious modification of the old faith: auricular confession, exorcism in baptism, saints' images in churches, and the wearing of chasubles, for example, were all retained in the Lutheran church of Brandenburg. When Elector Johann Sigismund in 1615 tried to have all saints' images and sidealtars removed from the Berlin *Dom*, which, after all, was his court church, there were riots in which even the elector's wife sided with the protesters.[22]

Thomasius believed the prince should enjoy the right to reform religious rituals in his lands, even against the will of the Lutheran church. The key to Thomasius's defense of the prince's rights was his transformation of the Lutheran concept of *adiaphora*, those religious rituals that were not considered strictly necessary for salvation. They were the result of human convention and belonged to the established practices of a particular human church. And yet, many Lutheran theorists argued, these indifferent[23] matters could not be changed or abrogated without the approval of the clergy.

The eminent Lutheran jurist Benedict Carpzov (1596–1666),[24] for example, wrote that while uniformity in the *adiaphora* was not necessary between different churches, within one church the *adiaphora* should be uniform and should not be changed without the approval of all three orders of the church, the laity, the clergy, and the magistrate.

The most important justification for protecting *adiaphora* to such an extent was *scandalum* (scandal), an offense to fellow believers, which was also a violation of charity and could be the occasion of sin in others.[25] The reason why the reformation or abolition of *adiaphora* could produce *scandalum* was that the "simple and unlearned"[26] among the parishioners were unable to distinguish between merely customary practices and those that were essential for salvation. Changing or abolishing *adiaphora* would shock and confuse them, because "they believe that there is much theological truth and orthodox religion" in them.[27] It would probably even lead them into sin, as their faith would be shaken by changes in practices they had thought necessary for eternal life. Only when there was a very strong reason for change (as in the case of the papal church) should it occur, and then only at a synod.[28] Even if a particular *adiaphoron* was not necessary to attaining faith and another ritual would serve the same purpose equally well, it was advisable not to change it precipitously, since "the canon in the exercise of *adiaphora* is charity; if we violate it, we sin by making unrestrained use of our liberty."[29]

The Lutheran church had to stand firm on these *adiaphora*, especially when it was under pressure from hostile confessions, as it had been from Catholics at the time of Charles V, and from the Reformed. It was then in particular that "a clear and constant profession of faith is required from us"[30] and "no ground is to be conceded to the enemies of the gospel, even in indifferent matters."[31] For otherwise the *infirmi* among the believers would be scandalized, begin to doubt the truth of their religious beliefs, and be led astray, into far more serious errors of faith.

Thomasius was critical of the orthodox argument that *adiaphora* had to be preserved to avoid scandal. Again, he considered this no more than a pretext for protecting the clergy's power over religious affairs and for excluding the Calvinist prince from them. He argued instead not only that the prince enjoyed the right to alter *adiaphora* but that nearly all ecclesiastical rituals were *adiaphora* and therefore subject to the will of the prince. In his *De Jure Principis circa Adiaphora* (*On the Right of the Prince in Indifferent Matters*) of 1695, for example, Thomasius wrote that Christianity, unlike Judaism, did not require elaborate ceremonial practices. When Christ came into the world, the "pomp of sacrifices and other rituals was abolished, *and all external ceremonies, with the exception of those that Christ specifically imposed on his disciples—for example, baptism, the Eucharist etc.—are indifferent matters.*"[32] The ceremonies that Christ did introduce were very few and simple,[33] and they were binding for humans because they were part of divine positive law, that is, the divine commands promulgated to humanity by specific acts of revelation. All other rituals were *adiaphora*, which were not required for salvation.

In the years following the publication of his dissertation on *adiaphora* in 1695, Thomasius even came to the conclusion that *no* ceremonies at all were commanded by God, and that therefore all forms of worship were *adiaphora*. The reason why he moved away from the idea that revelation required any ceremonial practices at all was that he abandoned the concept of a divine positive law on which these ceremonial laws rested. Positive law by definition had a punishment attached to it, but the existence of a punishment implied that the law was not necessarily in the subject's interest. For if it were, there would be no need for compulsion and the threat of sanctions, but only for persuasion. The reason for punishments in positive laws was that they were in the interest of the lawgiver, who wanted to make sure they were obeyed, but God could not derive any benefit from humans' performance of certain acts of worship and therefore had no interest in it.[34] Moreover, divine positive law was another instrument of "papalist" clergymen,[35] because it allowed priests to turn themselves into legislators who derived fictitious laws on ceremony from scriptural passages, although scripture was not intended to be a prescriptive law,[36] as Christ and the apostles only taught what could be done with a good conscience "and nothing more. They do not, however, coerce."[37] Priests, however, claimed that this advice in scripture was a divine command, supported by the threat of punishment, and the result was to strengthen clerical power over the laity.[38]

Thomasius's criticism of divine positive law thus eventually reduced all ceremonies to the status of *adiaphora*, human conventions, which were not essential for salvation. His view on ritual and its significance for faith was very similar to his conception of doctrine: forms of external worship, like doctrines, were exchangeable and no particular ritual was divinely prescribed. What mattered was whether the form of worship chosen was a sincere expression of the believer's love and veneration of God, that is, of the "inner worship" (*cultus internus*). The form of this expression was irrelevant, and the love toward God did not even have to be expressed in any outward signs of worship at all, since God did not profit from them and did not require them to judge the individual's state of faith.

However, although there was an infinite number of ways to worship God in an appropriate fashion, this did not mean that *every* form of worship deserved approval. There still remained a distinction between good and bad rituals, because rituals could be harmful if they encouraged the laity in the superstitious and "papalist" belief that their performance was in itself meritorious and would bring them closer to salvation:

> [E]ven if the so-called indifferent matters lie somewhere bet-
> ween precepts and prohibitions as intermediates, neverthe-
> less this middle position should not be understood as a single
> point, but with some latitude, so that it is now closer to a pro-
> hibition, now closer to a precept. . . . For what is conducive
> to edification or the purpose of Christian congregations, even
> if not necessarily, but by accident, is closer to the precepts of
> Christian religion; what, on the contrary, is an impediment to
> edification and worship is closer to being prohibited, and so
> it is praiseworthy to introduce the former and to abrogate the
> latter.[39]

When Thomasius defended the ruler's rights over religious ceremonies, he did not intend to imply that the ruler could impose ritual practices arbitrarily on his territory's church, but he did argue that the ruler should reform existing rituals that tended toward "papalist" superstition. As he put it in his 1695 dissertation on *adiaphora*, the *salus populi*, the well-being of the people, should be the supreme law (*suprema lex*). And the prince never cared better for this "well-being of his people" in indifferent matters than when he abolished superstitious ceremonies.[40] Thomasius thus presented interference by the ruler in the affairs of his territorial church as an act of a godly prince, concerned for his subjects' state of piety.

Thomasius's argument has often been seen as an example of a more secular conception of the role of the prince in ecclesiastical affairs, but the struggle against superstition is a purely religious concern.[41] How important, then, was the prince's secular power and authority for justifying his intervention in matters of religious ceremony? To a certain extent, Thomasius believed, the prince's secular office was a necessary condition of his interference. In his *On the Right of the Prince in Indifferent Matters* of 1695, Thomasius stated categorically that all external actions of citizens were subject to the regulations of the prince, to the extent that "*these actions are subordinate to the free will of the citizens both naturally and morally.* For it would be cruel to command subjects to do something *impossible*, and impious to command them to do something *immoral*."[42] As religious rituals were one form of external action that was neither impossible nor immoral, the prince did have the right to regulate ritual practices in his territorial church.

Thomasius also wrote that the purpose of the secular state was the preservation of public peace.[43] This meant that the secular prince was allowed to use coercion to prevent theological controversies from disturbing the peace of the commonwealth. This right did not restrict religious freedom because there was no reason why sincere religious belief should cause political unrest. Religion could not be the cause of sedition but only its pretext. "For, by the very fact that they stir up unrest in the commonwealth, they show sufficiently that true religion is nothing that they care

about or that is close to their heart."[44] The parties in a theological dispute
were free to hold their respective opinions without causing unrest or turning to persecution.[45] The right of the prince to suppress political unrest that
was theologically motivated, however, was a very limited right with respect
to religious affairs more generally. It allowed the magistrate to intervene
when religion was used as a pretext for sedition. But it was not sufficient
to permit him to reform rituals that were merely superstitious.

In general, there was no strong secular, political reason for the prince
to intervene in ritual practices. Thomasius always implied that the social,
moral, and political utility of religious ceremonies was very weak. Whether
or not an individual performed religious ceremonies was not significant for
civil peace. External acts of worship gave no indication to others of a person's state of heart, and it was possible for even the most godless individual to go through the external motions required by a particular ceremony,
without any sincere faith at all.[46] A far more certain sign of piety was a person's actual conduct in everyday life, whether he or she kept promises, did
good to others, and offended nobody, in short, acted according to the precepts of Christian charity. While true godliness was the foundation of sociability, it was not promoted by compelling people to attend religious
worship, for "there are many adults who attend church assiduously, but
lead a dissolute life before and after the service, enslaved to all their passions."[47] The failure to participate in divine worship gave no hint as to a
person's state of heart and thus as to his or her virtue and godliness. The
necessity or even the political and moral usefulness of external rituals could
not be proved with the resources of natural reason.[48] Thomasius was even
very critical of attempts to subordinate ceremonies to political calculations.
In his *Einleitung zur Sitte Llehre* of 1692 he wrote that

> it should be considered that if the secular interest of a com-
> monwealth is the true purpose of religious ritual one should
> have to say that divine service must differ according to the
> different republics and that the changeable interest of this or
> that republic must be the standard of a changeable divine
> service, which would seem very inappropriate and almost
> blasphemous.[49]

The right to purge the ceremonies of the church from superstition,
therefore, had to be legitimated on grounds other than secular interest or
divine command. This is unlike the argument made by Thomasius's older
friend, the jurist and philosopher Samuel Pufendorf, who argued that wor-
shipping God with external signs of reverence was an actual obligation
based on natural religion, an obligation that flowed from the recognition
by natural reason of God's omnipotence and the gratitude man was
bound to express toward his creator, though the specific form of worship

conducive to salvation had to be prescribed by revelation.[50] This natural duty to honor God in some fashion appropriate to his power and goodness allowed the secular sovereign to ban all forms of blasphemy, idolatry, which credited material objects rather than God himself with divine attributes, and atheism, which denied the existence of God or any of his essential attributes, such as his omnipotence. Humans might be hypocrites and worship was no certain indication of a reverence for God. What was certain was that blasphemers, idol-worshippers, and atheists did *not* honor God, as they should. As a consequence, they would not acknowledge themselves to be bound to fulfill the duties imposed on them by God. Among those were not only the duties of worship but also the duties of natural law, of which God was the legislator and which was essential to civic peace. This conferred the right on the secular legislator to punish those who violated the precepts of natural religion.[51]

Pufendorf's theory restricted the magistrate's right of intervention to narrower bounds than Thomasius, because Pufendorf granted this right only under the condition that natural religion was violated. If a ritual was indifferent in terms of natural religion, the prince could, in Pufendorf's opinion, neither order nor prohibit it. To Thomasius, by contrast, any obligatory ritual had to be commanded directly by God and anything left indifferent in terms of divine positive law could be subject to the prince's plans to eradicate superstition. The prince's powers over ritual were, therefore, potentially considerably greater in Thomasius's view than in the natural jurisprudential argument of Pufendorf's *De habitu religionis Christianae ad vitam civilem*. The prince, Thomasius concluded, could introduce the Gregorian calendar, decide whether instrumental music was permissible during services, or establish either confession in private or public confession.[52] Pufendorf and Thomasius are often presented as two similar critics of the Lutheran confessional state, but it is important to emphasize that Pufendorf was far more cautious than Thomasius when he defined the prince's rights over his territorial church, especially when it came to the rights of the Calvinist prince over the Lutheran church in his territory.[53] The reason for this appears to be a more skeptical attitude of Pufendorf than Thomasius toward Calvinism, which meant that he was less willing than Thomasius to allow the elector of Brandenburg to take part in the regulation of the Lutheran church's affairs.[54] Pufendorf might permit the prince to intervene on the basis of natural religion, but as soon as the minimal conditions were met, the prince's right to intervene ceased. If the Lutheran church in Brandenburg satisfied the minimal requirements of natural religion, the Calvinist elector could not impose his ideas concerning ritual on it.

Thomasius believed that indirectly it was in the prince's political interest to encourage true Christianity, because Christianity taught the elimination of the depraved passions, which were the main source of disturbance in the commonwealth.[55] The prince, however, could not establish true Christianity by legislation, or try to enforce Christianity because of its political benefits. Thomasius praised the example of the elector of Brandenburg, who had admonished his subjects to honor the Sabbath by interrupting their work and all trade on Sundays, especially at the time of divine services, and by closing public houses for the entire day.[56] These measures helped to strengthen piety, because they discouraged some of the more obvious vices, but to try and enforce a particular religious practice or belief, let alone piety itself, by laws was wrong and ineffective, because sincere Christian faith could not be brought about by the threat of force. In the *Vollstaendige Erlaeuterung der Kirchenrechts-Gelahrtheit*, Thomasius wrote that the prince should employ teachers who exhorted his subjects to recognize their corruption and to lead a Christian life, free of sin. But the prince did not do this as a prince. It was part of his duty as a Christian toward his subjects. Parents had exactly the same duties toward their children, and Thomasius even considered it preferable for parents rather than the prince to fulfill them.[57] Thomasius never advocated a "civic religion," a set of religious beliefs and practices that was designed to strengthen political loyalty. The prince was not allowed to instrumentalize religion politically: neither ceremony nor doctrine could have a legitimate political function, because this would subordinate faith to political interest.

Thomasius was not alone in looking to a godly prince to purge religious ritual of the vestiges of papalist superstition. When Spener left the court of the highly worldly Saxon elector and arrived in Brandenburg, he too was hopeful that his new prince would take a more active role in reforming his territory's church.[58] Another example is Thomasius's contemporary and colleague at the University of Halle, Johann Samuel Stryk. He was the son of Samuel Stryk, another jurist at the University of Halle and a colleague of Thomasius. In 1702, Johann Samuel Stryk published a treatise, *De Jure Sabbathi* (*On the Law of the Sabbath*), in which he put forward a defense of the reform of ritual by a godly prince that was in many ways very similar to the argument made by Thomasius.

The main danger of rituals, Stryk wrote, was that they encouraged superstition, that is, the adherence to them in the belief that they were an essential part of religion. The right and the duty of regulating these rituals and guarding against the growth of superstition lay with the prince. In general, the prince's rights over the church were founded on several principles. One of these was his role as secular head of the commonwealth. Because, Stryk argued, rituals were not prescribed by divine law and thus left to human disposition, the question of rites was left to the decision of the prince,[59] as the holder of *maiestas*. However, the possession of *maiestas* was only a necessary precondition for the prince's right over ritual; it was not sufficient to justify his intervention. For if it were enough, he could impose any rituals he liked on his subjects, a view Stryk clearly did not share. The prince's decisions in questions of ritual had to be guided by a number of principles, which guaranteed that they furthered the subjects' piety.

Like Thomasius, Stryk referred to the prince's duty to care for the *salus publica*, a duty that was not exclusively secular but required him "to conduct the subjects toward piety and arrange divine ceremony in the appropriate manner."[60] Secular rulers were, according to the Book of Wisdom, "prefects and vicars of the kingdom of God,"[61] who were entrusted with the task "of directing all actions of humans, including sacred affairs, in such a way that the kingdom of God is thereby furthered."[62] Stryk also drew on the classical passage from Paul's letter to the Romans, where the apostle declared that there was no power that was not from God and so "every soul is subject to the superior powers," including the magistrate, and various other biblical passages.[63] In order to fulfill his obligations toward the church, the prince had to study scripture, pray for illumination by the Holy Spirit, and be aware of the difference between the Old Testament law and the New Testament freedom of spirit (*libertas spiritus*). He was expected to lead by his own example, not only permit but encourage devotional gatherings (which, Stryk says, were very frequent at the time of the apostles), admonish subjects to observe Sundays and dedicate them wholly to sacred matters, and regulate "the place, time, and manner of divine worship."[64]

Like Stryk, Thomasius believed that no external cult was prescribed by God and that true faith was internal, requiring no external worship. And like Stryk, Thomasius also believed that rituals should if possible be reduced, though often this was not possible for pragmatic reasons, because of the superstitious attachment of the populace to them and the unrest that resulted from trying to remove them. The arguments of Stryk and Thomasius illustrate the continuing significance of justifications for the prince's right over the church that were not secular and were held even by those who are generally considered representatives of the early Enlightenment. It is arguable that Thomasius did "deconfessionalize" the rights of the prince over the Lutheran church, but not in the sense in which the term is commonly used: he did not separate secular politics from religion, but he defined religious belief in non-confessional terms as the faith of the heart, which transcended the doctrinal differences between the various sectarian religious communities. The prince's right to intervene in religious affairs rested on the fact that doctrinal purity was not essential to religious faith, contrary to the claims of the orthodox Lutherans, but was only a pretext for the clergy to exercise secular power under the mantle of piety. Thomasius's notion of "papalism," like "priestcraft," was thus intended to discredit orthodox Lutherans' defense of their refusal to grant the Calvinist prince any say in their church. Thomasius's justification of the prince's intervention in ritual rested on the conception of a godly prince, who encouraged the non-doctrinal faith of the heart, although he could never enforce it, and who purged the ceremonies of his territory's church from the remnants of superstition the Reformation had failed to remove.[65]

Part II

History

CHAPTER FOUR

ECCLESIASTICAL HISTORY AND THE RISE OF CLERICAL TYRANNY

The growth of clerical power and corruption, which led to papalism and made the Reformation necessary, had been a traditional subject in works of Lutheran historiography from the mid-sixteenth century onward. The common, orthodox view was that the decline had set in gradually, some centuries after the age of early Christianity, and that it culminated in the investiture contest of the eleventh century. The relationship between the church and the Christian emperors of late antiquity, however, had been exemplary,[1] and Luther's Reformation had returned church-state relations in Protestant lands to this pure state of the age of Constantine and Theodosius the Great. Thomasius expressed strong doubts about this conventional interpretation and questioned whether the Reformation had actually succeeded in restoring the relationship between prince and church to its proper balance. Although he praised Luther's achievements in general, he believed Lutheranism had not been purged of all the faults that had affected the church in the centuries before. In particular, modern orthodox Lutheranism continued to grant the clergy excessive influence on secular affairs and therefore was only another variant of historical "papalism." Thomasius also argued that the relationship between prince and church in late antiquity was not as uncorrupt as his orthodox opponents liked to suggest: papalism had already taken hold in the supposed golden age of the church's history under the early Christian emperors; it was the result of a corruption of faith that had begun even earlier, in the immediate post-apostolic era, and paradoxically was only made worse by the establishment of Christianity as the Roman Empire's state religion.

THOMASIUS'S HISTORY OF THE EARLY CHURCH

Thomasius's pessimistic view of the early Christian emperors seems to have formed sometime in the early 1690s, at the same time as the change in his notion of religious belief, to which it is closely related. In his *Rechtmäßige Erörterung* of 1689, for example, his defense of the marriage of the Lutheran Maurice William of Sachsen-Zeitz with a Calvinist princess, Thomasius had still regarded the state of church government under Constantine as exemplary. Thomasius wrote approvingly that at that time the right to declare a particular opinion to be heretical rested with the emperors, "though they drew on the clergy as ecclesiastical counselors in these matters."[2] This lasted until, "through the connivance and excessive respect of the emperors, the clergy and the popes gradually arrogated more rights than they were entitled to and finally usurped the rights over the church."[3] By the mid-1690s, however, there are signs of a greater skepticism. In 1695, for example, Thomasius wrote that his opponents continually appealed to the examples of the early Christian emperors, like Constantine and Theodosius the Great, even though these emperors, "not so much by their own fault as by that of the clerics they were burdened with, were responsible for many actions in the law concerning sacred matters that certainly cannot be defended."[4] In his *Das Recht evangelischer Fürsten in theologischen Streitigkeiten* of the following year, he said that "the world has been fooled for long enough by this prejudice in favor of existing authority, which declares the fortunate state of the Christian church under Constantine the Great."[5] In later writings, Thomasius even presented Constantine as an accomplice rather than a victim of the corrupt clergy, describing him in 1701 as "a prince who excelled more by his vices than his virtues,"[6] although orthodox Lutherans, like Thomasius's opponent Johann Benedict Carpzov,[7] considered him the outstanding example of a pious Christian prince.[8] In volume 1 of his *Observationes selectae* of 1700, Thomasius published three historical investigations of the time and character of Emperor Constantine the Great,[9] in which he argued that the adulatory accounts of Constantine's life were probably biased,[10] that Constantine himself, in all likelihood, was an impious, even criminal, tyrant, whose good deeds toward the church were restricted to material endowments and building projects, which only corrupted the church further,[11] and that he was, if baptized at all, not baptized as an orthodox Christian but as an Arian heretic.[12] The belief that the church had flourished under his reign and that the early Christian emperors in general had been the pious nursing fathers of the church was a myth and a relic of "political papalism."[13]

The core of the church's corruption in late antiquity was the same reduction of faith to a formulaic doctrinal orthodoxy that Thomasius had criticized in the Lutheran church of his own era. The original faith taught by Christ and the apostles was the faith of the heart, rather than the mind. What mattered was the yearning for regeneration, which came from God, rather than the profession of particular opinions. The corruption of faith, Thomasius believed, had already entered the church in the time of the pagan persecutions. Its origin was an almost natural and inevitable decline from the purity of the apostolic age, when saving faith was regarded as a work of the will rather than the intellect, and the sole criteria of faith were "love of one's fellow brethren and the fruits of the spirit, that is, charity, joy, peace, lenity, benignity, goodness, faith, amiability, and moderation."[14] This faith did not require doctrinal formulae: "it was sufficient to put forward the divine mysteries in any words whatsoever, as long as they did not detract from the spirit and its fruits."[15] From the second century onward, however, the basis of Christian faith was gradually reduced to doctrines, which were adopted by the intellect without any regard to the state of the heart,[16] and this marked the beginning of papalism with the emergence of a clerical caste, determined to use its religious authority to pursue secular ends. The tendency toward a more formulaic faith was also evident in the introduction of formalized rituals, which were designed to set Christians apart from members of other religions.[17] The cause of this development was probably the influence of "various professors of philosophy, Jews, Greeks, others accustomed in part to systematic doctrine and over-subtle speculations about God, in part to ceremonies and external rituals,"[18] which led to the identification of "orthodox" and "heretical" opinions.

The conversion of the emperors to Christianity made this corruption worse, because it created the possibility of an alliance between a corrupt clerisy and secular power. Usually, when one sect secured the support of the ruler, its opinions became "orthodox," while its opponents were labeled "heretics" who were to be subjected to "relegations and punishments."[19] In general, any sect, no matter what its opinions were, was likely to try to force its opinion on dissenters. When the Arians, for example, won the favor of Constantine's successor Constantius, they persecuted the former orthodox as ruthlessly as they themselves had been persecuted.[20] Which groups were defined as heretics, Thomasius wrote, depended on which faction was strongest at court at a given time. The point he wanted to make was that no sect could claim to represent the true faith, because the only matters that distinguished it from other sects were different opinions, which were irrelevant to faith.

There were other examples of a similarly skeptical view of the early Christian emperors, and Thomasius's criticisms have to be seen as one example of more general currents in Protestant ecclesiastical historiography. Thomasius praised Samuel Pufendorf, for example, for being one of the first to recognize that the age of Constantine was not the ideal to which the modern church should aspire. There was, however, an important difference between Thomasius's ecclesiastical history and that of Pufendorf, which reflected their religious differences. Pufendorf's analysis of the decline of Christianity was based on his belief that there was an orthodox doctrine, based on scripture.[21] He saw the cause of the church's decline not in the development of a rigid doctrinal orthodoxy, as Thomasius did, but in the abuse of disciplinary powers by the clergy, which Christians had exercised over their fellow believers under pagan rule. Before Constantine extended toleration to the empire's Christians, they had preferred to settle their disputes by appealing to the arbitration of their bishop, because they did not want to acquire a reputation for litigiousness among the pagans and because pagan morality and laws were too lax by Christian standards.[22] Nevertheless, the bishops at no point exercised coercive jurisdiction over the members of their church. They did not encroach on the rights of the pagan sovereign.

By the time the majority of the population and the Roman emperors had converted to Christianity, recourse to the authority of the bishops became superfluous, because now a Christian emperor could enforce the stricter moral and legal standards desired by Christians: "For this reason it became irrelevant, after all commonwealths together with their princes had embraced Christianity, because this sanctity of morals no longer served to shame the pagans, since after the disappearance of pagans all citizens aspired to the same purity in moral life."[23] There was no good reason to uphold the particular authority of the bishops. It was not an essential part of Christian religion and it could also threaten to usurp the powers of the sovereign, for "this [power of discipline] can easily be abused and grow into a sort of political power, severely restricting the sovereigns' powers."[24] The disciplinary practices of the church persisted, however, in the transition to Christian rule and became the foundation for the gradual usurpation of secular jurisdictional powers by the clergy. The early Christian emperors, Pufendorf argued, failed to assume the powers the Christian clergy had arrogated to itself in pagan times,[25] because the clergy could not be dislodged from the administrative functions it had assumed. Pufendorf writes that the Christian emperors were *novitii*, "novices," and could not deprive the bishops of their power, all the more so as the majority of the population was Christian,[26] and the Christian emperors did not realize that the primitive church's direction of itself was provisional and ought to disappear under a Christian magistrate.

Thomasius defined the corruption of the church in different terms from Pufendorf, that is, as the transition from a "faith of the heart" to a formulaic, doctrinal religiosity. Pufendorf also restricted the meaning of "papalism" to the Roman Catholic church and its institutions. Thomasius used it to describe institutionalized, repressive ecclesiastical sects more generally, including orthodox Lutheranism. In this respect, Thomasius's views were particularly close to those of mystical, spiritualist writers, who stressed that the end of the persecutions after Constantine's victory over Maxentius at the Milvian Bridge (312 A.D.) opened the doors of the church to opportunists and fair-weather Christians, who would never have endured the Christians' trials in the pagan era. Christian Hoburg (1607–75), for example, wrote that "when the pagan emperor [i.e., Constantine the Great] with his pagan mores, laws, and regulations entered the kingdom of Christ, Christianity became a Babel."[27] In Hoburg's *Der Teutsche Krieg*, in which he presented the Thirty Years' War as a divine punishment for the pitiable state of Christian faith, an interlocutor marvels: "I always thought that the church had, on the contrary, been miserable until then [the accession of Constantine]."[28] The response is that "the church was never more miserable than when it began to be able to breathe more freely under Constantine."[29] Joachim Betkius (1601–63) similarly traced the decline of the Christian church to the time when Christians were first granted toleration in the Roman Empire.[30] Phillip Jakob Spener was silent on Constantine, but his interests lay clearly with the primitive church before the conversion of the Roman emperors. Although Thomasius did not place quite as much emphasis on the Constantinian revolution, preferring to see the origin of the decline already in the primitive church, his ecclesiastical history followed this spiritualist tradition.[31] One of its most prominent representatives was the historian Gottfried Arnold (1666–1714), author of the *Unpartheyische Kirchen- und Ketzer-Historie* (*Impartial History of the Church and Its Heresies*), a work that Thomasius praised as the "best and most useful book with the exception of holy scripture."[32]

CHRISTIAN THOMASIUS, GOTTFRIED ARNOLD, AND THE RESPONSE TO WILLIAM CAVE

Thomasius had known Arnold at least since the early 1690s, when two short essays by Arnold appeared in journals edited by Thomasius.[33] In 1696, Arnold published his first major work on ecclesiastical history, *First Love of the Congregations of Jesus Christ* (*Die erste Liebe der Gemeinen JESU Christi*); this was followed by the more famous *Impartial History* in 1699. The central theme in Arnold's works was a critique of sectarian "orthodoxy" as a pretext for persecution. Arnold argued that the persecution of heretics under the early Christian emperors was not guided by piety, but motivated mainly by the envy, ambition, and other passions of the orthodox clergy, who measured faith by the profession of certain doctrines rather than by the spiritual unity of the apostles. Like Thomasius, Arnold argued that the very attempt to establish doctrinal orthodoxy and enforce it was an excuse for the clergy to persecute those they considered their opponents. The suppression of so-called heresies was no more than another example of the suppression of the weaker by the stronger, which entered the world with Cain's murder of Abel.[34] There was no self-evident Christian doctrine, particularly not in the first three centuries after Christ's death, when there was no agreement as to which texts were to be included in the Bible, and no scriptural norm of faith existed.[35] Faith at that time was measured in terms of the believer's spirituality. God's works and thoughts, moreover, were often too profound and mysterious to be grasped by human reason. The orthodoxy constructed by the *Kätzermeister*, the "heresy-mongers," mixed reason, pagan philosophy, and human authority with Christian religion.[36]

Paradoxically, Arnold argued that the age of pagan persecutions had been far happier for the church than that of the Christian emperors. Although it was natural to regard "the oppression of the first churches not as their proper condition and as that intended for them by God . . . because the human heart generally considers it an example of great beatitude and the supreme form of divine grace if the flesh is free of all or at least many sufferings,"[37] the contrary was true, because "the sufferings of the congregations tested their faith and strengthened the original love, whereas the security of the following centuries weakened and finally extinguished both."[38] The "supposed felicity under the protection, abundance, and splendor of Constantine and the following emperors"[39] was therefore "far removed from the original beatitude."[40] Gottfried Arnold continually stressed the isolation of the early Christian community as a result of persecutions, which discouraged membership but guaranteed the earnestness of those who did join.[41] The purity of the Christian congregation depended precisely on the fact that the truth of its teachings by itself was not so convincing that nearly everybody converted to it despite the prospect of martyrdom. Those who did convert were a minority, because most were deterred by the danger of persecution. The alliance of secular power and Christian religion did not consummate the felicity of the Christian church but overturned it.

The full title of Arnold's work also indicated that it was a response to the writings of the English theologian William Cave (1637–1713), whose *Primitive Christianity or the Religion of the ancient Christians in the first ages of the Gospel* (1673) was translated into German as *Erstes Christenthum oder Gottesdienst der alten Christen in den ersten zeiten des evangelii.*[42] Cave was not commenting on the situation in Germany but was concerned with the relationship of the Anglican Church to the English dissenters. Nevertheless, both Thomasius and Arnold interpreted William Cave's writings as an attempt to vindicate confessional orthodoxy and the suppression of dissent in general, not just in England. Cave had published several works on church history in the 1670s and 1680s. He was chaplain to Charles II and in 1684 was installed as canon of Windsor.[43] He was also one of the leading patristic scholars of his day and a stern opponent of dissenters. In 1685, Cave was one of the Anglican divines who authorized the republication of the Donatist tracts as a defense of the intolerance shown to dissenters by the Anglican Church in the Restoration period.[44] Cave's works were a defense both of the purity and of the Catholicity of the Anglican Church and the role of the clergy in it. In the dedication of his *Ecclesiastici* to the archbishop of Canterbury, he drew an explicit parallel between the doctrinal disputes and heresies within the early Christian church and the disputes of his own day. Now as then, altar was erected against altar and the result was dissension and unrest in the state and lack of respect for the clergy.[45]

Like orthodox Lutherans in the German territories, Cave wanted to present Emperor Constantine as a model for the government of the church, which, in Cave's case, was that of the Anglican Church of the Restoration period. As a result, he described the relationship between the Christian church under the pagan emperors and that after the Constantinian revolution quite differently from Arnold or Thomasius. Cave did not emphasize the opposition of Christianity to the world and secular society under the pagan emperors, but its triumphant progress within it. Cave claimed that Christianity had spread rapidly despite, and even as an inadvertent result of, the persecutions: Christians of all ages and both sexes withstood the cruelest and most terrifying torments without renouncing their faith.[46] This convinced others of the truth of Christian teaching, because it was apparent that only divine assistance could have enabled the martyrs to endure the pains they did.[47] The numbers of the Christian congregation grew, in spite of the persecutions by Nero, Domitian, Decius, and Diocletian. Tertullian declared that were the Christians to withdraw from the empire, the remaining pagans would be surprised how few they themselves were.[48]

Constantine's victory over Maxentius at the Milvian Bridge in 312 A.D and his decision to tolerate and protect the Christian faith did not mark a reversal in the condition of Christianity, as it did to Arnold, who maintained that toleration opened the Christian church to those who were weak in their faith and adopted it mainly for the sake of political expediency.[49] To Cave, the triumph of Constantine represented the culmination of the progress of Christianity, which required a godly prince to guard it and help in the administration of its external affairs. While Cave acknowledged that Constantine was not baptized until shortly before his death in 337 A.D., Cave's portrayal of the emperor is an enthusiastic advertisement of Constantine as the godly prince. Constantine supported the church and was respectful toward it. He presided at the Nicene Council on Arianism (325 A.D.).[50] He also passed several measures to end the reign of paganism as the public religion of the Roman Empire.[51] Constantine, Cave wrote in the preface to his *Ecclesiastici*, was the "Nursing Father to the Church. . . . he guarded it with Wise and Prudent Laws, enrich'd it with an immense Bounty and Munificence, honour'd and rever'd its Bishops, encourag'd and nobly provided for its Clergy."[52] Christianity did not depend on the assistance of a secular power to triumph over paganism. The adoption of Christianity as the empire's public religion only consummated a development independent of secular interest and complemented Christianity's successes in conversion with its external flourishing: "the *Christian Religion* made its own way into the world, and unassisted by any Secular Power or Interest, triumpht over all the opposition that was made against it."[53]

Cave's history also offered a justification of some degree of religious coercion, an argument that would have been particularly repugnant to both Arnold and Thomasius. Even after the adoption of the Christian religion by the emperors, many pagans refused to follow suit and remained faithful to their old beliefs. At first, Constantine attempted to convert these Gentiles by "patience and persuasion and by all the Arts of Levity and Gentleness," but "finding the greatest part perverse and obstinate, he proceeded to rout Idolatry by rougher methods."[54] This, however, raised the objection that conversion by force created hypocrites, who went through the external motions of adherence to the Christian faith without believing any of it.[55] But while he admitted that the understanding could not be compelled, Cave, like many other Anglicans, believed that force could be an occasion for ridding oneself of false beliefs and recognizing the truth.[56]

In the case of paganism, there is also a constant emphasis on the depravity of pagan ritual, which depended on being performed either at night or in the hidden recesses of temples to which only the priests had access. Once these were opened to the public eye, their perversity was exposed and even pagans were repelled. Paganism's persistence rested to a great extent on deceit. Believers had to be "bewitched and seduced."[57] It was only because its rituals were performed in secret that it could continue to be accepted. Before the pagan emperor Julian the Apostate, for example, left for his decisive battle against the Persian king, he withdrew to a temple. After his defeat and death, the doors of this temple were flung open. Inside, the Christians found the corpse of a woman, suspended from the ceiling by her hair, whose stomach had been slit open for the priests to consult her entrails about the outcome of the battle.[58] Pagan religion rested on deceit, which could be exposed only by force, and then conversion was almost automatic, because the corruptness of pagan religious practice was evident, once held up to the public eye. All that the Christian prince appears to be doing is to remove the impediments to realizing the perversity of pagan religion. Religious coercion in this sense helps self-evident truth to triumph.

PIETIST ECCLESIASTICAL HISTORY: JOACHIM LANGE

Thomasius's views also set him apart from Pietist Lutherans in Halle, who did not share his radical skepticism about all forms of doctrinal orthodoxy.

Joachim Lange (1670–1744), for example, professor of theology in Halle, drew a distinction between orthodoxy, which he wanted to retain, and "pseudo-orthodoxy," which he attributed to his traditionalist opponents such as the theologian Samuel Schelwig (1643–1715) or Johann Benedict Carpzov.[59] Pseudo-orthodoxy stood for an overemphasis on doctrine and neglect of purity of life. But while Lange was sympathetic to the insistence on holiness of life, he was also careful to distance himself from the "enthusiastic" implication that doctrine was therefore secondary or even superfluous.[60] Like Thomasius's other Pietist critics in Halle, such as Justus Joachim Breithaupt and August Hermann Francke, Lange was concerned to mediate between formulaic orthodoxy and the "enthusiastic" extreme represented by Thomasius or Arnold. In a piece on Arnold's *Kirchen- und Ketzer-Historie*, for example, Lange praised Arnold in very carefully qualified terms, saying that while Arnold's intentions were good, he had perhaps sometimes taken a too favorable view of some of the heresies in the early church.[61]

Lange was perhaps more similar to Pufendorf, in that he believed that some of the so-called heresies in the past were declared to be heretical only because they had opposed papalism, but this did not imply that orthodoxy as such was false. Papalism had gradually emerged from the time of the first Christian emperors onward. The reasons for this emergence were the negligence of the emperors as well as the increasing ambition of the bishops, which expressed itself in a luxurious lifestyle and an increasingly hierarchical structure of ecclesiastical orders. Orthodox doctrine was also corrupted by the addition of articles based on human opinion rather than revelation. These new articles were usually decreed and pronounced as binding at church councils.[62] However, doctrine itself was not a sign of corruption but an essential part of Christian faith.[63] This is clear especially from Lange's account of some of the heresies in the early church, such as those of the Arians, Photinians, and Nestorians, which he condemned explicitly as doctrinal aberrations.[64]

Lange therefore did not believe, as Thomasius did, that heresy itself did not exist and was only an invention of the sect that happened to be wielding secular power at the moment. But like Thomasius he did believe that the accusation of heresy was used as a pretext for persecution and, in any case, he considered violence and force inappropriate means to convince others of their errors.[65] In addition, religious error was not sufficient for heresy, which required, according to the traditional formula, that the heretic also refused obstinately and maliciously to accept the truth when it was presented to him or her. Lange implied that corrupt clergymen persecuted even those who had adopted false opinions in good faith.[66]

Thomasius's ecclesiastical history, therefore, reflected and was intended to support his critique of Lutheran orthodoxy. Modern orthodoxy constituted another example of the *fides cerebrina*, the intellectualist, doctrinal faith that had led to the emergence of the papal church in late antiquity. Thomasius's ecclesiastical history is also important to understanding his opinions on the most important body of law from late antiquity, which continued to be used in the modern Holy Roman Empire, Justinian's *Corpus Iuris Civilis*.

CHAPTER FIVE

THE HISTORY OF ROMAN LAW

Thomasius argued that the *Corpus Iuris Civilis*, compiled under Emperor Justinian in the sixth century A.D., was an important example of the growth of clerical power. Roman law was widely used in legal arguments in Thomasius's time and although legal historians have tended to focus on its decreasing importance in this period, numerous contemporary jurists continued to defend its usefulness and equitability.[1] In 1717, the Dutch jurist Wilhelm Best gave a public oration "On the Equity of Roman Law and the Pleasure of Studying It."[2] Thomasius's colleague at the University of Halle, Samuel Stryk, claimed that almost all European kingdoms esteemed the *Corpus Iuris* "on the most equitable grounds on which jurisprudence rests" and drew on it "whenever the particular laws of the kingdom were insufficient."[3] Leibniz, in a letter to Hermann Conring, said that the rules of strict natural justice harmonized perfectly with the maxims in the last title of Justinian's *Digest, De regulis juris.*[4]

Thomasius's more critical attitude toward Roman Law is usually seen either as an example of an early "Germanism" in legal theory, that is, the consciousness of a national legal culture, which prohibits the use of the foreign *Corpus Iuris Civilis* in German courts,[5] or as a reflection of Thomasius's natural law theory, in which he is said to have rejected Roman law whenever it conflicted with the precepts of natural law. However, an important but neglected reason for Thomasius's criticisms of Justinian's *Corpus Iuris* is that he believed its compilation coincided with the corruption of Christianity in late antiquity and was affected by it. At the beginning of his essay on the title *De Summa Trinitate* from Justinian's *Codex*,[6] he commented that the *Corpus Iuris* was full of the "fruits of Papist religion."[7] The essay then continued with an account of the decline of the church from the charity and piety of the early Christians, which set in soon after the apostolic age, once Christians had begun to debate doctrines, as if faith consisted in an intellectualist orthodoxy and not in purity of heart. It was not evident that Christians in the age of the apostles "defined their confession of faith in specific formulae,"[8] since the *expositiones* and *confessiones fidei* attributed to the church fathers of that age were spurious. Before Constantine, the supreme mystery of Christianity, the Holy Trinity, was not "reduced to a formula or technical terms, and the fathers of the primitive church made use of phrases [in speaking of the Holy Trinity] that would not have been tolerated after Constantine."[9] The title *De Summa Trinitate* in the *Codex* of Justinian was an example of the way in which faith was reduced to the profession of particular opinions, instead of the purity of the heart which was the true essence of Christian faith. Throughout the *Corpus Iuris*, Thomasius believed, were similar examples of the clergy's influence. The clergy had, in late antiquity, turned the *Corpus Iuris Civilis* into an instrument of the very same papalism or Papo-Caesarism he criticized in the orthodox Lutheran church of his own age.

ROMAN LAW IN SEVENTEENTH-CENTURY GERMANY

The authority, utility, and applicability of ancient Roman Law had been the subject of debate among German jurisprudents for some time before Thomasius. Other authors on this subject were, for example, the Helmstedt philosopher Hermann Conring, author of the famous *On the Origin of German Law* (*De Origine Iuris Germanici*) of 1643, the jurist Johann Schilter, who published a work on the *Practice of Roman Law in the German Court* (*Praxis Juris Romani in Foro Germanico*),[10] Johann Kulpis (*De Germanicarum Legum Veterum Origine*),[11] and Thomasius's colleague in Halle, Samuel Stryk (*Specimen Usus Moderni Pandectarum*).[12]

It has been argued that these views reflected an increasing awareness of the historical particularity of Roman law and its inapplicability to Germany in the seventeenth century.[13] Jurists were indeed well aware that their own age differed in many respects from ancient Rome, but there is little indication that this caused them to doubt whether Roman law could be applied at all to their own age. As Douglas Osler has commented with reference to an earlier French jurist, Guillaume Budé, "there was no contradiction between interpreting the Digest in the light of the history, languages and literature of Antiquity, and in regarding it as a work of authority."[14] The same holds true for German jurists of the late seventeenth century. If the differences in historical circumstances were taken into account and the original intention of the legislator and the real meaning of the law behind the words of the law were made clear, the *Corpus,* they argued, could in many cases be applied to their own age. As Samuel Stryk observed with reference to Roman public law: "you must not cling to the words of the law or base your application on them, but pay attention to the original intention of the legislator, when he disposed of public affairs. . . . Not everything will be applicable today, but most matters will be."[15]

The problem many jurists saw was that the *Corpus Iuris* had been understood in a narrowly literal sense, without regard to the legislator's intention or the law's *ratio*. Johann Samuel Stryk, Thomasius's colleague in Halle and son of Samuel Stryk, wrote that it was the jurist's duty to explain the law, "and to put forward its meaning and sense; here one must have recourse to the reason [*ratio*] of the law as its soul, and if this is not found to be expressed in the law itself, one must look for it by other means and on this basis finally a judgment on the entire law is to be made: this concerns Roman laws most of all."[16] The excessively literal interpretation of law and the failure to extract the essence, the *ratio*, from its shell of words was often characterized as a "scholastic" attitude. Thomasius's contemporary in Halle, the jurist Justus Henning Boehmer, for example, wrote that the art of grammatical interpretation, which concerned itself with the correction of corrupted passages and the clarification of obscure and ambiguous passages, was forgotten by the medieval glossators and had to be revived by humanists such as Erasmus, Reuchlin, and Alciatus.[17]

One area in which jurists urged particular caution in the use of Roman Law was that of public law and the empire's constitution, because the constitution of late classical Rome differed significantly from that of the modern Holy Roman Empire.[18] Many jurists and philosophers drew on the Aristotelian argument that laws had to be adapted to the constitution of a polity.[19] Though Conring's *De Origine Iuris Germanici*, for example, has been praised by later legal historians for its refutation of the Lotharian legend, the story that Roman law had been adopted as imperial law by Emperor Lothair III in 1137,[20] Conring's central point was that Roman law had been framed for a political constitution different from that of the modern empire, and therefore it could not be applied to modern Germany without qualification. As Stryk wrote in his *Specimen Usus Moderni Pandectarum*, it was clear that "many matters pertaining to the Roman state were put forward in Justinian's *Corpus Iuris*; but whether these laws should be applied to decide controversies concerning the modern constitution of the empire is a problem that has been the subject of exhaustive disputes by certain doctors," including Hermann Conring.[21] Stryk explained that "when the form of the commonwealth or its mode of administration begins to be different [from what it originally was], the necessity of public well-being requires that the existing constitution be buttressed by new laws and that that which was once constituted is either removed entirely or qualified by prudent advice in such a way that it does not obstruct government, but rather conserves and furthers it."[22]

The jurist Johann Schilter commented that confusion would result from the attempt simply to replace German law with Roman law "without paying attention to the diversity in principles and the reason of the law,"[23] and that the confusion became worse the more the laws extended to "public law and the constitution."[24] Now that the constitution was different from what it had been in the ancient Roman Empire, nobody, Schilter continued, who had "political prudence" (*prudentia civilis*), bound themselves to unconditional obedience toward Roman law, unlike the medieval glossators,[25] whom Schilter criticized for what he regarded as their naïve, literal understanding of Roman law.

The opposite extreme, in Schilter's opinion, to blind adherence to the *Corpus* was to reject it completely, a sin that was the result of the "envy and suspicion of [the empire's] estates against the emperors, as if the latter intended to transform the constitution of the *Respublica*, exchange German liberty for the inanities of a Roman Senate, and plainly erect a Justinianic form of domination,"[26] a fear he suggests is excessive. However, Schilter does argue that when Emperor Maximilian I introduced Roman law as the law of the *Reichskammergericht* in 1495, he aimed to restrain his subjects, not in order to establish a tyrannical government over them, but to use Roman law to balance the older, more bellicose German law and control the citizens of the empire for the sake of peace.[27] Schilter's interpretation of the introduction of Roman law probably reflects the association of the *Reichskammergericht* and its use of Roman law with the end of the era of feudal strife and the establishment of the "Eternal Peace" (*Ewiger Landfrieden*) in 1495.[28]

Another example of a similar interpretation by a contemporary of Thomasius is Johann Kulpis's *De Germanicarum legum veterum, ac Romani juris in republica nostra origine, auctoritateque praesenti dissertatio epistolica* (*On the Origin and Present Authority of the Old German Laws and Roman Law in Our Commonwealth*).[29] The Romans, Kulpis wrote, were used to a "fully monarchical government, while we had to preserve a certain liberty, which was governed magnificently by our laws; when those foreign laws took their place by usurpation, it could not but happen" that they caused confusion in the legal profession. The application of the *Corpus* to controversies in the modern empire led to "miserable verdicts in controversies on public matters, to the detriment of the common good and contributing to civil war and the destruction of the commonwealth itself."[30] To remedy this, certain interpreters of law who, Kulpis observes a little contemptuously, wanted to be considered particularly prudent, added "glosses and six hundred other interpretations," thus obscuring the original Roman law, which he regards as one of the most equitable codes of law ever compiled. Kulpis is criticizing not so much the use of Roman law itself but what he thinks is the crude manner in which the scholastic glossators have applied it to the modern empire. He concludes with an appeal to study Roman law according to the example of "our better Doctors, solidly not vulgarly" and predicts that this will benefit the commonwealth.[31]

The debate over the compatibility of Roman law and the modern constitution of the empire was particularly significant from the 1630s onward, because the Austrian Habsburgs had been widely suspected of trying to impose absolute dominion over the estates of the empire in the Thirty Years' War, through the Edict of Restitution (1629) and the Treaty of Prague (1635), for example. As the above quotation from Schilter illustrates, Roman law could be seen as an imperial instrument of absolute dominion. The publication of Conring's *De Origine Iuris Germanici* in 1643, when peace negotiations were beginning to get under way, was probably not coincidental but a contribution to a highly topical question, the relationship between emperor and estates in the empire after the Thirty Years' War.

Jurists therefore did not criticize the appeal to Roman law as such, but its crude, "scholastic" interpretation, which did not take into account the fact that the literal meaning of the laws might not reflect their *ratio* accurately and also the fact that the laws of the *Corpus* were designed for a political commonwealth with a constitution radically different from that of the Holy Roman Empire. Thomasius similarly blamed the "amorphous chaos"[32] of modern interpretations of Roman law on the "scholastic" glossators who were "endowed with supreme diligence, but destitute of all knowledge of letters and history."[33] In Thomasius's case, however, the criticism of these "scholastic" interpretations of Roman law was also based on his notion of orthodox papalism, which had emerged in late antiquity, at the time when the *Corpus Iuris Civilis* was being compiled.

"PAPALISM" AND THE CORRUPTION OF THE *CORPUS IURIS CIVILIS*

Thomasius's view of the relationship between the rise of clerical power and the corruption of the *Corpus Iuris Civilis* is illustrated particularly well in a university disputation published in 1706, the *De Aequitate Cerebrina Legis Secundae Codicis de Rescindenda Venditione.*[34] The subject of the disputation was the *laesio enormis*, which originally granted the seller of a piece of land the right to rescind the contract of sale if the price for which the land had been sold was half or less of the just price. By the time Thomasius was writing, jurists had extended the *laesio enormis* to include the buyer's right also to demand a rescission of the sale, if he had paid either one-and-a-half times or twice (there was some disagreement on this) the just price.[35] The term *laesio enormis* itself did not appear in the *Corpus* and had been coined by the medieval glossators, but the doctrine it signified rested on two laws from the *Codex Justinianus*. One of these was the so-called Second Law (*Lex Secunda*) to which the title of Thomasius's disputation referred.[36] The other was the eighth law in the same title in the *Codex*. Both were attributed to Emperor Diocletian and dated to the end of the third century A.D.

Thomasius was very critical of the *laesio enormis,* and a case has been made by some legal historians that Thomasius was opposed to it on the basis of his theory of natural law.[37] Klaus Luig, for example, has argued that Thomasius's natural law theory required him to reject the *laesio enormis,* because the *laesio enormis* violated the individualistic freedom of contract, which was part of Thomasius's natural jurisprudence. Thomasius thus considered the *laesio enormis* a case of iniquity or "false equity" (*aequitas cerebrina*), because it permitted one of the parties to a contract to annul the contract under certain circumstances, even if he or she had entered into it freely and without fraud.

The problem with this interpretation is that it is not clear Thomasius does consider the *laesio enormis* a violation of natural law, that is, an iniquity. Luig equated *aequitas cerebrina* with iniquity[38] and interpreted Thomasius's appeal to natural law as an attempt to prove the iniquity of the *laesio enormis.* Thomasius's definition of the term *aequitas cerebrina,* however, suggests that *aequitas cerebrina,* which literally means "false equity," is not the same as iniquity: "This false equity [*aequitas cerebrina*] differs from true equity in that it is not equity, but pretends to be, or is an irrational equity; *it differs from iniquity, in that not every iniquity is false equity* [*aequitas cerebrina*], *but only that iniquity that has an appearance of equity* [my italics]."[39] Thomasius's use of natural law was not intended to prove the *iniquity* of the *laesio enormis,* but its *aequitas cerebrina,* that is, the fact that there was no particular reason in equity or natural law for the *laesio enormis,* and that therefore its claim to be particularly equitable and to be based on natural law had to be either an error or a lie.[40] In terms of the principles of natural law, the doctrine of *laesio enormis* was not unjust, but it was incoherent, because prices depended on nothing but the free agreement of two parties to a contract of sale.[41] If the *laesio enormis* were to be plausible, prices would have to be inherent in the objects of the transaction, independently of the will of the contracting parties, but no means existed by which to determine such an inherent price: neither the good's substance, nor its essence, nor its quantity would serve this purpose. Although scarcity had a certain influence on the formation of the price, it did not determine the just price, since even a plentiful good might command a high price if someone freely agreed to pay it.[42] A good, Thomasius wrote, quoting a German proverb, was worth as much as a fool was willing to pay for it. The actual price agreed on by the seller and buyer *was* the just price, unless the agreement came about as a result of fraud or force.[43]

These arguments referred to the state of nature, without a sovereign or a civil law. In the transition to civil society its members could agree to give up their freedom of contract and adhere to a "just price" in all commercial transactions. This would not be contrary to natural law, but the problem was that the just price was impossible to determine. The legislator could set a price, a *pretium legitimum*, if public welfare required it, but this *pretium legitimum* had nothing in common with the just price of the *laesio enormis*: the *pretium legitimum* was a specific price imposed by the legislator, whereas the just price was usually interpreted as a range of fair prices. Any deviation, however small, from the *pretium legitimum*, was illegal, but it was only a deviation by half from the just price, which counted as a *laesio enormis*.[44] Scholastics often defined the just price as the *pretium commune*, the general market price based on the common opinion of buyers and sellers, but, as Thomasius argued, there was no reason why this should be binding on the basis of natural law, as the *pretium commune* did not depend on the will of the contracting parties. The notion of a *pretium commune* also raised practical difficulties, especially as it was not a specific price but a range of prices. The upper and lower ends of this range were not fixed, so that the calculation of a *laesio enormis*, a loss of half of the just price, became impossible.[45]

The true reason why the *laesio enormis* was wrong was that it was used to justify the usurpation of secular jurisdiction by the clergy on the grounds of *humanitas*, that is, humane principles. Supplementing the rigor of civil law with *humanitas* and similar principles was frequently presented as the task of canon law and the ecclesiastical courts. In the 1629 edition of his *Summa Iuris Canonici*, for example, Henricus Canisius at the university of Ingolstadt praised the utility of canon law, which could fill the gaps, the *lacunae*, left by civil law and correct it in all questions concerning *pietas*, *aequitas*, and *bona fides*.[46] On this basis, contracts of sale, Thomasius argues, were turned into cases that could be brought before an ecclesiastical court, as soon as one side claimed to have suffered *laesio enormis*. The *laesio enormis* thus also appeared in canon law as a matter in which a clerical court exercised jurisdictional powers.[47]

Thomasius was not the first to criticize the *laesio enormis* as a relic of papalism. More than thirty years before Thomasius's disputation, a certain Christian Friedrich Jan published a treatise in Wittenberg[48] in which he argued that fraud and error were sufficient to repeal unjust contracts. The purpose of the *laesio enormis*, he maintained, was to legitimate clerical, especially papal, interference in secular jurisdiction. Canonists justified this on the basis of the *denunciatio evangelica*, a "supplementary and subsidiary remedy of canon law, which comes to the help of the poor and of the suppressed by granting them the right of a renewed appeal"[49] to an ecclesiastical court in the case of an excessively harsh judgment by a secular court.[50] Jan sees the *laesio enormis* and other legal concepts as an attempt by the papacy to prepare the way for the reimposition of papal tyranny in Protestant territories.[51]

Thomasius combined this interpretation of the *laesio enormis* as an instrument of papalism with his particular criticism of religious orthodoxy and its emergence in the early Christian church. He argued that the textual basis of the *laesio enormis* in Roman law was corrupt and reflected the interference of the clergy in the compilation of the *Corpus Iuris Civilis* under Justinian. Until now, legal historical scholarship has treated Thomasius's argument for the corruption of the textual basis of the *laesio enormis* mainly as a contribution to philological scholarship on classical Roman law, but the textual analysis of the *Corpus Iuris* is also related to Thomasius's criticism of the *laesio enormis* as a legal rule. The two laws on which the doctrine of the *laesio enormis* rested, the C.4.44.2 and the C.4.44.8, had not been formulated by Emperor Diocletian toward the end of the third century A.D., at least not in their present form, which was the product of an interpolation by the compilers of the *Corpus* under Justinian in the sixth century A.D.

In order to understand Thomasius's philological analysis of the two laws, they are worth quoting in full:

> C.4.44.2. Rem maioris pretii si tu vel pater tuus minoris pretii distraxit, humanum est, ut vel pretium te restituente emptoribus fundum venditum recipias auctoritate intercedente iudicis, vel, si emptor elegerit, quod deest iusto pretio recipies, minus autem pretium esse videtur, si nec dimidia pars veri pretii soluta sit.
>
> [If you or your father sold a thing of a higher price for a lower price it is equitable that you either recover the farm you have sold, after restoring the price to the buyers, with the assistance of the judge's authority or, if the buyer so chooses, you recover what is lacking from the just price. The price is considered too little if one half part of its true price was not paid.]
>
> C.4.44.8. Si voluntate tua fundum tuum filius tuus venumdedit, dolus ex calliditate atque insidiis emptoris argui debet vel metus mortis vel cruciatus corporis imminens detegi, ne habeatur rata venditio, hoc enim solum, quod paulo minori pretio fundum venumdatum significas, ad rescindendam emptionem invalidum est. quod videlicet si contractus emptionis atque venditionis cogitasses substantiam et quod emptor viliori comparandi, venditor cariori distrahendi votum gerentes ad hunc contractum accedant vixque post multas contentiones, paulatim venditore de eo quod petierat detrahente, emptore autem huic quod obtulerat addente, ad certum consentiant pretium, profecto perspiceres neque bonam fidem, quae emptionis atque venditionis conventionem tuetur, pati neque ullam rationem concedere rescindi propter hoc consensu finitum contractum vel statim vel post pretii quantitatis disceptationem: nisi minus dimidia iusti pretii, quod fuerat

tempore venditionis, datum est, electione iam emptori praestita servanda.

[If you or your son sold your farm on your instructions, fraud from the guile and insidious actions of the buyer must be proved or fear of death or imminent torture of the body shown if the sale is not to be regarded as valid. The mere fact that you show the farm was sold for a slightly too low price has no force for setting aside the sale. Clearly, if you had considered the substance of the contract of buying and selling, and that the buyer comes to the contract hoping to buy more cheaply, and the seller to sell more dearly; and that only after much argument, with the seller gradually reducing what he demanded, and the buyer increasing what he offered, do they agree to a settled price; then you would truly see that neither good faith which protects the agreement of buying and selling nor any reason allows a contract definitely agreed on whether at once or after much haggling over the price to be set aside: unless less was given than half of the price that was just at the time of the sale, when the choice previously given to the buyer must be observed.]

The phrase at the end of the Second Law ("The price is considered too little if one half part of its true price was not paid") was probably a gloss, a later addition, which changed the meaning of the original law. Whereas the original *Lex Secunda*, Thomasius believed, rescinded *all* contracts of sale in which there was any deviation from the just price, the gloss restricted the rescission to cases in which the actual price was one half or less of the just price. The end of the Eighth Law was also to be explained as a later addition, because the phrase "unless less was given than half of the price that was just at the time of the sale, when the choice previously given to the buyer must be observed" was an exception to the freedom of contract and contradicted the categorical assertion of precisely this freedom in the rest of the law. If this exception at the end was treated as a later addition, then the meaning of the original Eighth Law became almost the opposite of that of the Eighth Law in the *Corpus*, and, instead of limiting the freedom of contract to cases in which the actual price did not deviate by half or more from the just price, the original Eighth Law would have asserted the validity of *all* contracts concluded without fraud or coercion!

The original Second Law and Eighth Law, therefore, were, in Thomasius's opinion, mutually contradictory: the original *Lex Secunda* allowed the rescission of contracts of sale for deviations from the just price, whereas the original Eighth Law asserted the validity of all contracts of sale agreed to freely by the parties involved, whatever the price of the transaction. Diocletian had intended to repeal the Second Law and replace it with the Eighth Law. The compilers of the *Corpus*, however, did not realize this and tried, instead, to reconcile the two laws by adding the glosses about the deviations by half or more of the just price at their end. This, to Thomasius, was the origin of the doctrine of a *laesio ultra dimidium* or *laesio enormis*, a loss of more than half of the just price. Before the compilation of the *Corpus* under Justinian, none of the several imperial rescripts repealing Diocletian's rescript on the just price mentioned the concept of a *laesio* higher than half of the just price. This lent support to the conjecture that the *laesio enormis* was unknown in Roman legal theory before Justinian.[52]

The interpolation of Diocletian's two laws, which produced the incoherent doctrine of a *laesio enormis*, was no accident but a reflection of "papalism." It could occur only because of the unfortunate condition of the age in which Tribonian compiled the *Corpus* under the direction of Emperor Justinian and in which the false opinions that sustained the hold of the clergy on the laity's mind had already become established: "[I]gnorance of justice and equity reigned, and everywhere the clergy appropriated this doctrine and put it forward, not according to the rules of right reason" but as their self-interest dictated them to do. To persuade the laity of their authority in matters of justice, the clergy claimed that correct knowledge of the laws of morality required knowledge of scripture, which they alone were entitled to interpret. The laity dared not protest, because "they had in the course of several centuries been led in part by fear, in part by the insidious inculcation of blind obedience to believe that credulity was the highest of the laity's virtues, and that the teachers inculcating these beliefs were infallible."[53] The decline of religion and learning in late antiquity allowed the clergy to insert the *laesio enormis* into secular legislation and undermine the jurisdictional and legislative authority of the secular sovereign.

There were several other legal problems, Thomasius believed, that papalism had used to influence the jurisdiction of the secular magistrate.[54] Usucaption, the acquisition of a title or right to property by uninterrupted possession for a prescribed term, for example, was made dependent on good faith. The person in possession of the particular property had to believe genuinely that its owner had abandoned it. The presence or absence of good faith, however, was determined by an ecclesiastical court, so that the clergy, in effect, decided whether a usucaption was valid or not.[55] Last wills also benefited the clergy, because pious bequests were the clergy's "main means of acquisition,"[56] but they were not based on natural reason, because the death of a person also extinguished all of his or her natural rights. Thus, it was impossible to dispose of property after death unless the civil legislator allowed for it.[57] The legal doctrine on oaths, as Thomasius claimed in his *De desertione ordinis ecclesiastici*,[58] concealed a similar *arcanum* of clerical power.

The very last university disputation over which Thomasius presided in Halle reiterated the connection between papalism and the *Corpus Iuris*

Civilis. This was the *De singulari aequitate legis unicae Codicis quando Imperator inter Pupillos etc. cognoscat etc., eiusque usu practico.*[59] The law discussed in this disputation allowed widows, orphans, and certain other persons to appeal to an ecclesiastical court in particular cases. The jurist Jacobus Gothofredus described the law as a "most equitable and humane . . . constitution of Constantine the Great,"[60] which he introduced out of a spirit of Christian mercy (*misericordia*). However, it had been shown that Constantine was no pious prince "but a depraved emperor,"[61] who was so confused by the controversies between the orthodox and the Arians that he did not know whether to regard the doctrines of the Council of Nicaea or those of the Arians as true. And

> through his lack of prudence and his adoption of the distinction between the internal and the external power of the church, the clergy (also the orthodox clergy) began to lay the foundations for exempting itself from the power and command of the secular magistrate and for using and abusing the power of the secular prince as its secular arm, to exercise any kind of tyranny.[62]

Aequitas cerebrina was one of papalism's favorite means of concealing its injustice behind a mask of piety and mercy. In one passage of his dissertation on the *laesio enormis*, Thomasius listed twelve papal *arcana*, secret strategies to promote the rule of *aequitas cerebrina*. Thomasius declared he would not be surprised if "the pillage, the destruction, in one word, the innumerable and unspeakable injuries that the Protestant commonwealths have been suffering for two centuries" were attributable primarily to this false equity.[63] The "regicide in France"—Thomasius was probably referring to the assassination of Henri IV by Ravaillac in 1610, which had been popularly ascribed to the Jesuits, acting on instructions from the pope—was another example of *aequitas cerebrina*. Papalism's most important means of spreading *aequitas cerebrina* was control of the education system. The *laesio enormis*, for example, was taught at the universities, most of which had originally been papal foundations and, even if they had been reformed, had not always rid themselves of all remnants of papalism: "Most Protestant academies were once papal, and they have not at the time of the Reformation been entirely cleansed from all ferment of papal doctrine. But it is known that the tiniest piece of ferment can infect the rest."[64] The academies were instituted at the height of the investiture contest. Their purpose was to persuade the laity, including rulers, of the "sanctity and equity of the church's canons and the law named after them" through false teaching.[65] Thomasius's criticism of Roman law thus formed part of his broader critique of the state of secular learning and of faith at Lutheran universities. Roman law was taught without awareness of the "papalist" remnants in it; it reflected the corruption of faith from late antiquity, and was designed to support the clerisy's influence on secular power and jurisdiction. History revealed that the *Corpus Iuris Civilis* was another example of "papalist" ideology, which combined corrupt faith with the distortion of law and philosophy.

PART III

NATURE

CHAPTER SIX

NATURAL LAW (I):
THE *INSTITUTES OF DIVINE JURISPRUDENCE*

Thomasius's interest in the reform of the corrupt will-as-desire was not important only because of religious faith or the influence of the clergy on secular jurisdiction. Thomasius also believed that temporal morality and happiness were based on the same reformed state of the will as religious belief, because a pious individual was free from the corrupting passions, which were the cause of sin and unease in the unregenerate. When the "scholastic" orthodox theologians reduced faith to doctrinal opinions in the intellect, this affected their moral philosophy, too, because it led them to ignore the importance of the will-as-desire for achieving moral virtue.

In his first work on natural law, the *Institutes of Divine Jurisprudence* of 1688, Thomasius had not yet adopted this belief in the importance of the human will-as-desire, but by the time he published his second treatise on natural jurisprudence, the *Foundations of the Law of Nature and Nations*, in 1705, the reform of the human will-as-passion had become central to his theory of moral conduct. This transformation of Thomasius's natural jurisprudence was to some extent a reflection of the changes in his notion of faith and his anthropology during the 1690s. It was, however, also symptomatic of a much broader trend in the moral philosophy of the early Enlightenment and the status of the passions within it. This was a development from a belief that actions motivated by passions were necessarily opposed to morality to a belief that moral actions were themselves motivated by certain kinds of passions.[1] Samuel Pufendorf, for example, had argued in his *On the Law of Nature and Nations* of 1672 that the subject of natural jurisprudence was laws imposed by God on humanity. The passions, Pufendorf believed, were not part of this morality but an obstacle to it, because they distorted the judgment by the intellect and restricted the freedom of the will, which was essential for the ability to choose what was morally good. Later theorists, however, such as Thomasius in his *Foundations* of 1705 or Thomasius's pupil Johann Jacob Schmauss (1690–1757),[2] argued that morality was, in some sense, the product of the natural operation of the human passions. They provided the necessary motive force for action, and, if functioning properly, did not disrupt virtue but conducted humans toward it. As a little-known member of the St. Petersburg Academy of Sciences, for example, put it in 1744, "the obligation that accompanies the laws of nature cannot consist in anything but an inseparable force of the passions, which naturally carries us toward that which provides us with satisfaction."[3] Eventually, this development turned moral theory into part of a culture of *Empfindsamkeit* (sensibility), in which the education of an individual's feelings or passions was essential to the formation of his or her moral personality.[4] Thomasius's two main works on natural law exemplify this transition from an earlier, Pufendorfian natural jurisprudential tradition, focused on natural laws as commands, to one in which the emphasis is on the beneficial contribution of the passions to moral conduct. As we shall see, this change in Thomasius's moral philosophy also had important implications for the relationship between morality and nature, in effect turning moral philosophy into a form of the study of human nature. In this chapter I shall focus on the *Institutes*, before turning, in chapter 7, to an examination of Thomasius's moral philosophy in the 1690s, leading to the publication of the *Foundations* in 1705.

The Controversy with Valentin Alberti

The *Institutes of Divine Jurisprudence*, first published in 1688, were a defense of Pufendorf's *On the Law of Nature and Nations* (*De Jure Naturae et Gentium*) against its orthodox Lutheran critics.[5] One of the most formidable and perceptive was Valentin Alberti, a professor at the University of Leipzig and author of the *Compendium Iuris Naturae Orthodoxae Theologiae Conformatum* (*The Handbook of Natural Law according to Orthodox Theology*).[6] Pufendorf had responded to Alberti's criticisms in a number of university dissertations, collected under the title of *Eris Scandica* (*Scandic Quarrel*) and published in 1686, to which Alberti replied with the *Eros Lipsicus* (*Lipsian Love*) of 1687. Thomasius's *Institutes* of 1688 were a contribution to this ongoing debate.

One of the main areas of disagreement between Thomasius and orthodox opponents like Alberti concerned the use of divine revelation, in particular the Ten Commandments, as a source of natural law. Alberti argued that Adam and Eve were created with innate notions (*notitia naturalis*) of good and evil, which were part of a divine image (*imago Dei*) in prelapsarian human nature. Original sin extinguished certain parts of this divine image, such as man's immortality in the state of innocence, and damaged others, such as the natural knowledge of good and evil, which was to a great extent lost. God had, however, revealed in scripture at least some of the moral precepts that had been self-evident to humans in the state of innocence, so that revelation supplemented humans' imperfect natural knowledge of morality after the Fall.

Alberti believed that the moral principles founded in pre-lapsarian human nature were not always applicable to the state of sin in the same way as they had been to the state of innocence, because the Fall had introduced situations, institutions, and customs unknown in paradise. Slavery and political society, for example, were introduced after Original Sin, but were subject, nonetheless, to the same natural law that had prevailed in the Garden of Eden. Natural law in the state of innocence also forbade humans to harm each other, but it did not have to prohibit them from returning an injury, as natural law in the post-lapsarian world did, because humans in the state of innocence never gave cause for it. To those aspects that were specific to the post-lapsarian world, the natural law was applicable *normaliter*, as a norm that had to be adapted to the particular circumstances of the state of sin. In those matters that had not been changed by the Fall from Grace, its precepts were applicable directly, or *formaliter*, as Alberti expressed it.[7] Thomasius, however, argued that Alberti's theory confused reason and revelation. Revelation did provide precepts that were morally binding on humans, but these precepts were part of divine positive law, not natural law. One example was the prohibition of polygamy, which could not be demonstrated from natural law but was based on universal divine positive law, that is, a law God had given to all of humanity and made known through revelation.[8] The purpose of divine positive law was not to restore humans' knowledge of a natural morality. It was an addition to it, which humans could not have known on the basis of natural reason, either before or after the Fall from Grace.

The different opinions on the use of revelation as a source of natural law reflected a basic disagreement over the nature of moral principles. Thomasius objected in particular to Alberti's argument that these were *a priori* truths and that God had commanded humans to act according to them because they were morally good *per se*, not that they were morally good because God had commanded them. Alberti's view implied that God only enforced a standard of right and wrong that existed antecedently to his will, an "eternal law" (*lex aeterna*), as Alberti and similar theorists put it.[9] In that case, Thomasius argued, God would not be the true legislator of natural law, as he ought to be, because he would be acting according to a law instead of defining it. In reality, God did not command or prohibit certain actions because they were good or bad *per se*; these actions were good or bad only because he commanded or prohibited them. Like Pufendorf,[10] Thomasius in the *Institutes* argued that moral qualities (*entia moralia*), were not inherent in certain actions but were imposed on a morally indifferent natural world in an act of free will by agents like God or, in the case of human law, the sovereign. A law was "the command of a superior obliging his subjects to institute their actions according to this command."[11] Moral action was characterized by conformity to the will of a superior, not to a standard of *a priori* reason. Blasphemy, for example, considered physically, was nothing but the articulation of certain sounds. A witness quoting a blasphemous remark was not committing a crime. Theft, considered physically, was nothing but "extending one's hands to another thing."[12] Natural law was God's will in relation to humans, insofar as this will was made known to them through natural reason rather than revelation.

Although natural law was the product of God's free will, it was not arbitrary. It was adapted to human nature, because God would not have contradicted himself by giving humanity laws that were not suitable for the human nature he himself had created. This natural law was not promulgated by God as positive law. Humans arrived at it through the observation of their own nature, from which they deduced the precepts God must have given to humans.[13] That humans owed their existence to God and should obey his commands could also be shown with the help of reason. Everything was caused by something else, and thus it was necessary to posit a first cause to avoid an infinite regression. This first cause was God.[14] Humans had to obey God because he by definition enjoyed the power to command his creation. If he did not do so, then he could not be God, the omnipotent creator of the world.[15]

The central principle of the law of nature was that of sociality and was evident from man's God-given rational nature. Human reason consisted in thought (*cogitatio*); thinking, however, was the connection of one term with another and one proposition with another. The latter was termed ratiocination and was a form of speech, whether it remained internal, that is, within the mind, or was uttered aloud. The acts of reason, therefore, were such that they were designed to be communicated to other humans.[16] Thus, *"there is no reason without speech, no use for speech outside of society, and reason does not exercise itself prior to society."*[17] To describe human nature as rational was the same as describing it as social, and the preservation of sociality was thus the central precept of natural law, commanded by God. Had God not wanted humans to do what conformed to sociality, he would not have endowed humans with a nature capable of ratiocination.[18] It was also evident from human nature that God wanted humans to preserve sociality by living according to a law, because the physical weakness (*imbecillitas*) of humans was so great that they "would necessarily perish, if other humans were not obliged [by a law] to succor [them]."[19] Secondly, unlike beasts, humans were characterized by a great diversity of minds and inclinations, which required laws to guide them in such a way that they promoted public peace.[20]

Thomasius's theory of natural law in the *Institutes* also required the freedom of the human will to choose between particular courses of action. This freedom of the will was necessary for humans' ability to regulate their actions according to the will of a superior and the moral qualities attached by this superior to particular physical actions or states of affairs. Again, the similarity to Pufendorf is evident.[21] Human actions were not governed by physical necessity. The material world was ruled by determinate relationships between bodies, but the human mind was not subject to them. The will, Thomasius argued in agreement with Descartes,[22] was located in the mind (*mens*) and was free from the necessities of material nature; it could choose or reject a certain course of action, depending on whether this action had had a positive or negative moral quality imposed on it. All other parts of creation, from stones to animals, Thomasius maintained, were incapable of this kind of choice.

In the state of innocence, this freedom of the will had been perfect. In post-lapsarian man it was subject to the influence of passions like avarice, ambition, and lust. "The human will lost much of its freedom, so that, in this state, it is almost completely inclined toward evil, because the passions incite man and cause him to be beside himself, and certainly constantly gnaw at their reins."[23] Yet, even this corruption of the will was such "that it retains at least the power to restrain the external actions effectively."[24] Otherwise, actions could not be imputed to their agents and the foundation of morality would collapse.[25] If humans did not retain at least the liberty to restrain their external actions, "man would punish man in vain."[26] Thomasius at this point was still far from defining the will itself as a passion or desire, as he did from the mid-1690s onward.

Not all human actions were suitable to be directed by laws. Some actions human nature "initiates as its own";[27] others "it has in common with beasts and plants."[28] Only those actions humans could either choose or reject freely were imputable to them and thus could be the subject of legislation. Whenever an object affected the external senses, it activated what Thomasius called the "first operation of the intellect" (*prima intellectus operatio*), in which the intellect "simply perceives the objects affecting the external sense organs, forming some sort of proposition on their nature or goodness from the properties affecting the external senses, or form[ing] confusedly ideas of the objects that have already been perceived by the senses before."[29] This initial perception was then received by the appetitive faculty (*appetitus*), which either immediately gave a command to the body's locomotive powers or passed the perception on to the second operation of the intellect, which "ratiocinates about the truth of these propositions and the goodness of the object, as well as, by further meditation in a discourse, on the ideas."[30] After ratiocination, the will chose a course of action and ordered its execution by the body's locomotive powers. Only those actions referred to the "second operation of the intellect" were subject to humans' will. If the *appetitus* receiving the first operation of the intellect immediately gave an order to the body's locomotive powers, this was not a free choice. An example was a reflex, such as lifting an arm to ward off a blow.[31]

NATURAL LAW AND THE DIVINE WILL

Thomasius believed that the "scholastics" like Alberti had used revelation as a source of natural law because they misunderstood its foundation: it was not based on innate principles of reason in human nature, which had been blurred by original sin and had to be restored by revelation, but was an expression of the divine will, which had to be reconstructed empirically, from the observation of actual human nature, created by God, not from revelation. The "scholastic" belief in *a priori* moral truths meant that God was not the legislator of natural law, or at least not a legislator in the sense in which Thomasius used the word, of a "superior obliging his subjects to institute their actions according to this command."[32] Alberti's argument that God only enforced existing principles of an eternal law (*lex aeterna*) when he gave humans natural law also implied that this eternal law, according to which God acted, and the natural law of humans were closely related to each other, perhaps even identical:

> Therefore, as God does, whatever he does, according to the norm of his divine sanctity, goodness, wisdom, and justice, and so subordinates himself by his own free will to an eternal law, it is necessary that the natural law that guides the actions of humans is also constructed according to this archetype; and so it is necessary that to conform with right reason is the same as to conform to divine justice and sanctity.[33]

The problem with this view was its implication that God's motives were at least similar to those of human actions and could be understood with the help of human reason. God's decisions, however, were inscrutable,[34] and all that humans could know was that he must have wanted them to conform to certain laws, because this was implied by their nature as God had created it. Thomasius's argument in the *Institutes* was an example of the same theological voluntarism that underpinned his critique of orthodox Lutheran theology at that time. In the *De felicitate subditorum Brandenburgicorum*, for example, he had observed that it was the application of human reason to questions of faith that caused the confusion over the meaning of scripture and the bitter disputes between the different confessions. The use of rationalist argument in debates about scripture had, he believed, been introduced by the clergy in order to distort the true meaning of scripture and substitute its own gloss, thereby legitimating its power over the laity. The same belief that human standards of reason were inapplicable to discussions about God and his decisions was central to Thomasius's defense of his natural law theory against orthodox Lutheran theorists such as Alberti. It was impossible to assume that human rational principles could be applied to understanding the reasons for God's actions.

Alberti replied that Thomasius had misunderstood his explanation of the nature of moral truths. Although they were *a priori* truths, the eternal law (*lex aeterna*) on which they were based was not "either external or prior to God"[35] or "antecedent to every free act of [God's] will,"[36] as Thomasius suggested,[37] but identical to God's own essence, in particular his intellect. God therefore was not subordinate to the eternal law in the sense that a human was subject to a law, because God "while he is by supreme right exempt from all law, is a sort of law unto himself."[38] The *lex aeterna* was antecedent to God's specific acts of volition, but it was not a set of eternal verities independent of him and did not restrict his freedom, because it was part of himself:[39] he always acted "in conformity to his practical intellect,"[40] in which "what is called the eternal law is said to consist,"[41] because it was a logical impossibility for God to act contrary to his own essence, not a restriction of his free will or omnipotence.

The principles of morality in humans were part of the divine image, which was a reflection of this divine essence and dependent on it, just as the reflection of light in a mirror depended on the source of the light. Although the source of light, God, had remained unchanged by the human choice to sin, human nature was now incapable of receiving this light as it had before the Fall from Grace. This relationship between God and the divine image in man and the difference between the pre- and the post-lapsarian states are illustrated particularly well by the frontispiece to the second edition of Alberti's *Compendium*. In the left half of the engraving is an image of man in the state of innocence. He is almost entirely naked and is standing in a lush and fertile countryside. He holds a level and a mirror, the frame of which bears the inscription *imago Dei*. The mirror itself reflects a bright beam of light that emanates from the Hebrew letters for God at the top of the page. Facing him on the right half of the page stands a man after the Fall from Grace, elegantly dressed in baroque clothes. Although he holds a mirror and a level like the man in the Garden of Eden, the mirror is cracked and the level is battered and broken in several places. The mirror's frame reads *Reliquiae*, that is, *imaginis divinae*. Although a second beam from the Hebrew word for God reaches the broken mirror, it is reflected only dimly. The representative of post-lapsarian human nature is surrounded by a bleak landscape, dotted with gnarled and leafless trees before a barren mountainside.

Natural law thus was derived from eternal law and dependent on it. The two laws were part of a hierarchical order of all being, at the apex of which stood God, while all levels below him were emanations or derivations of his essence. Alberti's conception of the hierarchical dependence of natural law on eternal law, the two of which are not identical, is strongly reminiscent of neo-Platonist patterns of argument, so that it is not surprising to find Alberti referring to a very neo-Platonist passage in Thomas Aquinas's *Summa Theologiae*, in which Aquinas declared that "as therefore the eternal law is the reason according to which the supreme ruler rules, it is necessary that all principles of rule that are in inferior beings are derived from the eternal law."[42] This derivation of human morality from God's eternally true justice precluded all "moral indifferentism" (*Indifferentismum Moralem*), which Alberti considered characteristic of Pufendorf and his followers, who, he said, claimed that "everything can be either commanded or prohibited by God indifferently"[43] and that natural law was defined only by God's will. Instead, "moral principles, too, must be considered necessary, but because of their conformity to this same law [the *lex aeterna*]."[44]

The error in Thomasius's argument was to assume that if the content of natural law was necessary and not at the disposal of God's arbitrary will, God was subordinate to it. Although God could not have created human nature differently or given natural law a different content, this did not remove the independence critical to divinity. That humans were rational beings was "necessary in an absolute sense,"[45] but nevertheless "the rationality of man *depends on God*, no less than man himself [my italics]."[46] The essences of all creatures were lower-order derivations from God's essence within the great hierarchy of being. Even though human nature, natural law, and creation as a whole could not be otherwise, they were thus also subordinate to and dependent on God. Alberti drew an important distinction between dependent and independent absolute necessity. The necessity of the essences of created beings was absolute only because it was dependent on the essence of God, who was eternal and unchanging. God alone enjoyed independent absolute necessity, while dependent absolute necessity pertained to the essences of creatures: "created essences . . . are indeed necessary, but because of their conformity to eternal law."[47] Both forms of absolute necessity were opposed to hypothetical necessity, because hypothetical necessity was conditional on something that was not necessarily the case. In Alberti's opinion, theorists like Pufendorf or Thomasius confused God's independence from his creation with arbitrariness of volition.

Alberti, therefore, had never intended to deny the omnipotence of God but conceived of God's role as legislator of natural law differently from Thomasius, believing that because the eternal law was God's essence, and natural law was derived from eternal law, natural law depended on God "with respect to its existence, like an effect from its cause."[48] This was the sense in which God was the cause of natural law. Its moral obligation was then added to it by God in the form of a *vis obligandi*, which was to be enforced in the afterlife. In this sense, "ratione moralis obligationis" ("by virtue of the moral obligation"), God was not the efficient cause but the legislator of natural law. The human legislator's function was to add the *vis obligandi* to what was right in human positive law, which "as far as its existence goes, or it is written, originates with the jurists; insofar as it has the power to obligate, from the magistrate himself."[49] The difference between God and human jurists was that jurists determined what was in itself just, whereas God's essence was the source of what was just.

Probably Alberti's strongest objection to Thomasius's Pufendorfian, voluntarist theory of natural law was that it reduced God to a tyrant and that it turned natural law into an arbitrary command, which had its origin only in the divine will, not in an absolute norm such as God's holiness, justice, or goodness. Thomasius's argument, however, was that it was nonsensical for humans to speak of God's justice and his other qualities: God's essence was incomprehensible to humans and any description of it would be only an inappropriate projection of human qualities onto divine nature. To describe God as just or holy at all was permissible only because these terms were used in revelation. It was, therefore, clear that God found them acceptable, but they were not an accurate description of his being.[50]

Nevertheless, the theoretical problem of God's tyrannical power remained. Several years later, Leibniz commented on this aspect of Pufendorf's natural jurisprudence and offered a more sophisticated version of the criticisms Alberti had expressed.[51] Leibniz's derivation of natural justice from God's rationally founded justice was consciously opposed to the voluntarism of both Hobbes and Pufendorf. While Hobbes equated God's right with his overwhelming power (just as a single person in the state of nature who was more powerful than all other humans together would exercise full rights over them), Pufendorf based natural law on God's will. "Now then," Leibniz asked, "will he who is invested with the supreme power do nothing against justice if he proceeds tyrannically against his subjects; who arbitrarily despoils his subjects, torments them, and kills them under torture; who makes war on others without cause?"[52]

Leibniz argued that the voluntarist position of thinkers like Pufendorf also led into self-contradiction. Pufendorf had declared that obedience to a superior who gave law required a just cause to justify the superior's power. In that case, however, justice was antecedent to the will of the superior and not its product:[53]

> God is praised because he is just. There must be, then, a certain justice—or rather a supreme justice—in God, even

though no one is superior to him, and he, by the spontaneity of his excellent nature, accomplishes all things well, such that no one can reasonably complain of him. Neither the norm of conduct itself, nor the essence of the just, depends on his free decision, but rather on eternal truths, objects of the divine intellect, which constitute, so to speak, the essence of divinity itself.[54]

Leibniz's critique of Pufendorf could be directed equally well against Thomasius's argument. In the *Institutes*, Thomasius had written that the first practical principle on which natural law rested was "obey the person who has the power to command."[55] This followed, first, from the definition of the *imperans*, that is, someone "who has the power to oblige another."[56] Second, it followed from the definition of law as "a command of an *imperans* obligating his subjects."[57] If a law did not have to be obeyed, it would be no law. Finally, the principle that the *imperans* had to be obeyed followed from the definition of obligation, because no obligation could exist if subjects did not owe obedience to their superior *imperans*. From Leibniz's perspective, however, there was no intrinsic reason why any *imperans* should be obeyed. Pufendorf and Thomasius had failed to provide any grounds for obedience to an *imperans*.

There is, however, no sign of a critical engagement by Thomasius with this particular problem in his natural law theory after 1688, although Schneewind has suggested that it is this problem that caused the changes in Thomasius's natural law theory in the 1690s. Schneewind refers, in particular, to a passage from the *Foundations of the Law of Nature and Nations* (*Fundamenta Juris Naturae et Gentium*) of 1705, where Thomasius criticized the notion of God as a despot.[58] However, the notion of a despotic God that Thomasius criticized in this work is different from the notion criticized by Leibniz in his "Opinions on the Principles of Pufendorf." A despotic God, Thomasius writes in the *Foundations*, is a God who inflicts "arbitrary external punishments"[59] on transgressors of natural law. "Arbitrary" punishments, in the sense in which the term is used by Thomasius, were those that are not the natural consequence of a transgression, as, for example, a hangover is the consequence of heavy drinking, but are imposed outside of the normal course of nature. True punishments, Thomasius argued in 1705, were not part of natural law, for "each punishment is inflicted visibly, but the evils that God ordained for the transgressors of natural law come secretly, that is, in such a way that the connection of the evil with the sin is not visible, even though the evil itself may be visible."[60] When, in the *Foundations*, he criticized the notion of a despotic God, he criticized the idea that God directly punished transgressors of natural law by some act that was outside the usual course of nature and a clear sign of divine anger. He was not criticizing the belief that the content of natural law was a product of God's arbitrary free will, as Leibniz did. This is also clear from the fact that Thomasius did not refer to Pufendorf's voluntarist theory or his own, similar position in the *Institutes*, but to "scholastic philosophy" as an example of belief in a despotic God, although the "scholastics" held the view that God *did* act according to eternal principles of justice.[61] Thus, the change in Thomasius's natural law theory was not a response to Leibniz's criticism of the belief that natural law was based on the divine will, but reflected, first, the changes in his notion of human volition, which were part of the development of his religious thought. Second, they were connected to the theoretical question of punishments in natural law, which he raised in the passage from the *Foundations*, quoted above, and which will be the subject of chapter 7.

CHAPTER SEVEN

NATURAL LAW (II):
THE TRANSFORMATION OF CHRISTIAN
THOMASIUS'S NATURAL JURISPRUDENCE

The question of punishments in natural law had already posed a problem
to Thomasius in the *Institutes* of 1688, and it is at least in part the theoretical challenge associated with punishment that caused him to refine and
modify his natural law theory after 1688. Laws, he had argued in the
Institutes, were expressions of the will of a superior who punished all trans-
gressions of his law. The problem in the case of natural law is that there
are no evident divine punishments. Although acting contrary to natural law
may sometimes prove a disadvantage, it is not invariably followed by an
unmistakable sign of divine anger. A thief is not struck by lightning. And
unless it is clear that the evil following from a transgression of natural law
is a punishment inflicted by the superior, the punishment does not fulfill its
purpose of signaling God's displeasure to his subjects. As Thomasius himself wrote, "if God does not care about the affairs of humans, there will be
no ruler and, therefore, nobody to be obeyed."[1]

It could be argued that divine punishments were not inflicted immediately because they were reserved for the afterlife. Leibniz, for example,
admitted that the transgressors of natural law had not always received their
punishment in temporal life, but he insisted that humans were able to
know on the basis of reason that God would punish them for their tres-
passes in the afterlife. "One cannot doubt," Leibniz declared, in his
"Opinion on the Principles of Pufendorf," "that the ruler of the universe, at
once most wise and most powerful, has allotted rewards for the good and
punishments for the wicked, and that his plan will be put into effect in a
future life, since in the present life many crimes remain without punishment
and many good deeds without recompense."[2] For this it was necessary to
assume that the existence of an afterlife and the immortality of the soul
were truths of natural reason, like natural law itself. Without the natural
knowledge of the immortality of the soul, it was impossible to conclude
that punishments in the afterlife formed part of the system of natural

jurisprudence, insofar as it was founded on natural reason alone. Leibniz did believe that the immortality of the soul was a rational truth, which did not require revelation and had already been known to certain pagan philosophers,[3] but this opinion was not universally accepted. The first chancellor of the University of Halle, Veit Ludwig von Seckendorff, wrote that although the wisest pagans always suspected the existence of a life after death, they possessed no proof for it. Life after death was not a rational truth but was made known to humanity in Christian revelation. Those pagans, therefore, who acted morally, even when this was contrary to their own self-interest, lacked the assurance that their actions would eventually be rewarded.[4]

Like Seckendorff, Thomasius could not argue that punishments in the afterlife were part of a system of natural law founded on reason, because he had denied that the immortality of the soul was known to natural reason. The belief that natural reason knew anything about the soul was a scholastic error.[5] All human knowledge had to be based on experience, for "we declare that all thoughts are created by things that affect the senses, wherefore it is necessary that those things that are perceived by the senses are also those that ratiocination has as its object."[6] Humans, however, had no sensory experience of the soul as an entity existing apart from the body after death. Without the assurance of an afterlife, however, obligation in temporal life seemed reduced to Epicurean utility. As Seckendorff argued, most pagans followed their corrupt desires and obeyed morality only out of fear of punishment by the temporal magistrate, because they did not know of life after death.[7] In a letter to Bierling, Leibniz wrote that

> I find it very bad that celebrated people, such as Pufendorf and [Christian] Thomasius, teach that one knows the immortality of the soul, as well as the pains and rewards which await us beyond this life, only through revelation. . . . All doctrines of morals, of justice, of duties which are based only on the goods of this life, can be only very imperfect. Take away the [natural] immortality of the soul, and the doctrine of providence is useless, and has no more power to obligate men than the gods of Epicurus, which are without providence.[8]

The most notorious modern Epicurean, at least in the eyes of his German contemporaries, was, of course, Thomas Hobbes.[9] A fictive interlocutor in the *Institutiones* accuses Thomasius of Hobbism, that is, of adopting Carneades' opinion that "utility is the mother of what is just and equitable, and nature does not know just from unjust," which "the Epicurean Thomas Hobbes revived for the greatest part."[10] Utility, Thomasius replied, could not be the motive for individuals' obedience to the precepts of natural law. In order to distinguish himself from Hobbes, it was important for Thomasius to deny that humans entered into society out of necessity and individual self-interest, and only in order to escape the dangers of the state of nature. They entered society, he argued, because their rational nature informed them that God had wanted humans to live in society.[11] Individual utility, clearly, could not be the basis for obedience to natural law, because what was useful to an individual was not necessarily morally good. But if neither a clear threat of punishment nor utility impelled humans to it, the motivation for obeying the natural law of sociality remained very weak. Although the common utility of humanity was served by sociality, this common utility could contradict some forms of individual utility. "Not everything that is useful [to particular individuals] is honest, but everything that is honest is also useful [to humanity in common]."[12]

RATIONAL LOVE AND NATURAL LAW

It is probably in response to this dilemma, the need to find a motivation for obeying natural law while steering clear of Hobbesian self-interest, that Thomasius developed an interest in a mainly French tradition of writing on rational or reasonable love as an ethical principle. His interest manifested itself at about the same time as his first work on natural law, the *Institutiones*, was published. The January 1688 edition of Thomasius's *Monatsgespräche* contained an article on *raisonnable Liebe* ("reasonable love"), in which a cavalier, representing Thomasius, explained that rational love was not a carnal desire but an "honest passion." Both Leibniz and Thomasius admired the didactic love novels of the French authoress Madeleine de Scudéry.[13] Thomasius also referred to Molière's comedy on the miser in his preface to the *Einleitung zur Sitten Lehre*[14] and described the person guided by rational love as an *honnête homme*,[15] the term used by Jansenist thinkers, including the Duc de la Rochefoucauld in his *Maximes*.[16]

This rational love included self-love, that is, a desire for self-preservation and felicity, for conserving and improving the powers of human nature, the physical health of the body, the body's locomotive powers and sensory abilities, the powers of human reason and will. A person who pursued these goods enjoyed tranquility of mind (*Gemuethsruhe*) because these were the true goods of human nature.[17] Many people were, however, guided by a perverted, irrational form of self-love. They were ignorant of the nature of true goods and pursued *Scheingueter*, false goods, which promised felicity but led to misery. False goods were, for example, wealth, physical pleasure, and honor, which were also the origins of the main human vices of avarice, lust, and ambition.[18]

It is already possible to see how this notion of rational love could later be fused with Thomasius's spiritualist conception of religious faith as a state of the will and a form of love. Before about 1693, however, Thomasius still explained disordered self-love as due to false beliefs in the intellect, rather than to the state of the will-as-desire. Morality thus required the *emendatio intellectus*, the liberation of the intellect from prejudices and false opinions. Anyone who enjoyed the *Gemuethsruhe* that came from rational self-love also sought "to unite himself with others who enjoy a similar tranquility," because similar people attracted each other.[19] Rational love of self was also rational love of fellow humans whose minds were directed toward the same goods, so that rational love also strengthened the sociality that Thomasius had identified in the *Institutes* as God's central command in natural law. Each human being had to realize that "the law of nature was founded in the general felicity of the human race; therefore he had to consider it a good thing to institute his life according to God's will, because the general happiness included his own particular happiness."[20] Rational self-interest and the love of others led toward that which God had enjoined in natural law. Tranquility of mind, brought about by rational self-love and the love of others, and the commands of natural law were complementary, and self-interest, understood correctly, did not contradict sociality but furthered it. The problem was that many if not most human beings held wrong opinions about their self-interest and pursued various false goods like honor or wealth, which then caused conflicts between them. Rational self-love, as opposed to corrupt self-love, was such that it was not only compatible with sociality but encouraged it. The distinction between rational and irrational self-love allowed Thomasius to explain why obeying natural law was in each individual's true self-interest, despite the fact that so many believed they had to pursue their self-interest by violating natural law.

The parallels between Thomasius and French writers on this subject are often striking.[21] Jacques Abbadie, a Swiss Protestant who lived in France until the Revocation of the Edict of Nantes in 1685 and spent the last years of his life in exile in Holland, Ireland, and Germany, is an example.[22] In 1692, he published his influential treatise, *L'Art de se connoitre soi-même* (*The Art of Self-Knowledge*). The title itself is reminiscent of the full title of a moral philosophical treatise by Thomasius, the *Practice of Moral Philosophy* (*Ausübung der Sitten Lehre*)[23] and his emphasis on self-knowledge as the basis for moral improvement. In his *Art of Self-Knowledge,* Abbadie asserted that all human action was motivated by a desire for happiness, a self-love, that led humans to virtue or, if it was disordered, toward vice. At the same time, self-love could lead to the love of fellow human beings. Virtue and enlightened self-interest were therefore identical. As Abbadie wrote, "[i]n general, vice is a preference for the self over others, and virtue seems to be a preference for others over oneself. I say 'seems to be,' because in fact virtue is only one way of loving the self, much more noble and sensible than all the others."[24]

However, if rational love was advantageous as well as moral, why then did so many people refuse to follow it, even if they were informed of their errors and the truth was simple to understand? In the *Ausübung der Sitten Lehre*, written between 1693 and 1696, Thomasius commented that it would be natural to assume that the majority of humans lived in happiness, as God had given them reason and they desired happiness. The opposite, however, was the case.[25]

In earlier works, such as the *Einleitung zur Sitten Lehre* or the *Introductio ad Philosophiam Aulicam*, Thomasius explained irrational love as caused by prejudices in the intellect and the force of habit. To what extent, however, could habit and prejudice be used to explain irrational love, without denying the freedom of the will, which was the foundation of moral imputation in law and in religion? How could an individual be punished for violating a law or be denied salvation by God for false beliefs, if his actions had been guided by false opinions that he was not free to reject because habit or prejudice made him adhere to them? If habit and prejudice were not strong enough to prevent rational love, the question arose why rational love was so neglected. But if prejudices were strong enough to prevent rational love, then humans were not free to choose between true and false opinions and their actions could not be imputed to them. Thomasius's response to this dilemma after about 1693 was to abandon his previous theory of the freedom of the will and the entire moral theory that had been founded on it.

Rational Love and the Reformation of the Will

In 1696, Thomasius published the *Ausübung der Sitten Lehre*, which reflected his new conception of the will as desire rather than as a capacity for choice, and his new, deep skepticism about the usefulness of the intellect for achieving rational love and thus morality. The reason for this insufficiency of the intellect was that the good or evil nature of something was not a "speculative truth," that is, a truth that could be determined by the intellect. The recognition of good and evil was a "moral truth," a question of the ends toward which volition was directed. Humans considered everything desired by their will to be good, everything shunned by it to be evil. A person would pursue the true good only if his will was informed by rational love, not the love of false goods, but this did not depend on the intellect. As in the earlier *Einleitung*, Thomasius posited three kinds of irrational love, ambition, avarice, and luxury, to which rational love was opposed as a fourth type. In the *Ausübung*, however, these forms of love did not reflect opinions in the intellect but were four distinct types of human volition, each of which directed the activity of the intellect toward a particular favored object. The desires of the will were prior to the opinions in the intellect. The end of human love was not prescribed by the intellect; rather, the intellect was the instrument with which the will pursued its aims.

Thomasius's notion of the will-as-desire in his moral philosophy was the same as that which became central to his conception of religious faith. The specific activity of the will was not free choice between the available courses of action but either desire or its negation, aversion. If the will were free and truly indifferent toward the available courses of action, it would be impossible for it to come to a decision. The decision of an indifferent will in favor of one action rather than another would have to be determined by something other than the will itself. The will would require a higher will to direct it one way or the other, but if this second will is also free and undetermined, this leads to a regression *ad infinitum*, a point very similar to Hobbes' criticism of the scholastic conception of the independence of the will.[26]

Particular desires in the will had their origin in sensory impressions that produced an "extraordinary convulsion of the life-spirits in the blood."[27] Whether a sensory impression produced such a "convulsion" depended on both the cause of the impression and the nature of the heart on which the impression was made. The heart of an avaricious man, for example, would be moved by the sight or clinking sound of coins, a sensual person by the sight of a sumptuous meal, and an ambitious character by outward signs of honor. The result of these sense impressions was pleasure or, in the case of deprivation, pain. If the pleasure or pain was not present but prospective it brought forth hope or fear. Such sensations of pleasure and pain or hope and fear led to a movement of the will directing the agent's actions toward its desired objects and away from their opposites, and this activity of the will was the nature of passion.[28] Thomasius therefore rejected the theory of the freedom of the will he had articulated in the *Institutiones*. He now pronounced Pufendorf's theory too scholastic and too close to the scholastic theory of the freedom of the will, in particular, whereas his own present theory cohered better with the Protestant emphasis on the weakness of the human will.[29] The will was not intrinsically indifferent, although it might be indifferent toward certain things that its passions neither feared nor desired. An ambitious man, for example, might be indifferent to drink, gambling, or prostitutes.

With his new theory of volition, Thomasius also moved away from his earlier Pufendorfian theory of moral imputation, which had depended on the indifference and inner freedom of the will. Both Pufendorf in the *De Jure Naturae et Gentium*[30] and Thomasius in his *Institutiones* had described bad actions as imputable to their authors because the will was free to choose between good and bad actions. Although the will was distracted by the passions, this only made free choice difficult, not impossible.[31] From the mid-1690s onward, however, Thomasius described the will as a determinate desire, directed to a specific end and unable to choose between different actions on the basis of rational argument. If the will, however, was unable to choose, what was the purpose of laws? Thomasius replied that the fear inspired by the punishment joined to the law overrode all other desires and fears contrary to it. Humans, he wrote in the *Ausübung*, might not be free to choose, but they were free to fear.[32]

This led to certain problems concerning moral responsibility. If an agent could not choose between one action and another, the question was how this agent could be considered answerable for whatever he or she did. Thomasius's colleague Johann Franz Buddeus (1667–1729) objected that it was not possible to uphold moral imputation without the freedom of the will.[33] To understand Thomasius's solution, it is first necessary to consider his conception of voluntary actions more closely. The will, Thomasius writes, could be in four states: hope, anxiety, sadness, or joy, which could be reduced to one, hope (*spes*). Anxiety arose at the possibility of a hope being disappointed, sadness was the feeling brought about by such a disappointment, joy the feeling brought about by the fulfillment of a hope. Hope was the expression of love, that is, a desire for something. The objects of desire were determined by the passions and their proportionate strengths in a person's heart. Their choice was never free in the sense of indifference to several courses of action. A person's choice, to Thomasius, could be free only in the sense that the intention of the will and the outcome of the action harmonized. Thomasius described this freedom of the will as *spontaneum*, spontaneous. "There are two forms of spontaneity; it is either free (extrinsically) when the will impels the body's locomotive powers without external stimulus either to the first volition, or hope, and without fear; or it is coerced, when the will is necessitated and coerced to do something by the external stimulation of either hope or fear."[34]

The important point was that even the second type of action, which the will was made to perform by the external stimulation of either hope or fear, was free in the sense of being *spontaneum* and, therefore, imputable. All that was necessary for an action to be imputed was an agreement (*complacentia*) between action and the agent's intention. If someone wanted to drink medicine and took poison by mistake, this action was involuntary with respect to the poison. If, however, somebody wanted to kill an enemy and mistakenly killed a friend, then he was, of course, guilty of murder.[35]

In the case of a *spontaneum coactum*, the will had been "necessitated and coerced extrinsically by the excitement of hope or fear,"[36] but even an action committed out of fear was imputable, because intention and action harmonized. Why, Thomasius asked, "must an action to which the human will has been coerced invisibly and by fear not be considered voluntary, when it is considered a voluntary action if the primary human will or its inborn desire is made to act by an external stimulation of its *potentia*, for example, by friendly persuasion, the offer of a reward, etc., as the reason is the same in both cases, that is, a coercion of the will."[37] "So peace treaties extracted by war, actions conforming to law, even if they proceed from the fear of (further war or) punishment, are, by common consent voluntary and are imputed."[38] There were, however, certain exceptions. Promises made to robbers out of fear, for example, were not imputed. The reason was that a legislator had "the [rightful] power to instill [fear],"[39] while a robber did not. Similarly, the actions of a slave commanded by his master were not imputed to the slave.

"Scholastic" moral philosophy, as Thomasius understood it, assumed that man was an *animal rationale*, that the intellect was the defining part of human nature, and that the will was free. Although Thomasius had held this conception himself in the *Institutiones* and even the *Einleitung* of 1692, he was now arguing that the "scholastic" philosophy of the traditional Lutheran universities overestimated the importance of reason in human nature. The general but mistaken belief in rationality as the essence of humanity was the reason for moral philosophy's lack of success thus far in leading humans toward felicity and virtue. The conclusions of reason always remained dependent on the orientation of the will and could not change it. Reason, by itself, was also incapable of understanding the nature of man's infelicity. It could lead humans to a recognition that they were miserable and radically incapable of achieving virtue by their own efforts, but it could not lead to a knowledge of why this was so and how it might be corrected.[40] The scholastics' focus on the intellect was also another of papalism's instruments to further the influence of the clergy on secular affairs. "The common doctrine of the internal freedom of the will is the principal fulcrum of the Papist doctrine of acquiring eternal salvation through good works."[41] It was another attempt by papalists, whether they were orthodox Lutherans or Roman Catholics, to establish *fides cerebrina*, that is, a faith based on an intellectual understanding of certain so-called orthodox doctrines, not on the purity of the will.

THE RELATIONSHIP OF RATIONAL LOVE TO CHRISTIAN LOVE

The relationship of rational love to Christian love was a particularly important question in the moral reform of human nature. In Thomasius's later work, such as the *Ausübung der Sitten Lehre*, rational (or reasonable) love and Christian love had become identical, but they were not the same in his earlier moral philosophical writings. In the *Einleitung zur Sitten Lehre* of 1692, for example, Thomasius had defined rational love as a stepping-stone in the progression toward Christian love. Although it was possible to love fellow humans and even God rationally without loving them in a Christian manner, it was impossible for Christian love to exist without rational love. At that time, Thomasius still drew a sharp distinction between rational and Christian love, a distinction corresponding to that between reason and revelation. Thomasius's declared aim in the *Einleitung zur Sitten Lehre* was to direct humans toward rational love, not Christian love. There were, he wrote, three types of human beings in the world, beasts, humans, and Christians. Bestial human beings were raised to the human level by the right use of natural reason, while the sincere adoption of Christian faith advanced them to the Christian state. His aim was to raise bestial humans to the level of "human humans," who used their rational faculties without prejudices.[42]

Thomasius was critical of attempts by authors like Johann Ludwig Prasch (1637–90) to present rational love and Christian love as essentially identical or, at least, as no more than two degrees on a continuum. In the *Commentatio de Lege Caritatis* (1688), Prasch maintained that *caritas,* the love of God and of other humans commanded in the Bible, constituted the principles of natural law.[43] In particular, Prasch objected to Grotius's opposition of natural law to charity in the *De Jure Belli ac Pacis.*[44] The precepts of natural law, Prasch wrote, were founded on principles of charity, not distinct from them as Grotius had argued. Grotius had failed to realize that human self-interest, from which he aimed to derive natural law,[45] was a mark of the human *status corruptus* and, because of this, not the basis of natural law.[46] God was love (*agape*) and man had been created in God's image. Therefore, man was, by nature, destined for love. Furthermore, a natural harmony among humans obligated them to mutual charity. The biblical moral law (*lex moralis*) merely repeated the principles of the natural law of charity. Prasch did separate a *caritas Christiana* from the *caritas communis* of natural law, but only as an extension that was different in degree, not radically distinct. While common charity was the foundation of natural justice among all human beings, Christian charity prevailed among Christians and extended beyond common charity to include, for example, patience and humility. Both Christian charity and common charity, however, were forms of charity and, to this extent, based on the same principle.

Thomasius's notion of rational love, in his early writings, did not exclude all love of God since natural reason could recognize God as author of creation and exact love for him on that basis, but this rational love of God differed from the Christian love of God and of fellow humans taught by revelation. Prasch's theory suffered from the same error as Alberti's moral philosophy. It implied that the difference between rational and revealed knowledge was one of degree rather than kind. Thomasius promptly criticized Prasch's *De Lege Caritatis* in his *Monatsgespräche* of February 1689, to which Prasch replied with his *Kurtze Gegen-Antwort auf Herrn Christian Thomas Einwürffe wider seine Schrifft Vom Gesetz der Liebe*.[47] Thomasius's view of the relationship between rational love and Christian love is summarized particularly well by a passage from his *Einleitung zur Sitten Lehre* of 1692:

> The greatest felicity consists in the love of God and one's neighbor. And although rational love is not as perfect as Christian love, rational love is, so to speak, a stage through which it is possible to reach Christian love, and as he who does not love God does not love his neighbor, so he cannot love others in a Christian manner, if he does not love them rationally.[48]

After 1693, however, the changed relationship of will to intellect in Thomasius's thought also necessitated a different conception of rational love. Reason, Thomasius now maintained, was incapable of leading humans even to temporal felicity, which depended on the correction of the will. Although reason led humans from the state of bestiality to that of humanity, those in the state of humanity had not achieved rational love but only recognized their misery. The fulfillment of man's natural powers of reason was not rational love but the realization that reason was inadequate to achieve virtue and felicity.

"Rational" love now depended on attaining the state of Christian faith, in which the will-as-desire was directed toward God, and rational (or reasonable) love and faith now were not distinct but identical. The redirection of the will from temporal goods toward God came about not through a single act of free choice but through a long struggle by the contrite soul, which culminated in a reform of the believer's entire nature and his or her spiritual rebirth. This remained true even after Thomasius revised his theory of regeneration and the will-as-desire around 1703 to avoid the accusation of enthusiasm. He continued to regard rational love as the love toward God.[49] Rational love, he now argued, consisted in maintaining a balance between the three passions of lust, ambition, and avarice, not in a fourth form of love that suppressed the other three. It is this definition of rational love on which Thomasius's second main work of natural law, the *Fundamenta Juris Naturae et Gentium*, is based.

It has been argued that Thomasius's theory in the *Fundamenta* is incoherent, because it is not clear how people can ever be sure they are not acting under the influence of passions.[50] If all people consider the object of their desire to be good precisely because they desire it, it seems impossible for a person under the influence of the passions to distinguish between rational love and corrupt love. All people will be convinced they are acting correctly, because their ambition, avarice, or lust will blind them to the corruption of their own will. As Thomasius observes, "he cannot apply it [moral philosophy] as long as his judgment is corrupt concerning his own actions, in such a way that he does not realize he is ill. This is the cause of most quarrels, that someone wants to correct others but believes that he himself does not require correction."[51] How then could any agreement on what is moral be possible, if the person who is under the influence of his depraved desires is as certain of his moral rectitude as the wise man whose passions neutralize each other?

And yet, Thomasius clearly believed such a realization and improvement to be possible,[52] mainly because the passions were not active all the time. They might not only neutralize each other but in certain matters not interfere with a person's judgment at all. This was more likely to occur in judging the affairs of other people, in which we had no interest and which did not depend on our will.[53] When the actions of others did depend on our will or we favored or disliked these people, our judgment lost its impartiality again. But even in one's own affairs it was possible to arrive at an impartial position, since "all passions have their intervals of rest and there is no doubt that during these intervals reason is free to judge correctly of good and evil," though these occasions might be rare and elusive, as "certain passions move the blood in the heart so subtly that the movement of these passions can barely be noticed even by someone who is highly attentive." Therefore, "the difference between right and corrupt reason is also often realized only with difficulty" and "human reason cannot safely trust itself as long as it is not certain of this interval."[54] In these intervals of tranquility, however, man was able to form rational and moral judgments. Man driven by ambition or avarice or lust might think he was pursuing what is good, but in the intervals of tranquility he would realize that he had not been, and he could recognize his own foolishness.

This recognition of one's own foolishness (*agnitio stultitiae*) was the beginning of wisdom.[55] Once a person had realized that human nature was corrupt and that this corruption was a corruption in the will, not the intellect, the main obstacle to moral reform had been removed. It was because the foolish believed that "they are the most excellent and wise of all creatures"[56] and because "they seek the excellence of human nature before all other creatures in the intellect"[57] that they tried to achieve virtue and felicity through opinions in the intellect, when virtue and felicity actually depended on the reform of human volition. Insight into the nature of human corruption led to contrition. This prepared the way for regeneration, which was the foundation of faith and morality in equal measure, and which required the assistance of divine grace, though this was the universal grace of God, which was not supranatural but operated within the natural order.[58] Wisdom, Thomasius wrote, was a "habit of divine virtue and the most subtle spirit," which was attracted "by the magnet of prayer, so to speak," and through which "foolishness in us is suffocated and bound."[59]

MORALITY AND THE TRANSFORMATION OF HUMAN NATURE

The moral regeneration brought about by faith did more than change the individual's pattern of actions. It transformed his or her very nature. He or she, quite literally, became another human being. This belief distinguished Thomasius's view in the *Foundations* from his first work, the *Institutes*. There, morality had depended on the recognition of God's commands by the intellect and the decision to obey them by the will. Morality and the study of human physical nature were sharply distinguished. Laws, Thomasius wrote in agreement with Pufendorf, were impositions by moral agents on the physical world.

This view, however, changed because Thomasius began to present the passions, based in the will-as-desire, as *natural* properties of humans and part of their *physical* nature, so that the redirection of these passions from corrupt to good ends also meant the transformation of this nature. He now argued that Pufendorf had opposed the spheres of morality and nature to each other too much and that the character of laws as *impositions* on the physical world was an exaggeration.[60] Instead, moral philosophy was *part* of the study of the natural, physical world. All science was the study of *potentiae*, that is, the qualities, powers, or properties of natural bodies: mathematics was that of the *potentia* common to all bodies, quantity; astronomy studied the "powers of bodies in the heavens";[61] while physics concerned itself with the *potentiae* of earthly bodies.[62] Physics, therefore, comprehended moral theory, because human beings were earthly bodies, too, and the passions were the *potentiae* of human volition and the subject of moral theory.

By turning moral philosophy into a part of the study of human nature, Thomasius also provided a solution to the question of punishments in natural law, which had presented such a problem in his earlier natural law theory of the *Institutes*. A transgressor of natural law would not be punished in an obvious sense, as a criminal was punished by a human sovereign. Instead, God "has arranged nature in such a way that everything good carries its own rewards and everything evil its own punishments. There is, properly speaking, no difference between physical and ethical evil, e.g., if you drink or whore you will suffer from a hangover or syphilis."[63] These physical evils were not punishment in the exact legal sense, because "each punishment is inflicted visibly, but the evils that God ordained to the transgressors of natural law come secretly, that is, so that the connection of the evil with the sin is not evident, even though the evil itself is evident."[64] Unless the evil was clearly linked to the sin, it would not, as punishments should do, serve to dissuade the sinner from wrongdoing. Natural law, therefore, was the understanding of the natural properties of physical entities, and of the natural consequences of moral and immoral actions. Moral philosophy examined human beings as members of the natural world rather than as existing in a separate moral realm. Thus, Thomasius's natural philosophy was essential to his moral theory, and his interpretation of nature will be the subject of chapter 8.

CHAPTER EIGHT

THE INTERPRETATION OF NATURE

Thomasius published only one natural philosophical treatise, the *Versuch vom Wesen des Geistes* (*Essay on the Nature of Spirit*) of 1699, a work in which he described the Cartesians' mechanistic interpretation of nature as pagan and impious, and as a reflection of sinful pride in the powers of the human intellect. According to Thomasius, Cartesianism and orthodox Lutheranism shared one critical defect, however different they were in other respects: both placed too much emphasis on the intellect. They ignored the importance of the will-as-desire in their view of human nature and failed to recognize the need for a reform of the heart to acquire religious faith, virtue, and thus wisdom.[1]

Cartesianism in a strict sense was very rare at German universities around 1700,[2] but Thomasius was responding to a loosely Cartesian form of natural philosophy, which had established itself in the medical faculty of Halle, and which was represented especially by physicians such as Friedrich Hoffmann (1660–1742), whose so-called "iatro-mechanistic" theory of medicine treated the human body as a machine, composed of particles of inert, extended matter, whose movements were directed by the soul.[3] Hoffmann's ideas reflected the influence of physicians such as Hermann Boerhaave (1668–1738) in Leiden and Giovanni Borelli (1608–79), who interpreted diseases as the mechanical malfunctioning of this body-machine. Hoffmann's theory did not rest on the same neo-Platonic metaphysical foundation as Descartes' physics, but it was not uncommon for Cartesian physics to be used without Descartes' metaphysics.[4] Similarly, in the *Versuch*, Thomasius did not examine Descartes' metaphysics, but only the Cartesian definition of bodily entities as no more than passive, extended matter.[5]

Thomasius's own natural philosophy was hermetic and quasi-mystical. It explained natural phenomena as due to the operation of hidden forces of sympathy and antipathy, that is, attraction and repulsion, between material bodies. These ideas were closer to the theories of thinkers like Paracelsus (1493–1541) than to those of the figures that are more commonly associated with the Scientific Revolution and the Enlightenment, such as Robert Boyle or Isaac Newton. It is not surprising, then, that Thomasius's natural philosophy is often considered a curiosity, which is marginal to his main, "enlightened" philosophical interests, as an aberration in his personal intellectual history, and a work that is of little consequence to his later thought.[6]

The natural philosophy of the *Versuch*, however, continued to play a role in Thomasius's writings after 1699 and is more important for his moral philosophy than has usually been argued.[7] Thomasius himself described the theories in the *Versuch* as the basis for his moral philosophical views in the *Foundations of the Law of Nature and Nations* in 1705, where Thomasius explained that in his *Versuch vom Wesen des Geistes* he had refuted the *moral* theory of his first work on natural law, the *Institutes* of 1688,[8] which had been founded on a very different conception of nature.

THOMASIUS'S THEORY OF NATURE, CA. 1690: MIND, BODY, AND SUBSTANTIAL FORMS

Although Thomasius did not publish a complete treatise on natural philosophy before the *Versuch* in 1699, he discussed a number of natural philosophical questions in an earlier work, the *Introduction to Court Philosophy* (*Introductio ad philosophiam aulicam*), published in 1688, the same year as his *Institutes of Divine Jurisprudence*. Thomasius's main interest in the *Introduction* was to define a middle way between the philosophical schools of Aristotelianism and Cartesianism.[9] His attempt to reconcile the two systems was part of a more general debate in late seventeenth-century Europe over the respective virtues and defects of modern and ancient philosophy, the authority of new ideas in comparison to the authority of tradition, or, as Thomasius put it, over the "prejudices of the Cartesians and the ineptitudes of the Peripatetics," respectively. In the mid-1670s, for example, the question of the superiority of either Cartesianism or Aristotelianism had been the subject of a major controversy at the University of Leiden in the Low Countries.[10]

Thomasius focused in particular on Aristotelians' and Cartesians' respective conceptions of substance, that is, of the essence of physical entities. Descartes defined the substance of corporeal being in terms of spatial extension, for reasons that were linked to his epistemological skepticism. The observable properties of material bodies, such as smell, taste, and color, were, on the whole, an unreliable source of information about physical entities, because sensory data on them was subject to distortion and lacked certainty. Spatial extension, however, was a category of geometry and, as such, was objective, in a way that other sensible characteristics of corporeal matter were not.[11] Spatial extension could be defined in mathematical terms, which enjoyed self-evident, *a priori* truth-status, unlike other sensory data.[12]

Thomasius argued that Descartes' epistemological skepticism was unnecessarily extreme.[13] Although he conceded that the senses were sometimes deceived, he denied that they were totally unreliable. For although the senses might fail to perceive the nature of the object affecting them, there always had to be something causing the sense impression, so that the senses were trustworthy guides at least to the existence or nonexistence of objects. False impressions gained from one sense organ could also be corrected by the impressions gained from another. For example, by touching a stick that appeared bent in water, an observer could determine that it was straight. To abstract from all sensory impressions to establish the first principles of philosophy was unnecessary.[14]

Spatial extension was not privileged over other sensible properties of corporeal entities, as Descartes believed. It was only one characteristic of bodily entities, and "[i]t could be accepted that Descartes described body as an *extended* substance, if only he had not said that *extension* was itself the *substance* of body."[15] According to Descartes, extension was the *substantial* characteristic of corporeal entities on which all other properties of these corporeal entities depended. Being blue, hot, or sour were no more than ways, *modi*, of being extended in space,[16] but Thomasius believed that extension was a characteristic like any other, not the substance-defining property of corporeal being. Being extended in a particular way, for example, having a certain color or being cold, was a mode (*modus*) of being substance X.

Unlike Aristotelians, however, Thomasius also believed it was impossible for humans to say what the substance X of a bodily entity was. The substance was the cause of the particular combination of characteristics (*accidentia*) in any material body,[17] but sensory observation of these characteristics did not lead to any knowledge of this substance, which was hidden and evident to the senses only in its effects, not in itself. "And I feel indeed that there is *something* that causes this combination [i.e., of *accidentia*], but I do not know *why* there is this combination."[18] There was no possibility of knowing substance X by studying the characteristics dependent on it, because "our knowledge of the existence of any thing begins with the *accidentia*. . . . abstractions based on *accidentia* will always be abstractions of *accidentia*" and cannot provide a notion of the underlying substance itself.[19] Humans therefore had "no distinct and clear concept of any created substance,"[20] at least since the Fall from Grace. In the state of innocence, humans had been able to grasp, "so to speak, intuitively the natures, essences, and forms of created things that today are hidden from us or are perceived by us barely, or not even to that degree, even following the most laborious scrutiny."[21]

Thus, the properties of natural bodies were to be explained not in terms of the mere structure and motion of extended matter but as expressions of their concealed substances. Experience indicated, for example, that plants, animals, even stones and minerals were not automata, but contained a substantial vital principle (*principium vitale*). Anyone who observed stones, Thomasius claimed, noticed that even they in some sense "live, are nourished and grow."[22] Animals were distinguished from plants and stones by their powers of locomotion.

The main difference between humans and all other animals was that humans were capable of forming abstractions and of ratiocination.[23] This was evident from language, which was used by humans but not by animals as a means of communication. Humans could infer from this that they consisted of two parts: like all other created bodies, they possessed a material *corpus* with particular substantial properties, but what set them apart from the rest of creation was the possession of a nonmaterial *mens*. The human body was an "external substance, endowed with a vital principle that exercised its operations partly through internal, partly through external movement."[24] The *mens* was a "being that can think."[25] If these two components were considered in conjunction, it was possible to "give a clear definition of *man* in no other way than by saying that man is a locomotive corporeal substance endowed with the capacity to think."[26] This bipartite nature of humans was the precondition for their freedom of will, which was central to Thomasius's early moral theory in the *Institutes of Divine Jurisprudence* of 1688. Because humans consisted of a body and a *mens*, which was not subject to physical necessity, and volition was a form of thought in the *mens*, the human will was not determined but free to choose any available course of action.

The possession of a mind or spirit that was different in kind from material bodies distinguished humans from all other parts of material creation. The essence of this *mens* however, or of any purely spiritual beings, such as angels, was unknown to natural reason. Throughout his career in Leipzig and Halle, Thomasius believed that humans could have no natural knowledge of spiritual being. He was critical of both Lutheran scholastic pneumatology, that is, the branch of philosophy that concerned itself with spiritual being, as well as Descartes' definition of *cogitatio* as the substance of spirit. Descartes had arrived at his definition by the following argument: even if a person did not trust the senses and doubted the existence of the external world itself, including his or her own existence, this doubt was an act of thought that proved the existence of the person as a thinking subject, endowed with a mind.[27] Thought was the essence of the mind, because thinking was its necessary activity, which was independent even of the existence of an external world. The mind always thought, even in infants and during sleep. From the mind's opposition to the material world of *res extensae*, Descartes derived the immortality of the soul. Death was the destruction of the material entity of the body, which left the spirit unaffected.[28]

Thomasius believed, however, that the activity of the mind could not be abstracted from the sensory perception of an external world. It was only as mind receiving, contemplating, and remembering sensory impressions that humans were conscious of it at all. "Thought is an action of the mind, by which the human being or reason [*mens*] in the mind [*cerebrum*] in the form of a discourse or speech consisting of words affirms, denies, or asks something about the forms impressed on the mind [*cerebrum*] by the motion of external bodies through the sense organs."[29] Thinking, *cogitatio*, therefore, was not the *substantia* of the mind, that is, that which the mind was necessarily, as Descartes had supposed. It was only a *modus existendi*, a particular mode of existence peculiar to the mind in human beings, who were receiving sensory impressions from the external world. It was also the only *modus existendi* of the mind known to humans. It was only as mind united to a body fitted with external sensory organs that humans had any experience of the mind, for "as long as we conceive of mind in the form of thinking, we necessarily do not have a distinct concept of it independently of its reference to the body" and the sense impressions derived from the body's sense organs.[30] Therefore, natural reason could not conceive the *mens* as an immaterial being, which could exist separately from the human body. From this it also followed that humans, contrary to Descartes, could not know of the immortality of the soul on the basis of natural reason.[31]

THE NATURAL PHILOSOPHY OF THE *VERSUCH VOM WESEN DES GEISTES* (1699)

The clear separation of spiritual being from physical nature was part of Thomasius's moral theory around 1690 and reflected his strict, characteristically Pufendorfian, distinction between the moral realm of rational beings, endowed with a free will, and the material world, governed by laws of physical necessity. In the course of the 1690s, however, this distinction between the spiritual and the physical world began to blur, at the same time as Thomasius revised his notions of faith and the will and his moral philosophy.[32] From the mid-1690s, Thomasius argued that every natural phenomenon and even the existence of any corporeal matter itself required the combination of matter with a spiritual principle,[33] and that therefore not only humans but "*every* corporeal entity consists of matter and spirit."[34]

Scholastics and Cartesians failed to provide a coherent explanation of natural phenomena, because both ignored the importance of spirits for natural phenomena. The former explained natural phenomena in terms of substantial forms, the latter in terms of the size, figure, and motion of corporeal matter. Both restricted spiritual being to the human intellect.

Thomasius's new physics of spirits is datable to some time around 1693–94. In November 1694, the physician Friedrich Hoffmann published a defense of his iatro-mechanistic medical theory against Thomasius's new physics of spirits.[35] Matter, Thomasius now argued, underwent change and even existed only by virtue of an active principle of spirit, which took the place of the non-spiritual substantial forms (*formae substantiales*), the vital principle (*principium vitale*), and intrinsic locomotive powers in Thomasius's earlier works. Thomasius's new criticism of Cartesian physics rested on experimental evidence, which he appears to have collected in the mid- to late 1690s. One of the inconsistencies of Cartesian theory, Thomasius argued, was its explanation of suction as the result of pressure by "cylinders of air" (*cylindri aerei*). The concept of *cylindri aerei* was incoherent, and the "new philosophers" could not agree in which direction these cylinders pressed, whether up, down, or from all sides.[36] If air pressure pushed downward, it would be impossible to raise anything; if its pressure were directed upward, everything would drift toward the sun. If the particles of air that exerted the pressure moved in different directions simultaneously, they would be incapable of exerting pressure in any particular direction.[37] The failure of strictly mechanistic principles to explain natural phenomena caused the adherents of mechanistic philosophy to invent concepts such as the elasticity of air in order to cover their ignorance of the true causes of a phenomenon. In effect, they thereby surreptitiously reintroduced occult powers into their natural philosophy, after claiming to have banished them from it.[38]

Another example Thomasius gave of the shortcomings of mechanistic philosophy was an experiment with a cup of mercury, which was placed inside a larger vessel. A tube was inserted into the cup with mercury and all the air was sucked from both the tube and the outer vessel. When air was released back into the outer vessel, the mercury began to rise in the tube. To other natural philosophers, such as Robert Boyle, this was proof of air pressure and, therefore, of the materiality of air.[39] Thomasius believed it was more convincing to conceive air as a spirit, not as matter, and attributed the behavior of the mercury to the power of attraction (*attractio*) by the *Lufft-Geist* (air-spirit), which increased in strength when air was sucked from the tube or the vessel and the remaining air-spirit was spread over a greater space. The more the air-spirit expanded to fill a space the stronger was air's power of *attractio*. The expansion of the air-spirit did not happen by itself but required another force, that of a second spirit, light. The forces of light and air were opposed to each other: the former caused expansion, the latter attraction and contraction.

There were other experiments that, Thomasius believed, proved that suction was not caused by air pressure, but by an inherent power of attraction in air. If one conducted the experiment described above, waited for the mercury to rise in the tube, and then prevented communication between the air pump and the tube, the column of mercury would drop. If the valve that controlled the flow of air between the tube and the pump was reopened, the column would go up again. "Thus it is possible, therefore, to let the mercury in the tube dance up and down by turning the valve."[40] Because the air pressure on the mercury remained the same, it could not explain the rise and fall of the level of mercury in the glass cylinder. Only the power of the air-spirit to attract other objects, a power that increased when the spirit expanded to fill a larger space and was the stronger the larger the space that exerted this force, could explain the movement of the mercury. Restoring communication between the glass cylinder and the pump resulted in a larger space, which pulled at the mercury with greater strength and, therefore, was able to make it rise higher in the cylinder. Closing the valve between pump and cylinder reduced the size of the space filled with expanded air, diminishing the strength of the force attracting the mercury.

Another experiment used by Cartesians to demonstrate the existence of material air pressure was turned into an argument against it by Thomasius. A bottomless brass cup was connected to an air pump at one end. The other was covered by a glass disc, stuck to the rim of the cup with wax. If air was sucked from the cup, the glass disk broke. If two glass disks were placed above each other, the inner disk was shattered first. Thomasius concluded that the power of suction must be attributed to the *attractio* exerted by the rarefied air. If external pressure were the cause, the outer disk would break before the inner one did.[41]

Thomasius was not the only philosopher to criticize the narrow definition of corporeal entities as *res extensae*. Leibniz, for example, also wrote that because matter was a passive principle, it could not extend itself but required an active principle to extend it.[42] Where Leibniz and Thomasius differed, however, was in their conception of these active principles. The active forces with which Leibniz explained physical motion were within bodily matter and could not exist apart from it in the same way as Thomasius's spirits. Leibniz's model of nature was another version of corpuscular mechanics. It was similar to Descartes' ideas in that all natural phenomena were produced by the movement of pieces of extended matter and the modifications of their movements by collisions between them.[43] Thomasius's theory was more similar to Henry More's "Spirit of Nature" than to Leibniz's *vis activa*, as Thomasius attributed motion and corporeal extension to certain spirits that extended matter, formed it into corporeal entities with specific properties, such as taste or color, and directed its motion through forces of attraction and expansion.[44]

These Thomasian spirits could exist apart from matter and were extended in space, unlike Descartes' *res cogitans*, which had no spatial extension. Thomasius believed that spirits' extension in space and their ability to exist outside of corporeal matter was evident on the basis of reason. It was generally agreed that no space in the world could be filled with nothing. Descartes had concluded that everything was filled with matter and that spirits did not occupy space, but Thomasius replied that if everything were filled by matter, physical motion would be impossible: "And so there could be no motion if everything were full of matter and there were no spirit that moved matter and in which matter was moved; for it is contrary to all sensory experience to say that I can move many contiguous bodies by moving one or a part of them, if all spaces are occupied."[45] The particles of prime matter had to be either

> round and rounded, or with corners. In the first case, small spaces would have remained between these particles, which would have been occupied either by nothing, or by this nobler being [that is, spirits], or by other pieces of matter. If there was nothing in these spaces, this would be absurd; the second assumption would prove the existence of our spiritual being, but the third would make all physical movement impossible.[46]

Therefore there had to be immaterial beings with spatial extension that filled the voids between material bodies. There also had to be a force that held the particles of prime matter together. Common sense and experience indicated that large bodies could not be formed simply by compressing smaller pieces of matter but had to be made to cohere from within by a spirit.[47] And even if bodies were formed by the compression of smaller parts of matter, there had to be something continuously pushed these particles together externally, so that the existence of spirits in nature was not disproved.[48]

As Thomasius had said in his *Introductio ad philosophiam aulicam* of 1688, reason knew nothing about the nature of spiritual being. Contrary to the arguments of various theorists, such as the Cartesians, scholastic metaphysicians, Henry More, and Leibniz, Thomasius believed that reason on its own could not, for example, know of the immortality of the soul, that is, its continued existence after the material body had disintegrated.[49] This was in contrast to Leibniz, who had argued that God had instituted creation according to principles that were not only rational but also accessible to human understanding. Although these nonmaterial causes of natural phenomena were themselves invisible, humans could form a rational concept of them.[50] Thomasius, however, had always insisted on the inscrutability of God, the incomprehensibility of his being and his decisions to human reason. Natural knowledge of the invisible causes of natural phenomena therefore could not go beyond very limited conclusions based on sensory observation. The observation of an effect could not yield a necessary conclusion about its cause, because the same effect could be caused differently in different instances,[51] and even when the effect of one particular cause was known, the reverse conclusion, that every effect of this particular kind was always due to the same type of cause, was not necessarily true. Though natural philosophers like Robert Boyle and Henry More, for example, might agree on the phenomenon to be explained, their interpretations of its cause often differed.[52] It was also impossible to know whether every relevant circumstance had been considered in the explanation of a particular phenomenon.[53] A single circumstance could change the effect of a particular cause. To be able to formulate universal and necessary propositions, humans would have to make every observation that can be made, but "the entire human race cannot have this wealth of experience, let alone one human being."[54]

Knowledge of the spiritual principles underlying physical nature thus had to be based on revelation, not sensory observation or reason,[55] and Thomasius turned, in particular, to the account of creation in the book of Genesis, like several other, mainly spiritualist, theorists before him: the German mystics Jacob Böhme and Valentin Weigel, the Englishman Robert Fludd in his *Philosophia Moysaica*,[56] and the Moravian John Amos Comenius in his *Physicae ad Lumen Divinum Reformatae Synopsis* are examples.[57] The central principles of this "Mosaic Physics" were based on verses one through ten of the first chapter of Genesis:

1   In the beginning God created the heaven and the earth.

2   And the earth was without form, and void and darkness was upon the face of the deep. And the spirit of God moved upon the face of the waters.

3   And God said, Let there be light; and there was light.

4   And God saw the light, that it was good: and God divided the light from the darkness.

5   And God called the light day, and the darkness he called night. And the evening and the morning were the first day.

6   And God said, Let there be a firmament in the midst of the waters, and let it divide the waters from the waters.

7   And God made the firmament, and divided the waters which were under the firmament from the waters which were above the firmament: and it was so.

8   And God called the firmament heaven: and the evening and the morning were the second day.

9   And God said, Let the waters under the heaven be gathered together in one place; and let the dry land appear: and it was so.

10   And God called the dry land earth; and the gathering together of the waters he called seas: and God saw that it was good.[58]

From this passage, Thomasius derived the existence of the two main spirits in nature, light and air: Light caused warmth and expansion, while air was cold and caused contraction. The human *anima* was not a separate type of spirit, as Thomasius had claimed in the *Institutiones* or the *Introductio ad philosophiam aulicam*, but a composite of these two spirits of air and light, which were released after a person's death.[59]

NATURE AND MORALITY

This natural philosophical theory of attraction was important for Thomasius's moral philosophy, because it offered a physical explanation for the nature of the human will as desire or love, that is, as a form of attraction, which Cartesian physics failed to provide. In his preface to Poiret's "*De eruditione solida, superficiaria et falsa*," for example, the text that signals Thomasius's new anthropology and religiosity, Thomasius praised Poiret for his defense of a principle of attraction (*attractus*) in physical nature, contrary to the opinion of the Cartesians, who reduced all natural phenomena to the effects of *pulsio*, collisions between extended pieces of matter.[60]

The nature (*potentia*) of humans was their attraction to those particular goods that they believed furthered their self-preservation. This attraction or desire, which was based in the human will, was either the worldly love of the unregenerate or the pure love of the regenerate, which was directed toward God and fellow humans. It was also an example of the more general principles of attraction and repulsion, or sympathy and antipathy, throughout the natural order:

> The plants and trees sense their vital sap, suck it into themselves, grow, thereby produce fruit and seeds; their love and hate or their desires are described in many thousands of examples by those who have written on the sympathy and antipathy between things. For their sympathy is nothing other than the love of the spirit of plants, minerals, and animals, and antipathy is their hate.[61]

The difference between human love and the forces of sympathy operating in the rest of nature was that the objects of human love could vary within the human species, from one individual to the next and within any period of time, whereas the objects of the love or sympathy of all other creatures were uniform and constant within each species. The reason was that the desires of the human will had been in disorder since the Fall from Grace, when man's will, which had been intended to guide his actions with rational love toward care for himself and benevolence toward his fellow human beings, had been corrupted by the passions of ambition, lust, and avarice. The proportionate strengths of these three passions differed from one person to the next and even within one person over time. Because the passions guided the will and the will was the main part of human nature, the varying strengths of the passions meant that humanity did not have a uniform nature or essence, so that "the animals of one species have the same desires throughout their life, while among humans there are as many desires as there are people and a person within a quarter of an hour is torn by so many desires conflicting with each other and made restless."[62] Although love was the generic essence of human nature, insofar as regenerate and unregenerate characters were guided by different objects of love, they had different specific natures, so that "the regenerate and the unregenerate differ as to their species."[63] There was thus no single human nature and it was certainly not that of an animal endowed with reasoning powers (*animal cogitatione praeditum*) as university philosophy, whether Cartesian or scholastic, maintained.[64]

Humans' corrupt and divergent wills undermined the original harmony of human social life, as they led humans into conflict with one another. This was unlike, for example, animals of one species, who never came into conflict and always pursued their true self-interest, because their love directed them to what was good for themselves and furthered their self-preservation. Humans' corrupt will, however, caused them to pursue false goods, which, instead of preserving them, shortened life and lessened its felicity: "The power of the heart is such that while animals are not by nature enemies, one human by nature does not love another, but hates many, and while the desires of animals are directed toward the preservation of their faculties, the spirit of humans yearns for preservation, but all human desires ruin them."[65]

Humans, Thomasius concluded, were less wise and more foolish than, for example, bees or spiders.[66] Wisdom, that is, the pursuit of what is truly good for a creature, depended on the correct orientation of this creature's love or desire. It was not achieved by the intellect, contrary to the claims of academic philosophers. "The spirit of metals, plants, and animals cannot produce syllogisms and chimeras. . . . But it produces diamonds, rubies, cedars, elephants, and your intellect cannot create a louse. It [the spirit of metals, animals, plants] draws conclusions that preserve and sustain its corporeal existence," while the conclusions of human reason were often fruitless and counterproductive. A stone, which did not act against its own interest, was wiser than a human being who was led to self-destructive behavior under the influence of the corrupt passions.[67]

Thomasius's contemporaries were quick to detect and to criticize the intended religious implications of this argument about wisdom: if this ordered love, which in humans was the foundation of Christian faith, depended as little on the intellect in human nature as it did in the nature of plants or bees, then the adoption of an orthodox doctrine by the intellect contributed nothing to Christian faith, either. Thomasius's theory of sympathy and antipathy in nature was directly opposed to his orthodox opponents' insistence on doctrine as a precondition of Christian faith. In Leipzig, the orthodox clergyman Albrecht Christian Roth denied that it was possible, as Thomasius had done, to equate sympathy in nonhuman nature, among plants or bees, with love in the "kingdom of the intellect" (*regnum intellectuale*) to which humans belonged. The possession of an intellect, Roth argued, *did* constitute a critical distinction between human and nonhuman nature.[68] Religious faith began with *notitia*, the understanding in the intellect of the message of salvation offered by Christ. In the believer, *notitia* was followed by *assensus*, intellectual assent to the truth message. From this sprang *fiducia*, trust toward God.[69] Thomasius, in Roth's opinion, downplayed the importance of the intellect in human nature in order to disparage doctrinal orthodoxy. Thus, Thomasius's interpretation of nature was another example of his religious "Enthusiasterey."[70]

Thomasius's hermetic natural philosophy was not the only example of its kind in Halle around 1700. While some physicians at the University of Halle, including Friedrich Hoffmann (1660–1742), put forward a very different, mechanistic theory of human nature, there was a rival school of medicine, represented by Georg Ernst Stahl (1659–1734), that was much closer to Thomasius's ideas.[71] In an essay, one of Stahl's pupils, Michael Alberti, referred with approval to Thomasius's criticism of mechanistic explanations in nature.[72] Like Thomasius, Stahl argued that the body was not a purely material being, whose functioning depended on the mechanical interaction of its different parts. The movements of the body's organs required the presence of an active, intelligent spiritual principle, which was part of them and not an external operator, or, to use Robert Boyle's metaphor, the person in the "manned boat."[73] Stahl's theory was not identical to that of Thomasius in every respect, but like Thomasius, Stahl believed that the state of the soul, especially the passions, had a direct effect on physical health. Every corrupt passion produced its particular disease. A person with a choleric temperament, for example, suffered from severe headaches, insomnia, and catarrh. These symptoms might be accompanied by a tendency toward emaciation and consumption.[74] Sanguine personalities abandoned themselves wholly to bodily pleasures, and as a result ruined their digestion, contracted gout, arthritis, kidney stones, and *lues venerea*, and suffered from paralysis and strokes.[75] Phlegmatic characters lacked all energy, resolve, and constancy in their endeavors and avoided all unnecessary exertion. Their specific complaints were diarrhea, dull headaches, dizziness, lassitude, inflammation of the eyes, poor hearing, and an addiction to sleep.[76] Regulating the passions, therefore, was essential to sustaining physical health. Stahl gave the example, common in hermetic literature, of the effects of the passions of an expectant mother on her unborn child. Stahl said a pregnant woman was so terrified by a statue representing Christ's Crucifixion, in particular by the deformity of one of the soldiers gambling for Christ's clothes, that her child born half a year later was afflicted with a physical deformity similar to that of the soldier.[77] Religious faith was the means of regulating the passions and therefore also of maintaining health.

Thomasius's hermetic theory of nature, therefore, was an integral part of his religious and moral philosophical preoccupations. It helped to explain the nature of the human will as desire and the physical effects that corrupt desires had on human nature. This theory was not an intellectual aberration but reflected his general religious and philosophical concerns about orthodox Lutheran "scholasticism." Like Cartesians, scholastic Lutherans failed to explain the nature of the human will as desire and overestimated the importance of the intellect in human nature.

CONCLUSION

REASON AND FAITH IN THE
EARLY GERMAN ENLIGHTENMENT

In this book, I have shown that Thomasius's religious beliefs are an important part of his thought, and that they must inform the interpretation of his program for a more general intellectual reform and renewal, on which his reputation as an "enlightened" philosopher mainly rests. Although faith and philosophy were distinct spheres, Thomasius believed that they were, at the same time, closely dependent on each other. A false conception of religious faith threatened to corrupt philosophy. The problem with traditional, orthodox Lutheran theology and its emphasis on doctrine was that it led believers to overestimate the importance of the "head" in relation to the "heart" in human nature. It produced false "scholastic" and pedantic learning and neglected the true wisdom, which required humans to recognize that the source of their moral corruption was the will-as-desire, not the intellect. Although Thomasius's notion of faith did not determine every aspect of his ideas on morality, nature, and history, none of these areas can be explained entirely without it. It was part of his criticism of orthodox Lutherans' "papalism" and their refusal to grant the Calvinist elector of Brandenburg any say in the administration of their ecclesiastical affairs. Thomasius's history of the church was primarily about the origins of false religious orthodoxy, based on doctrine, which was the foundation of the clergy's authority and power over laymen. His history of Roman law also reflected his preoccupation with the rise of this false orthodoxy, which made use of a distorted version of Christian religion to justify priests' influence on secular jurisdiction. Thomasius's increasing emphasis on the importance of the passions in his theory of natural law and moral philosophy was closely related to the change in his notion of faith from a theological to an anthropological voluntarism. And his hermeticist interpretation of nature, which explained natural phenomena with reference to powers of sympathy and antipathy between natural bodies, was, as orthodox Lutherans recognized and pointed out, designed to furnish his heretical notion of the will-as-desire with a natural philosophical foundation. The reform of faith and the criticism of formulaic, orthodox Lutheran religion were inseparable from Thomasius's insistence on the need for a general reform of learning. He did not aim to preserve secular reason from any connection with a particular form of religious faith, but to protect religion from corruption by *false* philosophy, and philosophy from corruption by *false* religion. His indifference toward theological doctrine did not reflect indifference to the truth of religious belief; it meant only that religious truth was defined not in doctrinal terms but—no less narrowly—as a state of the human will.

The case of Christian Thomasius raises important questions about the relationship of religion to enlightened thought. In general terms, the importance of religious thought in the Enlightenment has been recognized for some time.[1] Peter Gay's description of the Enlightenment as the "rise of modern paganism"[2] is no longer widely accepted, and it has become common to speak of a "theological" or "religious" Enlightenment, a "middle way" between the extremes of anti-Christian rationalism and traditional religiosity. David Sorkin, for example, has described this "theological Enlightenment" as the use of the "new science" and of mathematics to reform theology, and as an attempt to reconcile reason with revelation, an attempt that generated tensions but was on the whole successful.[3] The notion of a "theological" or "religious Enlightenment" in this sense, however, does not apply to Thomasius. There is also no single "rational" philosophy in the German Enlightenment. The meaning of the term "reason" itself varied from one thinker to the next and over time. And it is questionable whether any significant thinker of the German Enlightenment before about 1730 considered the reconciliation of reason and religion to be a problem at all, which had to be overcome. "Reason" in roughly the first quarter of the eighteenth century in Germany was not regarded as a critical faculty that could be the measure of revealed truth. The question with which theorists were concerned was rather to what extent rational philosophy could play a role in supporting or explaining truths of Christian faith. The two possible alternative arguments were either that reason provided additional grounds for the belief in certain truths of revelation or that it had to be excluded from arguments about revelation because of its weakness.[4] Thomasius emphasized the weakness of human reason. He was not an "enlightened" thinker in a stereotypical sense, a philosopher showing particular confidence in the powers of secular rationality, but he believed that reason was too feeble to play any role in religious belief and argument.

These views on the limitations of human reason illustrate the idea that "reason" was not a central and self-evident principle, around which the early Enlightenment formed, but a contested notion whose meaning was debated primarily in relation to religious questions. Like Thomasius, another figure of the early Enlightenment, Samuel Pufendorf, stressed the inscrutability of God's nature and his decisions to human understanding, and the irrelevance of rational philosophy to the interpretation of revealed doctrine. Natural reason only provided humans with some limited knowledge of God as the origin of all things and of all motion in the world. Reason was also capable of seeing that God was not a brute force but intelligent, determining itself to act. Creation itself testified to the greatness of its author. It was also rationally evident that man was the particular concern of this author of creation because the condition of mankind was much better than that of all other creatures. For this reason, man owed God veneration. Rational argument would also lead to the conclusion that God must be perfect and eminent to the highest degree, but beyond this, reason could not establish any further truths.[5] It could not be used to interpret the revealed truths in scripture. The incarnation of the Son of God, for example, "far exceeds all Reach of Humane Research, so it is not fitting that we should dare to plunge our Curiosity further into it, than so far as the Sacred Scripture leads us, and as may suffice to understand the Office of the Saviour."[6] The same principle applied to the union of God and man in Christ, which also exceeded the comprehension of human reason. All metaphors that were used to describe this relationship had to be taken "with due Qualifications,"[7] and much of the contention over the person of Christ could be avoided "if Men would confine themselves within the bounds of this Simplicity, and not let their Curiosity proceed to those Matters which do not concern that Office."[8] The different confessions would not be reconciled on the basis of reason, but on the basis of scriptural revelation, without the aid of rationalist argument, because scripture was a self-evident text, if only it was examined dispassionately. Thus, Pufendorf's emphasis on the separation of reason from religion was not a defense of the secular autonomy of reason but a statement that the reconciliation of the different Christian confessions must not be attempted through the application of human philosophy to scripture.

Pufendorf and Thomasius believed that truth in Christian religion depended on *excluding* rationalist argument from debates over revelation, but one of the most famous philosophers of the early Enlightenment, Gottfried Wilhelm Leibniz, defended the opposite view. He maintained that reason constituted the instrument with which to arrive at a consensus over the meaning of scripture and to reconcile the different confessions into which Western Christendom had been divided by the Reformation. Reason to Leibniz was not distinct from scriptural argument but a means to demonstrate its truth and to explain its meaning. The difference between human and divine rationality was a difference only of degree, and God's decisions could, at least to a limited extent, be understood by humanity with the help of its rational powers. Leibniz's argument was directed primarily against Pierre Bayle and his rejection of all truths of reason in matters of faith, although it was equally applicable to Pufendorf and Thomasius. Bayle compared reason to a runner who did not know when to stop, because it would inquire into matters about which it had to remain ignorant, that is, the mysteries of Christian faith, which were inscrutable to human reason. The very essence of faith was to be a belief that man held firmly even though it could *not* rest on the reassurance of a rational conviction.[9] Leibniz, however, argued that the difference between divine and human understanding was not one of kind but only of degree. God and humans shared the same standard of rationality. In God's mind were eternal quasi-geometrical truths, many of which were accessible to the human intellect. Humans could also use their understanding of these verities to confirm the truth of certain revealed doctrines. This did not mean that only those doctrines that could be explained by human reason, were acceptable as God's intellect was infinitely superior in degree to human reason. It did, however, mean that it was possible through rational argument to achieve a consensus on parts of revealed doctrine.

Bayle believed that God could not be described as a rational being in these terms, for if he could, then it was impossible to explain the presence of evil in the world. God moved in mysterious ways, and humans were not able to understand the purposes of divine providence from their finite perspective. Leibniz's very different solution to the question of evil was the argument of the *Theodicy*.[10] Though God necessarily wanted the good absolutely, in the created world there were limits on the coexistence of different instantiated ideas: the existence of one good might be incompatible with the existence of another. In these cases, God would choose the lesser evil. It was these limits imposed by the *compossibilitas*, the possible simultaneous existence in reality of different ideas, that accounted for the existence of injustice and evil in a world created by a supremely just God. The existence of evil thus reflected the necessary imperfections of a created world, not God's lack of goodness or power.

The role of scriptural revelation was diminished to some degree in Leibniz's thought.[11] God's goodness, which inspired humans' love for him, was taught no less by reason than by scripture.[12] Christ's teachings revealed principles of natural religion, based on reason, that had already been known to individual wise pagans before Christ, though the public religion of the pagans had always corrupted the divine light of reason with "ridiculous and absurd" ceremonial,[13] and the wise pagans had refrained from speaking openly about natural religion, out of fear of being executed like Socrates.[14] The role of Christ had been to promulgate the natural religion of reason as public religion, in a way that was accessible to lesser minds.[15] To the monotheism established by Moses, Christ added the ideas of the natural immortality of the soul, as a rational substance, which can be the subject of divine justice, and of charity guided by wisdom as the foundation of law.[16] When the Roman Empire converted to Christianity, this turned the rational religion of the wise into public religion.

From the 1730s onward, a different conception of the relationship between religion and reason became increasingly prominent. In spite of their disagreements, neither Pufendorf nor Thomasius nor Leibniz had believed that reason could be used to *correct* what had been presented as revealed truth. This distinguished their ideas from currents in German deism after about 1730, which were the probably unintended product of Wolffian philosophy. Christian Wolff (1679–1754) had refrained from discussing revelation, but he had insisted that revelation by its very nature must conform to the standards of reason. The implications of this view became most obvious in the publication of the infamous Wertheim Bible of Johann Lorenz Schmidt in the mid-1730s. Schmidt's work was a systematic examination of the Pentateuch from a naturalistic, rationalist perspective: natural reason became the critical instrument with which to examine the truth of the text. Unlike Pufendorf, who had described the Holy Trinity as a mystery that could not be explained on the basis of human reason, Schmidt wrote that it was contrary to reason and therefore absurd.[17] Schmidt's views were highly controversial and resulted in a ban on the printing, distribution, and sale of the Wertheim Bible. Schmidt was arrested but escaped to Holland; he later returned to Altona, which was under Danish jurisdiction.[18] Schmidt was no atheist, but he argued that what had been presented as divine revelation was often the product of human invention, and that natural reason could expose the false authority of these man-made texts. Another famous example of this new, critical use of reason to question the authority of scripture as a historical text was the writings of Hermann Samuel Reimarus, which became the subject of the famous "Wolfenbütteler Fragmentenstreit" of the 1770s, in which the dramatist Gotthold Ephraim Lessing played a key role.[19] Thomasius, however, like his contemporaries, was far from subordinating revelation to rational argument in this way, as reason, however useful for certain purposes, was too weak and limited to judge revealed truth.

As we have seen, Thomasius from the mid-1690s onward was also skeptical about the extent to which reason guided human actions. His "enthusiastic" emphasis on the will-as-desire and its importance for human conduct may not seem particularly characteristic of the Enlightenment as it is often understood. But Thomasius's religiously motivated belief in the superiority of the pre-intellectual, spontaneous guidance of the "heart" over the reasoning of the "head" became a firm part of the culture of *Empfindsamkeit* or sensibility in the Protestant German Enlightenment from around the mid-eighteenth century. This rested on the belief that morality required the education of an individual's feelings, in such a way that they conducted him or her toward virtue. Thomasius's idea that true philosophy was about the reform of the will and the passions, rather than the conclusions of the intellect, was continued after his death by a flourishing and fashionable genre of didactic sentimental literature. It was a central concern of publications such as the *Moralische Wochenschriften*, the moral weeklies, which offered their readers practical advice on their conduct. Thomasian anthropology and moral philosophy provided these texts with a basic view of human nature and a toolbox of arguments about the passions and human characters, which were recycled in series of essays with advice to readers on day-to-day moral questions.[20] *Empfindsamkeit* has often been explained as a secularized form of Pietism,[21] but the case of Christian Thomasius indicates that the origins of this culture of sensibility are more complex. His religious beliefs were important for his views on human nature and human conduct, but they were not specifically Pietist. Thomasius's main contribution to the development of *Empfindsamkeit* was his fusion of an anthropology, which emphasized the role of the passions in human nature, with a natural jurisprudential tradition based on the principle of sociability and derived from Grotius and Pufendorf.[22]

Thus, Thomasius's religious beliefs are not only compatible with his central place in the early Enlightenment; they are essential to explaining it. And yet, like Newton's alchemical or theological interests,[23] they became an embarrassment to later authors who wanted to present Thomasius as the father of the German Enlightenment. Thomasius's "enlightened" interests in natural law and the critique of witchcraft trials, for example, began to be distinguished from his unfortunate sympathy for mystical and spiritualist religious views. His reputation as an "enlightened" philosopher was made to rest on his ability to turn philosophy into an intellectual pursuit that was independent from questions of religious truth. Religion, however, is central to understanding Thomasius's philosophy and his dissatisfaction with the state of learning of his age. The importance of the issue of religious truth in Thomasius's thought does not question his status as an "enlightened" thinker. It reveals the deeply religious preoccupations at the heart of the early German Enlightenment.

NOTES

INTRODUCTION

1. Ernst Bloch, "Christian Thomasius, ein deutscher Gelehrter ohne Misere," in Bloch, *Naturrecht und menschliche Würde* (Frankfurt am Main: Suhrkamp, 1985); Werner Schneiders, *Naturrecht und Liebesethik. Zur Geschichte der praktischen Philosophie im Hinblick auf Christian Thomasius* (Hildesheim and New York: Olms, 1971); Friedrich Vollhardt, ed., *Christian Thomasius (1655–1728). Neue Forschungen im Kontext der Frühaufklärung* (Tübingen: Niemeyer Verlag, 1997); Frank Grunert, *Normbegründung und politische Legitimität. Zur Rechts- und Staatsphilosophie der deutschen Aufklärung* (Tübingen: Niemeyer Verlag, 2000); Peter Schröder, *Christian Thomasius zur Einführung* (Hamburg: Junius, 1999).

2. "Wir alle verdanken ihm einen großen Theil unserer intellektuellen und materiellen Glückseeligkeit" (quoted in Martin Pott, "Christian Thomasius und Gottfried Arnold," in *Gottfried Arnold [1666–1714]*, ed. D. Blaufuß and F. Niewöhner [Wiesbaden: Harrassowitz, 1995], 247).

3. See the letter by Schiller to Goethe 29 May 1799 in *Briefe der Jahre (1798–1805)*, vol. 2 of *Der Briefwechsel zwischen Schiller und Goethe*, ed. S. Seidel, (Munich: Beck, 1985).

4. See, for example, Notker Hammerstein, *Jus und Histori. Ein Beitrag zur Geschichte des historischen Denkens an deutschen Universitäten im späten 17. und im 18. Jahrhundert* (Göttingen: Vandenhoeck und Ruprecht, 1972); see also, for example, Thomasius's comments in his *Dissertatio Iuridica Inauguralis de Aequitate Cerebrina Legis Secundae Codicis* (Halle: Salfeld, 1706), chap. I, §19. Thomasius's criticism of "scholastic pedantry" has contributed substantially to the negative view of the state of German universities around 1700, but it is part of the rhetoric of Thomasius's campaign against his academic opponents and should probably not be taken as an accurate description, as R. J. W. Evans has shown in "German Universities after the Thirty Years' War," *History of the Universities* 1 (1981): 169–89.

5. Schneiders, *Naturrecht und Liebesethik*, 239. This book remains one of the most important works on the thought of Christian Thomasius.

6. Ian Hunter, *Rival Enlightenments: Civil and Metaphysical Philosophy in Early Modern Germany* (Cambridge: Cambridge University Press, 2001), chaps. 4 and 5.

7.   Frank Grunert, "Antiklerikalismus und christlicher Anspruch im Werk von Christian Thomasius," in *Der Kampf der Aufklärung. Kirchenkritik und Religionskritik zur Aufklärungszeit,* ed. Jean Mondot (Berlin: Berliner Wissenschafts-Verlag, 2004), 41; see also his *Normbegründung und politische Legitimität,* 169–230.

8.   Two important exceptions are the articles by Friedrich de Boor, "Die ersten Vorschläge des Christian Thomasius 'wegen auffrichtung einer Neuen Academie zu Halle' aus dem Jahre 1690," in *Europa in der frühen Neuzeit. Festschrift für Günther Mühlpfordt,* ed. E. Donnert, vol. 4 (Weimar: Böhlau, 1997), 57–84, and Horst Dreitzel, "Christliche Aufklärung durch fürstlichen Absolutismus," in *Christian Thomasius (1655–1728). Neue Forschungen im Kontext der Frühaufklärung,* ed. Friedrich Vollhardt (Tübingen: Niemeyer, 1997), 17–50.

9.   See, for example, Brian Young, *Religion and Enlightenment in Eighteenth-Century England. Theological Debate in England, from Locke to Burke* (Oxford: Clarendon Press, 1998); Knud Haakonssen, ed., *Enlightenment and Religion: Rational Dissent in Eighteenth-Century Britain* (Cambridge: Cambridge University Press, 1996); David Sorkin, *The Berlin Haskalah and German Religious Thought* (London: Vallentine Mitchell, 2000); Hans-Erich Bödeker, "Die Religiösität der Gelehrten," in *Religionskritik und Religiösität in der deutschen Aufklärung,* ed. Karlfried Gründer and Karl Heinrich Rengstorf (Heidelberg: Schneider, 1989); Margaret Doody, "The Mystics' Enlightenment" (the Saintsbury Lecture, University of Edinburgh, 1 November 2002). The description of the Enlightenment as the "rise of modern paganism" derives from Peter Gay's work, *The Enlightenment: An Interpretation,* vol. 1, *The Rise of Modern Paganism* (New York: Knopf, 1966).

10.   Sorkin, *The Berlin Haskalah,* 17.

11.   J. G. A. Pocock, "Enthusiasm: The Antiself of Enlightenment," in A. J. La Vopa and L. Klein, eds., *Enthusiasm and Enlightenment in Europe, 1650–1850* (San Marino, CA: Huntington Library, 1998), 11.

12.   On "priestcraft," see Mark Goldie, "Priestcraft and the Birth of Whiggism," in *Political Discourse in Early Modern Britain,* ed. Nicholas Phillipson and Quentin Skinner (Cambridge: Cambridge University Press, 1993), 209–31.

13.   The two treatises are his *Institutiones Jurisprudentiae Divinae* (Frankfurt and Leipzig: M. G. Weidmann, 1688) and the *Fundamenta Juris Naturae et Gentium* (Halle and Leipzig: Salfeld and Groß, 1705).

14.   Martin Gierl, *Pietismus und Aufklärung. Theologische Polemik und die Kommunikationsreform der Wissenschaft am Ende des 17. Jahrhunderts* (Göttingen: Vandenhoeck & Ruprecht, 1997). For a recent discussion of Gierl's thesis, see James van Horn Melton, "Pietism, Politics, and the Public Sphere in Germany," in *Religion and Politics in Enlightenment Europe,* ed. James E. Bradley and Dale K. Van Kley (Notre Dame, IN: University of Notre Dame Press, 2001), 294–333. Research on the importance of the public sphere for the Enlightenment has drawn especially on Jürgen Habermas's 1962 work, *Strukturwandel der Öffentlichkeit* (translated into English as *The Structural Transformation of the Public Sphere* [Cambridge: Polity Press, 1992]). For a lucid and up-to-date general work on the role of a public in Enlightenment Europe, see James van Horn Melton, *The Rise of the Public in Enlightenment Europe* (Cambridge: Cambridge University Press, 2001). See also Hans-Erich Bödeker, "Aufklärung als Kommunikationsprozess," *Aufklärung* 2, no. 2, 1988: 86–111.

CHAPTER ONE

1.   According to the Julian calendar.

2.   Hans-Peter Schneider, *Justitia Universalis. Studien zur Geschichte des Naturrechts bei Leibniz* (Frankfurt am Main: Klostermann, 1967), 34.

3.   "[E]in berühmter Philosophe und Polyhistor" (Johann Heinrich Zedler, *Grosses vollständiges Universal-Lexikon,* vol. 43 [Leipzig and Halle: Zedler, 1743], col. 1603).

4.   Christian Thomasius, *De iniusto Pontii Pilatii iudicio* (Leipzig: Georg, 1675).

5.   Rolf Lieberwirth, "Christian Thomasius (1655–1728)" in *Aufklärung und Erneuerung,* ed. G. Jerouschek and A. Sames (Hanau: Dausien, 1994), 31.

6.   Ibid., 32; Gertrud Schubart-Fikentscher, "Christian Thomasius. Seine Bedeutung als Hochschullehrer am Beginn der deutschen Aufklärung," *Sitzungsberichte der Sächsischen Akademie der Wissenschaften zu Leipzig, Philologisch-historische Klasse* 119, no. 4, 1977: 7.

7.   Erik Wolf, *Grosse Rechtsdenker der deutschen Geistesgeschichte* (Tübingen: Mohr, 1963), 378.

8.   See the "Dissertatio Prooemialis" of his *Institutiones,* 1688, §16.

9.   Thomasius, *De crimine bigamiae* (Leipzig: Johann Georg, 1685).

10.   In the *De crimine bigamiae,* Thomasius set out to demonstrate that monogamy was not commanded by natural law. This is sometimes taken as an example of Thomasius's secularizing tendencies (see, for example, Bienert, *Der Anbruch der christlichen deutschen Neuzeit dargestellt an Wissenschaft und Glauben des Christian Thomasius* [Halle: Akademischer Verlag, 1934], 76), though it is not quite clear why, because Thomasius goes on to argue that all humans, Christians, Jews, and pagans, are obligated by universal divine positive law to practice monogamy (see *De crimine bigamiae,* §45: "Prohibet igitur Jus divinum toti generi humano latum utramque Polygamiam"). The disputation includes a historical account of the transmission of the prohibition of polygamy from the Jews to the ancient Greeks, Romans, and all other nations. The importance of nonrational religious revelation, in this instance, is increased, not diminished.

11.   See Samuel Pufendorf, *Samuel Pufendorf. Briefwechsel,* ed. Detlef Döring (Berlin: Akademie-Verlag, 1996), 153, for Pufendorf's first letter to Thomasius, probably written around May 1686.

12.   Quoted in Rolf Lieberwirth, "Die französischen Kultureinflüsse auf den deutschen Frühaufklärer Christian Thomasius," *Wissenschaftliche Zeitschrift der Universität Halle* 33, 1984: 63.

13.   Thomasius, *Institutiones,* 1688.

14.   Valentin Alberti, *Compendium Juris Naturae Orthodoxae Theologiae Conformatum* (Leipzig: Frommann, 1678).

15.   Johann Benedict Carpzov gave the funeral oration for Jacob Thomasius (Max Fleischmann, "Christian Thomasius," in *Christian Thomasius. Leben und Lebenswerk,* ed. M. Fleischmann [Halle: M. Niemeyer, 1931], 28–29).

16.   Heinrich Luden, *Christian Thomasius nach seinen Schicksalen und Schriften* (Berlin: Unger, 1805), 40.

17.   Ernest Gigas, ed., *Briefe Samuel Pufendorfs an Christian Thomasius* (Munich and Leipzig: R. Oldenbourg, 1897), 20, note 2.

18. For Thomasius's own account of his disputes with the university in Leipzig and with Masius, see his *Das Recht evangelischer Fürsten in theologischen Streitigkeiten*, in his *Dreyfache Rettung des Rechts evangelischer Fürsten in Kirchen-Sachen*, ed. Johann Gottfried Zeidler (Frankfurt am Main: Zeidler, 1701), 245.

19. Hector Gottfried Masius, *Interesse principum circa religionem evangelicam* (Copenhagen: Bockenhoffer, 1687).

20. On this dispute, see especially Frank Grunert, "Zur aufgeklärten Kritik am theokratischen Absolutismus," in *Christian Thomasius (1655–1728). Neue Forschungen im Kontext der Frühaufklärung*, ed. Friedrich Vollhardt (Tübingen: Niemeyer Verlag, 1997), 51–77, though Grunert may be overestimating the extent to which Masius's theory is a religious legitimation of political power, to which Thomasius responds with a secular political theory. Masius does not maintain that the prince must be Lutheran to be legitimate, but only that Lutherans alone acknowledge *maiestas* to be immediately from God and not mediated by the people. Masius's belief that *maiestas* comes immediately from God rather than indirectly, as Thomasius argues, is not, it seems, necessarily in itself a religious theory of political legitimation, especially as Thomasius regards the establishment of commonwealths with a sovereign as a divine command. God, Thomasius says, does not confer *maiestas* on an individual ruler, but he commands humans to form commonwealths in which one or several persons hold *maiestas*. Thomasius's purpose, it seems, is to steer a middle path between Monarchomach ideas and Masius's theory. On Thomasius's theory of *maiestas*, see his *Institutiones*, 1688, bk. 3, chap. 6.

21. On the origins of Calvinist Monarchomach theory, see Q. R. D. Skinner, *The Foundations of Modern Political Thought* (Cambridge: Cambridge University Press, 1978), vol. 2, chap. 9.

22. According to Gottfried Wilhelm Leibniz ("Monsieur Masius, concionateur du Roy de Dannemarc et autrefois de l'Ambassadeur danois de Paris . . ."), in *Leibniz. Textes inédits*, vol. 2, ed. Gaston Grua (New York: Garland, 1985), 887.

23. Grunert, "Zur aufgeklärten Kritik," 65.

24. Lieberwirth, "Christian Thomasius," 38.

25. Wilhelm Schrader, *Geschichte der Friedrichs-Universität*, vol. 1 (Berlin: Dümmler, 1894), 4.

26. *Leibniz. Textes inédits*, vol. 2, ed. Grua, 887.

27. The *Rechtmäßige Erörterung der Ehe-und Gewissensfrage, ob zwey Fürstliche Personen in Römischen reich, deren eine der lutherischen, die andere der Reformirten Religion zugethan ist, einander mit gutem Gewissen heyrathen können?* (Halle: Salfeld, 1689).

28. Lieberwirth, "Christian Thomasius," 37.

29. August Hermann Francke, "H. M. August Hermann Franckens . . . Lebenslauff," 1690/91, in *August Hermann Francke. Werke in Auswahl*, ed. E. Peschke (Berlin: Evangelische Verlagsanstalt, 1969), 16.

30. Heinrich Leube, *Orthodoxie und Pietismus. Gesammelte Schriften* (Bielefeld: Luther-Verlag, 1975), 172–73.

31. Leube, *Orthodoxie*, 175; Francke, "Lebenslauff," in *Werke in Auswahl*, ed. Peschke, 19.

32. "Es ist nicht genug in der Schrift zu kritisieren, sondern man mueste durch Les- und Forschung der Schrifft frömmer werden" (quoted in Leube, *Orthodoxie*, 179).

33. Leube, *Orthodoxie*, 177.

34. "[W]ie man eine Hand umwendet, so war alle meine Zweiffel hinweg, ich war versichert in meinem Hertzen der Gnade Gottes in Christo Jesu. . . ." (Francke, "Lebenslauff," in *Werke in* Auswahl, ed. Peschke, 27).

35. Johann Georg Walch, *Historische und Theologische Einleitung in die Religions-Streitigkeiten der Evangelisch-Lutherischen Kirche*, vol. 1 (Stuttgart-Bad Cannstatt: Frommann, 1972), 579.

36. See chapter 3, below.

37. Leube, *Orthodoxie*, 182.

38. Ibid., 195.

39. Ibid.

40. On this history of the dispute, see Frank Grunert, "Zur aufgeklärten Kritiks."

41. Published as "Meine zu Leipzig Anno 1689 gehaltenen Lectiones de praciudiciis," in Christian Thomasius, *Vernünfftige und Christliche aber nicht Scheinheilige Thomasische Gedancken und Erinnerungen über allerhand Gemischte Philosophische und Juristische Händel III. Theil* (Halle: Renger), 17–25.

42. Leube, *Orthodoxie*, 207.

43. T. Kervorkian, "Piety Confronts Politics: Spener in Dresden, 1688–1691," *German History* 16, no. 2 (1998): 145–64.

44. Lieberwirth, "Christian Thomasius," 38.

45. Quoted in de Boor, "Die ersten Vorschläge von Christian Thomasius 'wegen auffrichtung einer Neuen Academie zu Halle' aus dem Jahre 1690," 60.

46. Christian Thomasius, *De felicitate subditorum Brandenburgicorum*, 1690 (Halle: Grunert, 1749), §8.

47. Klaus Deppermann, *Der hallesche Pietismus und der preußische Staat unter Friedrich III. (I.)* (Göttingen: Vandenhoeck & Ruprecht, 1961), 89.

48. Ibid., 100.

49. Ibid., 102.

50. Ibid., 104.

51. Ibid.

52. "Man muß den Mann auf alle Weise sekundieren" (ibid.).

53. Ibid., 105–6.

54. "[A]ls worinnen das Fundament ihrer zeitlichen und ewigen Wohlfarth bestehe" (Christian Thomasius, *Bericht von Einrichtung des Paedagogii zu Glaucha in Halle/Nebst der von einem gelehrten Manne verlangten Erinnerung ueber eine solche Einrichtung* [Frankfurt am Main and Leipzig, 1699], §1).

55. Melton, "Pietism, Politics, and the Public Sphere in Germany," 324.

56. Carl Hinrichs, *Preußentum und Pietismus: der Pietismus in Brandenburg-Preußen als religiös-soziale Reformbewegung* (Göttingen: Vandenhoeck & Ruprecht, 1971), 381–83.

57. On the Peace of Westphalia, one of the standard works is still Fritz Dickmann, *Der Westfälische Frieden*, 2nd ed. (Münster: Aschendorff, 1965); see also the discussion of the religious provisions of the peace by Joachim Whaley,

"A Tolerant Society? Religious Toleration and the Holy Roman Empire, 1648–1806," in *Toleration in Enlightenment Europe*, ed. O. P. Grell and R. Porter (Cambridge: Cambridge University Press, 2000), 179–82.

58. On the "second reformation" in Brandenburg, see the excellent account by Bodo Nischan, *Prince, People and Confession* (Philadelphia: University of Pennsylvania Press, 1994), especially chaps. 5 and 6.

59. Nischan, *Prince, People and Confession*, 188.

60. Volker Press, *Kriege und Krisen* (Munich: C. H. Beck, 1991), 355.

61. Otto Hintze, "Die Epochen des evangelischen Kirchenregiments in Preußen," in *Regierung und Verwaltung. Gesammelte Abhandlungen zur Staats-, Rechts- und Sozialgeschichte Preußens*, vol. 3 (Göttingen: Vandenhoeck & Ruprecht, 1967), 61.

62. Hintze, "Die Epochen des evangelischen Kirchenregiments in Preußen," 75.

63. Rudolf von Thadden, *Die brandenburgisch-preußischen Hofprediger im 17. und 18. Jahrhundert* (Berlin: de Gruyter, 1959), 60.

64. Leopold von Ranke, *Preussische Geschichte* (Wiesbaden: Vollmer, 1957), bk. 2, chap. 4 ("Brandenburg im Gegensatz mit der Restauration des Katholizismus").

65. Nischan, *Prince, People and Confession*, chap. 4.

66. The literature on Pietism is vast and the following sections cannot claim to provide a complete survey of the entire scholarship on it. For an introduction, see Martin Brecht, ed., *Der Pietismus vom siebzehnten bis zum frühen achtzehnten Jahrhundert* (Göttingen: Vandenhoeck & Ruprecht, 1993).

67. William R. Ward, *The Protestant Evangelical Awakening* (Cambridge: Cambridge University Press, 1992), 57.

68. Mary Fulbrook, *Piety and Politics. Religion and the Rise of Absolutism in England, Württemberg and Prussia* (Cambridge: Cambridge University Press, 1983), chap. 2; F. Ernest Stoeffler, *The Rise of Evangelical Pietism* (Leiden: Brill, 1965), 8.

69. Udo Sträter, *Sonthom, Bayly, Dyke und Hall. Studien zur Rezeption der englischen Erbauungsliteratur in Deutschland im siebzehnten Jahrhundert* (Tübingen: Mohr 1987), 5–8.

70. Ibid., 8.

71. Ibid., 8–9.

72. Ibid., 5.

73. Ibid., 9.

74. Ward, *The Protestant Evangelical Awakening*, 48.

75. The date would be 23 January according to the Gregorian calendar.

76. Johannes Wallmann, *Philipp Jakob Spener und die Anfänge des Pietismus*, 2nd ed. (Tübingen: Mohr 1986), 1.

77. Ibid., 23.

78. Ibid., 8.

79. Ibid., 69.

80. Kervorkian, "Piety Confronts Politics." Kervorkian argues that Spener's criticism of the elector was one example among many throughout Europe of clerical criticism of the vices of courtly life. Thus it was not, Kervorkian suggests, a radical departure even from orthodox Lutheran tradition for Spener to attack the excessive drinking and dining, hunting, and other sins typical of the Dresden court.

81. On Luther's theological principles, see Skinner, *The Foundations of Modern Political Thought*, vol. 2, 3–12.

82. Martin Schmidt, *Der Pietismus als theologische Erscheinung* (Göttingen: Vandenhoeck & Ruprecht, 1984), 156–81.

83. Philipp Jakob Spener, "Pia desideria," 1675, in *Philipp Jakob Spener. Schriften*, vol. 1, ed. Ernst Beyreuther and Dietrich Blaufuß (Hildesheim and New York: Olms, 1979), 10.

84. Ibid., 15.

85. Ibid., 11.

86. Johannes Wallmann, "Labadismus und Pietismus. Die Einflüsse des niederländischen Pietismus auf die Entstehung des Pietismus in Deutschland," in *Pietismus und Reveil*, ed. J. van den Berg and J. P. van Dooren (Leiden: Brill, 1978), 141–68.

87. Leube, *Orthodoxie*, 116.

88. Martin Brecht, "Philipp Jakob Spener, sein Programm und dessen Auswirkungen," in *Der Pietismus vom siebzehnten bis zum frühen achtzehnten Jahrhundert*, ed. Martin Brecht (Göttingen: Vandenhoeck & Ruprecht, 1993), 315.

89. Udo Sträter, "Aufklärung und Pietismus—Das Beispiel Halle," in *Universitäten und Aufklärung*, ed. Notker Hammerstein (Göttingen: Wallstein, 1995), 49–61. As Sträter points out, neither Francke nor Spener accepted the description of themselves as "Pietists," because the term implied separatism and the formation of a sect, similar to the Labadists.

90. Samuel Pufendorf, *The Divine Feudal Law*, ed. Simone Zurbuchen (Indianapolis: Liberty Fund, 2002), §54.

91. Ibid., §50.

92. Ibid., §54.

93. Ibid.

94. Ibid., §20.

95. Ibid., §54.

96. This has been pointed out by Detlef Döring in his *Pufendorf-Studien. Beiträge zur Biographie Samuel von Pufendorfs und zu seiner Entwicklung als Historiker und theologischer Schriftsteller* (Berlin: Duncker und Humblot, 1992), section 2.2.4.

97. On Seckendorff, see Michael Stolleis, "Veit Ludwig von Seckendorff," in *Staatsdenker in der frühen Neuzeit*, ed. Michael Stolleis (Munich: Beck, 1995), 148–71.

98. Veit Ludwig von Seckendorff, *Christen-Stat* (Leipzig: Gleditsch, 1685), chap. I, §2.

99. Ibid.

100. Leube, *Orthodoxie*, 181.

101. "Fellerus imprudens cecinit cum enim Pietistarum quod sectam indicare videtur nomen tota urbe sonare assereret" (quoted in Leube, *Orthodoxie*, 192).

102. Thomasius also pointed out that Spener had never intended to form a separate sect (Thomasius, *Versuch vom Wesen des Geistes*, 1699, 2nd ed. [Halle: Renger, 1709], "Vorrede" §8).

103. Sträter, "Aufkärung und Pietismus—Das Beispiel Halle," 51.

104. Ward, *The Protestant Evangelical Awakening*, 47; Heinrich Rotermund, *Orthodoxie und Pietismus* (Berlin: Evangelische Verlagsanstalt, 1959), 10, gives Löscher's motto as *Veritas et Pietas*. Löscher (1673–1749) also passed several typically "Pietist" measures when he was church superintendent in Dresden. He introduced

examinations on the catechism, reformed the school system in Saxony, and founded schools for the poor (Rotermund, *Orthodoxie*, 11).

105. "Obwohl von einem Menschen, bey welchem gar keine geistl. Früchte auff das rechte Wissen folgen, gesagt werden kan, daß der Wissende todt sey in Sünden, und sich bloß buchstäblich halte, so ist doch die Orthodoxie, die er hat, nicht todt, oder nur buchstäbisch, sondern wird im geistlichen Tod zurück gehalten" (Rotermund, *Orthodoxie*, 38).

106. See, for example, H. G. Neusse's statement that "irregenitis cognitio vera est omnino impossiblis" (quoted in Rotermund, *Orthodoxie*, 32, note 12).

107. Rotermund, *Orthodoxie*, 58.

108. Ward, *The Protestant Evangelical Awakening*, 49.

109. Martin Kruse, *Speners Kritik am landesherrlichen Kirchenregiment und ihre Vorgeschichte* (Witten: Luther-Verlag, 1971), 42–43; Joachim Whaley, *Religious Toleration and Social Change in Hamburg, 1529–1819* (Cambridge: Cambridge University Press, 1982), 29–32.

110. Brecht, "Philipp Jakob Spener, sein Programm und dessen Auswirkungen," 362.

111. Christian Friedrich Bücher, *Plato mysticus in Pietista redivivus* (Danzig: Reiniger, 1699).

CHAPTER TWO

1.   On radical enthusiastic sects in the *Reich*, see Hans Schneider, "Der radikale Pietismus im 17. Jahrhundert," in *Der Pietismus vom siebzehnten bis zum frühen achtzehnten Jahrhundert*, ed. Martin Brecht (Göttingen: Vandenhoeck & Ruprecht, 1993), 391–439; Barbara Hoffmann, *Radikalpietismus um 1700* (Frankfurt am Main: Campus-Verlag, 1996).

2.   On the reintroduction of metaphysics into Protestant university curricula, see Max Wundt, *Die deutsche Schulmetaphysik des 17. Jahrhunderts* (Tübingen: Mohr, 1939); Walter Sparn, *Wiederkehr der Metaphysik* (Stuttgart: Calwer Verlag, 1976).

3.   A revised and extended version of this chapter has appeared as "Enthusiasm and Enlightment: Faith and Philosophy in the Thought of Christian Thomasuis," *Modern Intellectual History* 2, 2 (2005): 153–77.

4.   "[H]i sunt *fructus philosophiae gentilis*, vel potius abusus, quod Scholastici mysteria fidei ex philosophia deducere instituerunt, & philosophiam normam fecerunt Theologiae, contra praeceptum Apostoli, qui Colossenses graviter monuit, ne patiantur se decipi per philosophiam & inanem fallaciam" (Thomasius, *Institutiones*, 1688, bk. 1, chap. 3, §65). The passage Thomasius is referring to is Colossians 2:8.

5.   "[D]ivinarum & humanarum rerum notitia" (Thomasius, *Institutiones*, 1688, bk. 1, chap. 2, §165). This is a definition that appears in Marcus Tullius Cicero's *De Officiis* (Oxford: Clarendon Press, 1994), I, 43.

6.   "[P]raedicata Philosophiae illius antiquae, quae ad instar Reginae se gerebat" (Thomasius, *Institutiones*, 1688, bk. 1, chap. 1, §166).

7.   "Philosophia hodierna, cui honesta ministerii gloria est relicta" (Thomasius, *Institutiones*, 1688, bk. 1, chap. 1, §166).

8. "[H]omines incauti Philosophiam gentilem Christianismo, lucem tenebris miscerent" (Christian Thomasius, *Introductio ad Philosophiam aulicam* (Hildesheim: Olms, 1993, reprint of 1688 Leipzig ed.), chap. 1, §57).

9. Brecht, "Phillip Jakob Spener, sein Programm und dessen Auswirkungen," 336; most recently, Friedrich de Boor has pointed out Thomasius's interest in sincere piety well before the beginning of his so-called "Pietist phase," which is dated to 1693 (see de Boor, "Die ersten Vorschläge," 78). According to Martin Gierl (*Pietismus und Aufklärung. Theologische Polemik und die Kommunikationsreform der Wissenschaft am Ende des 17. Jahrhunderts* (Göttingen: Vandenhoeck & Ruprecht, 1997), Thomasius shared no religious ideas with the Pietists, but was regarded as a Pietist by orthodox Lutherans because he sided with the Pietists in Leipzig in the late 1680s. Gierl argues that Thomasius's aim was to defend a new model of conducting scholarly controversies in the republic of letters and among theologians, the aim of which was not the pursuit of absolute truth, but the management of disagreements. It was this opposition to the orthodox claim to absolute truth rather than to the contents of this supposed truth itself, Gierl maintains, that led to Thomasius's alliance with the Pietist movement. Gierl's argument, however, appears to overemphasize the formal aspect of theological controversy and neglect Thomasius's ideas on faith and other religious questions, which were not only similar to those of Pietists in many respects but were commented on by orthodox Lutherans (see Albrecht Christian Roth, "Synopsis Errorum Thomasianorum in Theologia, Christologia at Anthropologia," 1699, in Roth, *Thomasius portentosus* ωσ εν συνο ψϵι & *suis ipsius scriptis de portentis illis convictus* [Leipzig: Albrecht Christian Roth, 1700]). Gierl maintains that the orthodox did not discuss Thomasius's conception of faith, regeneration, and similar questions, but this does not appear to be the case, as this chapter will illustrate.

10. "[V]iel frembdes/ unnuetzes und mehr nach der weltweißheit schmeckendes" (Spener, "Pia desideria," 23).

11. Spener, "Pia desideria," 5–6.

12. Thomasius, *De felicitate subditorum Brandenburgicorum*, 1690 (Halle: Grunert, 1749), §7: "[L]eguntur scripta *Domini Speneri* . . . praecipue vero ejusdem *pia desideria*, & non ita pridem typis impressa vere Theologica *praefatio, de impedimentis Studii Theologici*, quibus eo major applausus datur a desiderantibus redintegrationem sanctitatis Christianae, quo majori conatu ringunt & ora distorquent Pseudo-Apostoli."

13. "[P]lurima ex scriptis humanis, paucissima ex verbo Dei proferrent, loco Theologicarum doctrinarum Philosophicas inculcarent, & ad quemlibet locum quamlibet controversiam obtorto collo traherent, ut solum prurigini litigandi, calumniandi, atque disputandi possent satisfacere" (Thomasius, *De felicitate*, §8).

14. Thomasius, *Rechtmäßige Erörterung der Ehe- und Gewissensfrage*, chap. 1, §6.

15. Valentin Alberti, *Compendium Iuris Naturae Orthodoxae Theologiae Conformatum*, 2nd ed. (Leipzig: Jacob Fritsch, 1696).

16. On Leibniz's theory of volition, see Patrick Riley, *Leibniz' Universal Jurisprudence* (London: Harvard University Press, 1996), 47; on Hobbes, see Susan James, *Passion and Action: The Emotions in Seventeenth-Century Philosophy* (Oxford: Clarendon Press, 1997), 134–35.

17. Bruno Bianco, "Freiheit gegen Fatalismus: Zu Joachim Langes Kritik and Wolff," in *Zentren der Aufklärung*, vol. 1, *Halle. Aufklärung und Pietismus*, ed. Norbert Hinske (Heidelberg: Schneider, 1989), 111–55.

18. David Hume, *Treatise of Human Nature* (Oxford: Clarendon Press, 1978), 415.

19. "[R]egeneratio nihil est aliud, quam transitus ab amore creaturarum & sui ipsius ad amorem Dei per odium sui & indifferentiam creaturarum" (Christian Thomasius, "Dissertatio ad Petri Poireti libros de Eruditione solida, superficiaria et falsa," 1694, in *Programmata Thomasiana* [Halle and Leipzig: Krebs, 1724], §14). See St. Augustine, *The City of God* (Cambridge: Cambridge University Press, 1998), bk. 14, chap. 28.

20. On Thomasius's increasing interest in French literature on *amour raisonnable*, see Lieberwirth, "Die französischen Kultureinflüsse auf den deutschen Frühaufklärer Christian Thomasius," 63–73. On French Jansenist authors, see James, *Passion and Action*, chap. 10.

21. See Pott, "Christian Thomasius und Gottfried Arnold," 255.

22. Thomasius first described this tripartite human essence in an essay, "Partes hominis tres," in *Historia Sapientiae et Stultitiae*, ed. Christian Thomasius (Halle: Salfeld, 1693), vol. 3, chap. 3.

23. James, *Passion and Action*, 236.

24. Thomasius, *Von Der Artzeney Wider die unvernünfftige Liebe und der zuvorher nöthigen Erkäntnüß Sein Selbst. Oder: Ausübung der Sitten* Lehre, 1696, 4th ed. (Halle: Salfeld, 1708), 521.

25. "*[I]n qualibet creatura particulam divinam esse*" (Valentin Löscher [*praeses*], G. R. Habbius [*respondens*], *Deismus Fanaticorum* [Wittenberg: Gerdesius, 1708], 11). In a later passage (page 16) in the same piece, Löscher referred to Thomasius's *Versuch vom Wesen des Geistes* as an example of this Fanaticism. Deists, to Löscher, are those "[o]mnia, qui fingunt, esse creata Deum" (see the poem by Strunzius addressed to the *respondens*). See also Valentin Löscher's *Unschuldige Nachrichten von alten und neuen theologischen Sachen* (Leipzig: Grosse, 1702–19), vol. 3, 805, where Thomasius's *Versuch vom Wesen des Geistes* is presented as an example of this "Fanatical" belief in the world as "nichts anders als dessen [i.e., God's] ausgegangenes Wesen."

26. "Fanatici omnes, quotquot unquam existeterunt, hanc defenderunt sententiam, *Deum ex se ipso, sive ex sua essentia, hoc universum, & quicquid est in eo, creasse*" (Justus Wesselus Rumpaeus [*praeses*], D. Harder [*respondens*], *Ex Loco de Imagine Dei Quaestionum Recentiorum imprimis Pietisticarum Pentadem* [Greifswald: Adolphus, 1705], 8).

27. "Verbum igitur, Christus, spiritus, semen, lumen, Evangelium, stylo Fanaticorum, sunt unum & idem" (G. Wernsdorfer [*praeses*], J. A. Hillig [*respondens*], *De Verbo Dei Scripto, sive Scriptura Sacra* [Wittenberg: Gerdes, 1708], 14).

28. "Voluntas est norma & dux intellectus, non intellectus voluntatis. Ea scrutamur quae amamus, non ea amamus, quae scrutamur" (Thomasius, "Dissertatio ad Petri Poireti libros," §7).

29. "Alibi ostendi, hunc esse communem errorem Philosophiae gentilis, quo a Philosophia Sancta abiit" (ibid., §23).

30. "[C]ogitatio mera seu speculatio non est hominis essentia, sed pars igno-
bilior animae. Nobilior est voluntas tam in homine integro, quam lapso & regenito,
est enim voluntatis amare, non intellectus" (ibid., §17); see also §23: "essentia
hominis amor seu voluntas est."

31. Ibid., §19.

32. "[A]pud nos in confesso sit, nunquam inveniri veram fidem sine amore
Dei, nec amorem Dei sine vera fide." (Anon. [Gustav Phillip Mörl], *Repetitio
Doctrinae Orthodoxae ad Amicos quosdam scripta, de Fundamento Fidei occasione
cujusdam Disputationis halensis de Quaestione: An Haeresis sit Crimen?* [Leipzig:
Brandenburger, 1697], §11).

33. "[A]ttendamus . . . quomodo Diabolus per hoc dogma nostram fidem
evertere possit" (Anon. [G. P. Mörl], *Repetitio Doctrinae Orthodoxae*, §11).

34. "Nec enim cultus noster brutus esse debet, ut tantum colamus Deum &
Christum, ut ignari, quis sit, quem colamus, aut quomodo colamus, ut cur colamus,
sed debet esse λογικος & rationalis" (Joachim Fecht, *Scrutinium profligatae ex
Ecclesia Haeretificationis, Godofredo Arnoldo oppositum* [Rostock and Leipzig:
Russworm, 1714], 39).

35. Albrecht Christian Roth, *Thomasius portentosus* (Leipzig, 1700), 63–64.

36. "Deus est, qui justificat (justificat vero eum, qui est ex fide Jesu. . . .)"
(Anon [G. P. Mörl], *Repetitio Doctrinae Orthodoxae*, §6).

37. Roth, *Thomasius portentosus*, 36: "Sed illam ipsam fidem tamen, si justifi-
cationem ullam admittit, ex sua mente justificantem debebat dicere, h.e. regeneran-
tem & renovantem. Nam pro Synonymis haec habet."

38. Martin Heckel, *Staat und Kirche nach den Lehren der evangelischen
Juristen in der ersten Hälfte des 17. Jahrhunderts* (Munich: Claudius, 1968), 160.

39. "Res ergo postulat, ut *sententia* feratur *decisiva*, qua erroribus damnatis,
silentium eorum sive autoribus sive patronis imponatur, ipsa vero ad omnium noti-
tiam & cognitionem *publice promulgetur*" (Johann Benedict Carpzov, *De Jure decidendi controversias theologicas* [Leipzig: Tietze, 1695], Thesis 2, §2).

40. Carpzov, *De Jure decidendi*, Thesis 2, §2.

41. Ibid., Thesis 2, §3; see also Thesis 6, §1: the particular churches are held
together "consensu de doctrina Evangelii & administratione Sacramentorum," in
contrast to the universal church, which is simply the invisible community of the
saved.

42. See, for example, the definition by Georg Wernsdorfer (*praeses*), *De
Indifferentismo Religionum in Genere* (Wittenberg: Gerdes, 1707), §28.

43. Wernsdorfer (*praeses*), *De Indifferentismo*, §§79–95.

44. Fecht was responding to Thomasius's *An Haeresis sit Crimen* of 1697 (see
Joachim Fecht, *Scrutinium profligatae*, 15). Thomasius referred to Fecht in the pref-
ace to his *Versuch von Wesen des Geistes*, §5, when he spoke of the Rostock "Fecht-
Schule," a term that means either "fencing school" or "Fecht's school."

45. Johann Friedrich Mayer, *Eines Schwedischen Theologi Kurtzer Bericht von
Pietisten samt denen Königlichen Schwedischen EDICTEN wider dieselben* (Leipzig:
Gross, 1706). Although Mayer, an orthodox theologian at the University of
Greifswald, published his piece anonymously, the identity of the author was soon
known.

46. "[W]as fuer unbeschreiblich vieles Unheil aus der Redens-Art/Pietisten/herkomme" (*Der Theologischen Facultät auf der Universität zu Halle Verantwortung gegen Hn. D. Joh. Fried. Mayers / Professoris Theologi auf der Universität Greiffswald / unter dem Namen eines Schwedischen Theologi herausgegebenen so genannten kurtzen Bericht von Pietisten* [Halle: Waisenhaus, 1707], 23).

47. "[D]ie allergreulichsten Schwaermer und Verfuehrer" (*Der Theologischen Facultät auf der Universität zu Halle Verantwortung*, 22).

48. *Der Theologischen Facultät auf der Universität zu Halle Verantwortung*, 74 ("[W]eil sie auch den Glauben durchaus nicht im Verstande/ sondern bloß in dem Willen des Menschen suchen").

49. Ibid., 56.

50. Ibid., 81–82.

51. Ibid., 100.

52. Ibid., 103.

53. Ibid., 76–77. Francke defended himself similarly, writing that scripture was always "his rule and measure" ("Regul und Bleymaß"; see August Hermann Francke, *Aufrichtige und gruendliche Beantwortung eines an ihn abgelassenen und hiebey abgedruckten Send-Schreibens eines Christlichen Theologi der Professorum Theologiae zu Halle und seine eigene Orthodoxie in der Lehre I. Von der Rechtfertigung II. Von der wahren und realen Gottseligkeit Und III. Wie deren Grund allein in Christo zu legen sey betreffend* (Halle: Waisenhaus, 1706), 42.

54. See *Der Theologischen Facultät auf der Universität zu Halle Verantwortung*, 106: the orthodox say: "Gute Wercke sind nicht noethig zu Erlangung der Seligkeit, davon aber nichts gedencken/ wie es also zu verstehen/ daß keine wirckende oder vedienstliche Ursache der Seligkeit in den guten Wercken zu suchen oder zu setzen sey/ jedoch sey es an dem/ daß der allein seligmachende Glaube diese Eigenschafft habe/ daß er freylich nach vorher gegangener wahrer Bekehrung/ und nach der Vergebung der Suenden aus pur lauter Gnaden/ auch die guten Fruechte hervor bringen muesse."

55. See, for example, Francke, *Auffrichtige und gruendliche Beantwortung eines an ihn abgelassenen und hiebey abgedruckten Send-Schreibens eines Christlichen Theologi*, 23–24: "wir . . . bezeugen/ . . . daß die Busse und der Glaube der Menschen rechtschaffen und ungeheuchelt sey/ und die Rechtfertigung auch ihre Frucht beweise in einem geaenderten Sinn und gottseligen Leben und Wandel."

56. "Fides viva non est absque bonorum operum studio; sed justificat oram [*sic*, = coram?] Deo absque nostrorum operum subsidio" (Paul Anton, *Disputatio Hallensis prima de harmonia fidei quae justificat, & fidei, quatenus justificare dicitur* [Halle: Henckel, 1702], 48).

57. "Wie dem auch gedachter Thomasius in seiner Historia Sapientiae & Stultitiae vieler Haupt-Schwaermer Sache wieder die Rechtglaeubigen vertheidiget hat" (*Der Theologischen Facultät auf der Universität zu Halle Verantwortung*, 82).

58. Johann Friedrich Ludovici had published an *Untersuchung des Indifferentismi Religionum* in 1700 under the pseudonym Eric Fridlibius (= "Eric Peacelove").

59. *Der Theologischen Facultät auf der Universität zu Halle Verantwortung*, 87.

60. "[D]ie Pietisten einer goettlichen Lehre den Namen des Glaubens durchaus nicht geben wollen/ weil sie auch den Glauben durchaus nicht im Verstande/ sondern bloß in dem Willen des Menschen suchen und setzen/ siehe des Haellischen Professoris Thomasii" (*Der Theologischen Facultät auf der Universität zu Halle Verantwortung*, 74).

61. *Der Theologischen Facultät auf der Universität zu Halle Verantwortung*, 139: "daß also auf gleich Weise/ wie in andern Druckereyen die Censur denen Facultaeten/ nicht aber dem Directori des Waysenhauses oblieget."

62. "Sacra Scriptura iis constet vocibus & locutionibus, quae quam accommodatissime sint ad exprimenda ejusmodi notationes, per quas *objectum* infinitum concipiatur notitia *in tantum positiva* & vera, in quantum hanc Spiritus Sanctus in nobis, ut est captus hominum, producendam intendit" (Justus Joachim Breithaupt, *Observationes Theologicae de Haeresi juxta S. Scripturae Sensum* [Halle: Zeitler, 1697], 11).

63. Carl Hinrichs, *Preußentum und Pietismus: Der Pietismus in Brandenburg-Preußen als religiös-soziale Reformbewegung* (Göttingen: Vandenhoeck & Ruprecht, 1971), 378–79. On Francke's attempt to distinguish his own views on regeneration from those of more extreme, millenarian sects, see Melton, "Pietism, Politics, and the Public Sphere," 324.

64. Christian Thomasius, "Dissertatio nova ad Petri Poireti libros de eruditione triplici solida, superficiaria et falsa," 1708, in *Programmata Thomasiana* (Halle: Renger, 1724), §25; John Locke, *Essay Concerning Human Understanding*, 5th ed. (London: Awnsham and John Churchill, 1706), bk. 4, chap. 19.

65. "[V]ariis obervationibus pedetentim convictus essem, periculosam valde esse hanc viam, & ad Enthusiasmum ducere. . . ." (Thomasius, "Dissertatio nova," §34).

66. Sorkin, *The Berlin Haskalah*, 16–17.

67. "[N]ulla esset methodus transeundi ad statum sapientiae a statu stultitiae, sed omnis & tota emendatio esset plane supranaturalis ac miraculosa." (Thomasius, "Dissertatio nova," §30).

68. Locke, *Essay*, bk. 4, chap. 19, §14.

69. Thomasius commented on this in a footnote to §22 in the 1724 edition of his "Dissertatio ad Petri Poireti libros."

70. Roth, *Thomasius portentosus*, 39: "est hic error de homine ejusque tribus partibus inter πρωταψευδα Thomasii & inter principales, ex quo fere sequentes omnes promanant."

71. Löscher (*praeses*) and Habbius (*respondens*), *Deismus Fanaticorum*.

72. Rumpaeus (*praeses*) and Harder (*respondens*), *Ex Loco de Imagine Dei Quaestionum Recentiorum imprimis Pietisticarum Pentadem*, Quaestio 4, 15.

73. Thomasius, *Fundamenta Juris Naturae et Gentium*, 4th ed. (Halle and Leipzig: Salfeld, 1718), "Caput Prooemiale," §21, note. The change in Thomasius's anthropology and religious thought can be dated to the years between 1703 and 1705. In 1703 he first gave the lectures on which the "Caput Prooemiale" of his *Fundamenta Juris Naturae et Gentium* was to be based. In a footnote to the introductory chapter of his *Fundamenta*, he observed that "in the first dictations of this chapter," that is, in 1703, he had still distinguished a good divine spirit and an evil natural spirit in humans. When the *Fundamenta* were published in 1705,

however, he had already revised his view and rejected the idea of a separate divine *spiritus* in humans (see *Fundamenta*, 4th ed., page 3, and bk. 1, chap. 3, §§77–88).

74. "[O]ra Deum, . . . ut actiones tuas dirigat gratia sua & providentia, quo finem optatum in acquirenda felicitate adipiscaris" (Thomasius, *Cautelae circa Praecognita Jurisprudentiae* [Halle: Renger, 1710], chap. 2, §23).

75. Thomasius, *Cautelae*, §35.

76. "[C]ortex verborum" (ibid., §36).

77. "[A]pud Deum, tanquam cordium scrutatorem, plus operentur suspiria, quam multiloquium" (ibid., §32).

78. "Etsi enim sapientia tanquam habitus virtutis divinae, & subtilissimus Spiritus, penetrans omnia etiam Spiritus subtiles, (*Sap.* c. 7 v. 23) necessario prope sit omnibus hominibus, nemini tamen se obtrudit, neminemque cogit, sed attrahitur quasi magnete orationis, & conservatur, simul vero stultitia in nobis suffocatur & ligatur" (Thomasius, *Cautelae*, note a).

79. "Non meliorem librum vero studiosis sapientiae inveniet, qui ad veram naturae & sui ipsius cognitionem manuducat, quam scripturam sacram" (ibid., 33).

80. "Ergo . . . noxium est, si primo erronea principia de DEO, ejus operibus & creatures, de statu, essentia ac viribus humanis, de voluntate divina, de felicitate humana, de mediis eam acquirendi, ex scriptoribus paganis hauriat." (ibid., 34).

81. See, for example, Wernsdorfer (*praeses*), *De Indifferentismo*, §§80–95, where the author includes Thomasius in a list of religious enthusiasts.

82. For a discussion of Thomasius's "practical" orientation, see Frederick Barnard, "The Practical Philosophy of Christian Thomasius," *Journal of the History of Ideas* 32, 1971: 221–46, though Barnard interprets this practical orientation in rather modern terms.

83. Georg Forster, "Charlateneria eruditorum," in *Respublica litteraria. Die Institutionen der Gelehrsamkeit in der frühen Neuzeit*, ed. S. Neumeister and C. Wiedemann (Wiesbaden: Harrassowitz, 1987). In his 1702 edition of the *Introductio ad Philosophiam aulicam* published in Halle, Thomasius included a piece by the Franeker jurist Ulrik Huber on pedantry.

84. Thomasius, *Cautelae*, chap. 2, §8.

85. "[C]ognitio subtilis boni sufficiat, & quasi haec homines reddat felices" (Thomasius, *Cautelae*, chap. 1, §50).

86. "Haec ultima stultitia idea maxima est, quia fere incurabilis, fundata videlicet in universali doctrina scholarum felicitatem hominis dependere ab intellectu. Unde alibi diximus eruditos stultos esse majores reliquis" (Thomasius, *Cautelae*, note n).

Chapter Three

1. "[P]rimatum in Ecclesia et brachium seculare" (Thomasius, *De felicitate subditorum Brandenburgicorum*, §8).

2. On "priestcraft" in an English context, see Mark Goldie, "The Civil Religion of James Harrington" in *The Languages of Political Theory in Early Modern Europe*, ed. A. Pagden (Cambridge: Cambridge University Press, 1987), 19–24; and Justin

Champion, *The Pillars of Priestcraft Shaken* (Cambridge: Cambridge University Press, 1992).

3.   See, for example, Ian Hunter, *Rival Enlightenments*, 149, though he also draws attention to the limited nature of the "secularization" through positive law in the Peace of Westphalia (151). On these questions, see also Klaus Schlaich, "Der rationale Territorialismus. Die Kirche unter dem staatsrechtlichen Absolutismus um die Wende vom 17. zum 18. Jahrhundert," *Zeitschrift der Savigny-Stiftung für Rechtsgeschichte, Kanonistische Abteilung* 85, 1968: 269–340; and Christoph Link, *Herrschaftsordnung und bürgerliche Freiheit* (Vienna: Böhlau, 1979); Peter Schröder, *Naturrecht und absolutistisches Staatsrecht. Eine vergleichende Studie zu Thomas Hobbes und Christian Thomasius* (Berlin: Duncker & Humblot, 2001); Schröder, "Thomas Hobbes, Christian Thomasius and the Seventeenth-Century Debate on the Church and State," *History of European Ideas* 23, 1997, 59–79. For a different view, however, see the important article by Horst Dreitzel, "Christliche Aufklärung durch fürstlichen Absolutismus: Thomasius und die Destruktion des frühneuzeitlichen Konfessionsstaates," in *Christian Thomasius (1655–1728). Neue Forschungen im Kontext der Frühaufklärung*, ed. Friedrich Vollhardt (Tübingen: Niemeyer, 1997), 17–50; Thomas Ahnert, "The Relationship between Prince and Church in the Thought of Christian Thomasius," in *Natural Law and Civil Sovereignty. Moral Right and State Authority in Early Modern Political Thought*, ed. Ian Hunter and David Saunders (Basingstoke, UK: Palgrave, 2002), 91–105.

4.   See especially Whaley, "A Tolerant Society? Religious Toleration and the Holy Roman Empire, 1648–1806."

5.   See, for example, Karl Otmar von Aretin, *Das Reich. Friedensgarantie und europäisches Gleichgewicht 1648–1806* (Stuttgart: Klett-Cotta, 1986).

6.   See Hunter, *Rival Enlightenments*, 258–60.

7.   In his *Rechtmaeßige Eroerterung Der Ehe- und Gewissensfrage*, chap. I, §9: "so ist . . . nicht zu leugnen . . . /daß . . . allzeit bey denen Roemischen Kaysern gestanden . . . eine Decision oder Schluß/ was im Roemischen Reich fuer eine rechtglaeubige Lehre gehalten werden solte/ zufassen."

8.   "[U]t ejus Cleri velit dominari in conscientias, & habeat intentioni suae inserviens brachium seculare, vel Principis, vel majoris partis populi. Hoc est, ut intentionem dominandi habeat, & vires" (*De Jure Principis circa Haereticos* [Halle: Salfeld, 1697], §36).

9.   "Die Clerici haben die Kirchen-Busse in eine Straffe verwandelt. . . . die Kirchen-Buße ist ein gezwungen Werck/ denn sie wird den Leuten gleichsam durch ein Urtheil vom Consistorio zuerkant/ und offt durchs brachium seculare/ wenn man sie nicht in der Gemeine leiden wil/ exequiret" (Anon. and Christian Thomasius, "Vertheidigung des Regiments der Kirchen Jesu Christi aus dem Latein uebersetzt/ und durch stete Anmerckungen beantworte," in *Dreyfache Rettung des Rechts Evangelischer Fuersten in Kirchen-Sachen/ etc. Beyde letztere aus des Herrn Thomasii Lectionibus publicis mit Fleiß zusammen getragen von Johann Gottfried Zeidlern*, ed. J. G. Zeidler [Frankfurt am Main, 1701], 47, note g by Thomasius).

10.   Thomasius, "Das Recht evangelischer Fürsten in theologischen Streitigkeiten," 13. Satz, §§1–4.

11.   Heckel, *Staat und Kirche nach den Lehren der evangelischen Juristen in der ersten Hälfte des 17. Jahrhunderts*, 141; Theodor Reinking, *Conclusiones*

CCXC. de brachio seculari et ecclesiastico seu potestate utraque (Giessen: Hampel, 1616).

12. "[P]ro potestate, qui quisque horum ordine pollet" (Carpzov, *De Jure decidendi*, Thesis 6, §1).

13. Immediately after his death, Thomasius was remembered for his struggle against "Protestant papalism" (see the preface by Johann Peter von Ludewig to the *Consilia Hallensium Iureconsultorum*, vol. 1 [Halle: Renger, 1733], 39).

14. On responses to the Anabaptists in the Reformation, see, for example, Sachiko Kusukawa, *The Transformation of Natural Philosophy: The Case of Philip Melanchthon* (Cambridge: Cambridge University Press, 1995), 63. Carpzov wrote that "Fanatici autem cum Anabaptistis pro Statu *Democratico* pungent" (Carpzov, *De Jure decidendi*, Thesis 7, §5).

15. "Denn des Priesters Lippen sollen die Lehre bewahren/ daß man aus seinem munde das gesetz suche/ denn er ist ein Engel des Herrn Zebaoth" (Carpzov, *De Jure decidendi*, Locus 2).

16. Carpzov, *De Jure decidendi*, §3.

17. "[I]n explicando & praedicando Dei verba" (ibid., §7).

18. "[V]eluti arca quaedam in qua doctrina salutaris verbo accepta pura atque illibata instar thesauri pretiosissimi recondita" (ibid., §7).

19. "[Q]uatenus is [the magistrate] Ministerium ad decidendas controversias convocat, decisionem mandat, cognoscit, discernit, exequitur, modum etiam agendi praescribit" (ibid., Thesis 7, §I).

20. "Et breviter, Ecclesiasticus status debet consulere de persona idonea; popularis approbare, Politicus decernere" (Theodor Reinking, *Tractatus de Regimine Seculari et Ecclesiastico* [Basel: Genath, 1622], bk. 3, pt. 1, chap. 6, no. 17).

21. See Reinking, *Tractatus*, bk. 3, pt. 1, chap. 6, nos. 10–14; see also Carpzov, *De Jure decidendi*, Thesis XIV: "Summa omnium huc redit: Jus decidendi controversias Theologicas *radicaliter* est penes totam Ecclesiam, *quoad exercitium* a) penes Magistratum & Ministerium ecclesiasticum, quorum ille *decisionem extrinsecus promovet,* hoc *in decisionem formaliter influit,* Populo consentiente & approbante."

22. Nischan, *Prince, People and Confession*, especially chaps. 5 and 6.

23. "Indifferent" matters (*adiaphora*), which are not essential for salvation, are not to be confused with "Indifferentism" (*Indifferentismum*), the belief that *no* particular doctrines are essential for salvation.

24. Not to be confused with the author of the *De Jure decidendi controversias theologicas*, his nephew Johann Benedict Carpzov (1639–99).

25. This rested in particular on Matthew 18:6: "[W]hoever causes one of these little ones who believe in me to sin [*scandalizaverit*], it would be better for him to have a great millstone fastened round his neck and to be drowned in the depth of the sea." For a discussion of the medieval origins of the debates on *scandalum*, see in particular Ludwig Buisson, *Potestas und Caritas. Die Päpstliche Gewalt im Spätmittelalter* (Cologne and Graz: Böhlau Verlag, 1958).

26. "[S]implices ac indocti" (Benedict Carpzov, *Opus Definitionum Ecclesiasticarum seu Consistorialium* [Leipzig: Ritzsch, 1665], 366).

27. "[M]ultum veritatis theologicae ac orthodoxae Religionis subesse existimant" (Carpzov, *Opus Definitionum*, 368).

28. Ibid., 371.

29. "[I]n exercitio adiaphororum canon sit charitas, quam si violamus, intempestivo libertatis nostrae usu peccamus" (ibid., 369). Carpzov adds a quotation from Paul's letter to the Corinthians, 1 Corinthians 10:23–24: "Omnia mihi licent, sed non omnia conducunt: omnia mihi licent, sed non omnia aedificant" ("Everything is permitted to me, but not everything is useful: everything is permitted, but not everything contributes to edification").

30. "[P]erspicua & constans confessio a nobis exigitur" (Carpzov, *Opus Definitionum*, 369).

31. "[H]ostibus Evangelii in rebus adiaphoris non sit cedendum" (ibid., 369).

32. "Abolitus est sacrificiorum aliorumque rituum apparatus, *omnesque ceremoniae externae, exceptis illis, quae Christus specialiter Discipulis suis injunxit, e.g. baptismo, coena &c. sunt adiaphora*" (Thomasius, *De Jure Principis circa Adiaphora* [Halle: Christoph Salfeld, 1695]) chap. I, §2.

33. Carpzov, *Opus Definitionum*, §5.

34. See also the chapters on Thomasius's natural law theory below. God did impose certain ceremonial laws on the Jews after their exodus from Egypt, but these were exceptional and intended as a punishment for their idolatry, not as an example for any other group of people or nation, let alone Christians. See Christian Thomasius, *Vollstaendige Erlaeuterung der Kirchenrechts-Gelahrtheit oder Gruendliche Abhandlung vom Verhaeltniß der Religion gegen den Staat* (Aalen: Scientia-Verlag, 1981) reprint of 2nd ed., Frankfurt and Leipzig, 1740.

35. See his *Fundamenta*, 4th ed., 1718, 11: "[E]go assertiones doctrinales, ob quas antea legem divinam positivam universalem defenderam, hoc loco vel ostenderim falsas esse & ex reliquiis politicis Papatus ortas."

36. "[A]lles was gesagt wird/ vor Gesetze halten" (Thomasius's footnote in Anon. and Thomasius, "Vertheidigung," 80).

37. "[U]nd weiter nicht. Sie zwingen aber nicht" (ibid.).

38. "Das ist das Papale wesen/ wenn ein Lehrer begehret/ der Fuerst solle seine autoritaet conserviren/ und gleich wieder diejenigen die der Lehre nicht folgen/ die exekution ergehen lassen" (ibid.).

39. "Nam etsi, quae adiaphora dicuntur, inter praecepta & prohibita quasi intermedia jacent, tamen istud medium non intelligendum est in puncto, sed cum aliqua laxitate, ita ut modo prohibitioni modo praeceptioni sit propinquius . . . Nam quae aedificationem aut finem conventuum Christianorum, etsi non necessario promovent, sed per accidens, a praeceptis religionis Christianae propius absunt, quae e contrario impediunt, prohibitioni propriora sunt, adeoque illa laudabilius introducuntur, haec abrogantur" (Thomasius, *De Jure Principis circa Adiaphora*, chap. 2, §4).

40. "Quemadmodum autem Principis suprema lex est, aut certe esse debet, salus populi, ita & circa adiaphora salutem subditorum intendere debet, quo maxime facit, *si inutiles, & ad superstitionem magis, quam ad aedificationem inclinantes & disponentes ceremonias abroget*" (Thomasius, *De Jure Principis circa Adiaphora*, chap. II, §4). This was an allusion to Cicero's *De Legibus* (Marcus Tullius Cicero, *De Republica. De Legibus* [London: Heinemann, 1928], III, iii, 8).

41. Schlaich, "Der rationale Territorialismus. Die Kirche unter dem staatsrechtlichen Absolutismus um die Wende vom 17. zum 18. Jahrhundert"; and Link, *Herrschaftsordnung und bürgerliche Freiheit*, 261.

42. Thomasius, *De Jure Principis circa Adiaphora,* chap. 1, §8.

43. See Christian Thomasius, "Kurtze Lehr-Saetze vom Recht eines Christlichen Fuersten in Religions-Sachen," in *Vernünfftige und Christliche aber nicht Scheinheilige Thomasische Gedancken und Erinnerungen über allerhand Philosophische und Juristische Händel. Andrer Theil* (Halle: Renger, 1724), especially 2–7.

44. "Eo enim ipso, dum isti turbas excitant in Rep. satis indicant, veram religionem sibi curae cordique non esse" (Thomasius, *De Jure Principis circa Adiaphora,* chap. I, §8).

45. "[M]it gebührenden Zwangs-Mitteln" (Thomasius, "Das Recht evangelischer Fürsten in theologischen Streitigkeiten," 11. Satz).

46. Thomasius, *Vollständige Erläuterung,* 14.

47. "So finden sich auch viele erwachsene Leute, welche fleißig in die Kirche gehen, und dennoch so wohl vor als auch nach der Kirche ein liederliches Leben nach allen ihren Passionibus führen" (Thomasius, *Vollständige Erläuterung,* 35).

48. "[W]eder ex lumine Rationis, noch Revelationis" (Thomasius, *Vollständige Erläuterung,* 17).

49. "So ist auch hierbey wohl zu ueberlegen/ daß wenn das zeitliche Interesse des gemeinen Wesens der wahrhafftige Zweck des aeusserlichen Gottesdienstes seyn solte/ so wuerde man auch sagen muessen/ daß der Gottesdienst nach Unterscheid derer Republiquen auch unterschieden seyn/ und der veraenderliche Nutzen dieser oder jener Republique auch die Richtschnur eines daselbst veraenderlichen Gottesdienstes seyn muesse/ welches doch sehr unfoermlich und beynahe gottloß klingen wuerde" (*Einleitung zur Sitten Lehre* [Halle: Salfeld, 1692], 142). This is a point reaffirmed later in his *Vollstaendige Erlaeuterung,* 17 ("[S]o wohl der Cultus externus als internus soll allen Menschen frey seyn, und gehoeret dannenhero nicht ad Principem, so ferne er ein Caput Reipublicae ist.").

50. On these questions, see Simone Zurbuchen, *Naturrecht und natürliche Religion: Zur Geschichte des Toleranzproblems von Samuel Pufendorf bis Jean-Jacques Rousseau* (Würzburg: Königshausen & Neumann, 1991); Zurbuchen, "Gewissensfreiheit und Toleranz: Zur Pufendorf-Rezeption bei Christian Thomasius," in *Samuel Pufendorf und die europäische Frühaufklärung,* ed. Fiammetta Palladini (Berlin: Akademie-Verlag, 1996), 169–80.

51. Samuel Pufendorf, *De habitu religionis Christianae ad vitam civilem* (Bremen: Schwerdfeger, 1687), §§1–7.

52. See Thomasius, *De Jure Principis circa Adiaphora,* chap. 2, §§6, 7, 12. The last, in particular, is significant, given the context of the dispute over the confessional in Berlin and the fact that Thomasius's work is dedicated to Paul von Fuchs, the minister for ecclesiastical affairs in Brandenburg. On the dispute over confession, see Helmut Obst, *Der Berliner Beichtstuhlstreit. Die Kritik des Pietismus an der Beichtpraxis der Lutherischen Orthodoxie* (Witten: Luther-Verlag, 1972).

53. For literature emphasizing the continuity between Pufendorf and Thomasius, see, for example, Schlaich, "Der rationale Territorialismus. Die Kirche unter dem staatsrechtlichen Absolutismus um die Wende vom 17. zum 18. Jahrhundert," 320–21. Ian Hunter has also described Pufendorf and Thomasius as examples of a "civil Enlightenment," which is concerned with the regulation of political affairs on a non-religious basis (see Hunter, *Rival Enlightenments*).

54. Döring, *Pufendorf-Studien*, 100.

55. Thomasius, *Vollstaendige Erlaeuterung*, preface, §1: "Von der Christlichen Kirche und dero rechten Eigenschafften ist nicht zu zweiffeln/ daß sie den wahren Nutzen der Republiq befoerdere; Denn sie lehret ihre Glieder den Ehr-Geitz/ Geld-Geitz und Wollust/ als den eintzigen Brunnquell alles Ungluecks zu daempffen/ und durch die wuerckende Gnade Gottes in Heiligkeit und Gerechtigkeit zu leben/ woraus nothwendig auch die wahre zeitliche Glueckseligkeit muß hervorkommen/ weil alles Unheil in dem gemeinen Wesen seinen Ursprung hat von solchen Lastern/ wider die Christ-Lehre am meisten streitet."

56. "Dahin gehoeret das Christliche Edict unseres Gnaedigsten Chur-Fuersten von Heiligung des Sabbaths/ darinnen ernstlich anbefohlen wird/ an denen Sonn-Fest-Buß und Bet-Tagen nicht allein mit allen Handthierungen/ Verkauffen und Arbeiten/ sonderlich unter wahrendem Gottedienste einzuhalten/ sondern auch in den Schencken/ Bier- und Wein-Haeusern den gantzen Tag ueber keine Saefte zu setzen" (ibid.).

57. Thomasius, *Vollstaendige Erlaeuterung*, 32.

58. Kervorkian, "Piety confronts politics"; Kruse in his *Speners Kritik* writes that Spener had opposed princely interference in the church while he was at the court of the worldly Elector of Saxony, but began to favor it after moving to Brandenburg, where the elector showed a keen religious interest in the reform of the Lutheran church.

59. Samuel Stryk, *De Jure Sabbathi*, 5th ed. (Halle: Waisenhaus, 1715), 49.

60. "Primum est, ut subditi ad pietatem ducantur, & cultus divinus rite ordinatur" (ibid.).

61. "[P]raefecti regni Dei. & vicarii" (ibid., 52).

62. "[O]mnes hominum actiones, ac ita etiam negotia sacra eo dirigendi, ut iis regnum Dei promoveatur" (ibid., 52).

63. Ibid.

64. "[A]d locum, tempus & modum cultus divini" (ibid., 64).

65. On the importance of the reform of piety for Thomasius, see, in particular, Zurbuchen, "Gewissensfreiheit und Toleranz," 177; and Dreitzel, "Christliche Aufklärung durch fürstlichen Absolutismus," 45.

CHAPTER FOUR

1. See, for example, the praise of Constantine the Great in Matthias Flacius, Johann Wigand, Matthaeus Richter, Basilius Faber, et al., *Historia Ecclesiastica, integram Ecclesiae Christianae conditionem, inde a Christo ex Virgine nato, juxta seculorum seriem exponens* (Basel: Ludovicus Rex, 1624), Centuria 4, chap. 31.

2. "[W]iewohl sie die Clerisey disfals als Kirchen-Raethe gebrauchten" (Thomasius, *Rechtmäßige Erörterung der Ehe-und Gewissensfrage*, chap. 1, §9).

3. "[D]urch die conniventz und dem uebermaeßigen respect der Kaeyser die Clerisey und Paepste immer nach und nach/ sich mehr Recht als ihnen gehoerete/ hinaus nahmen/ und endlich die Jura Ecclesiastica an sich zogen" (ibid.).

4.   "[N]on tam vitio proprio, quam illorum Clericorum, quibus erant obsessi, multa *in jure circa sacra perpetrarunt, quae certe defendi nequeunt*" (Thomasius, *De Jure Principis circa Adiaphora*, chap. 1, §§6–7).

5.   "[M]an hat ja mit diesem praejudicio autoritatis, nemlich von dem glueck-seligen Zustande der Christlichen Kirchen zu Constantini M. Zeiten/ . . . die Welt lange gnug geäffet. . . ." (Thomasius, *Das Recht Evangelischer Fürsten in theologis-chen Streitigkeiten*, 5. Satz, §4).

6.   "Principem maiorem vitiis quam virtutibus" (Christian Thomasius, "Fundamenta Historica in Expositione Tituli Codicis de Summa Trinitate etc. Supponenda," *Observationes selectae ad rem litterariam spectantes*, vol. 2, *Observatio* 8 [Halle: Renger, 1700], §47).

7.   Carpzov, *De Jure decidendi*, Thesis 7, §3.

8.   See, for example, Carpzov, *De Jure decidendi*, Thesis 2, §3, where Carpzov refers to Constantine's contribution to ending the Arian controversy. For the opin-ion of the eminent orthodox theologian Johann Konrad Dannhauer (1603–66), see Kruse, *Speners Kritik*, 124–29. The significance of Thomasius's interest in Constantine is pointed out by Stefan Buchholz, "Historia Contentionis inter Imperium et Sacerdotium. Kirchengeschichte in der Sicht von Christian Thomasius und Gottfried Arnold" in *Christian Thomasius*, ed. Friedrich Vollhardt, 168–70.

9.   See Pott, "Christian Thomasius und Gottfried Arnold."

10.   Thomasius, "Fides Scriptorum Vitae Constantini Magni," in *Observationes selectae ad rem litterariam spectantes*, vol. 1, *Observatio* 22 (Halle: Renger, 1700); see also the following *Observatio* on Constantine's parents.

11.   Thomasius, "Fundamenta Historica in Expositione Tituli Codicis de Summa Trinitate etc. Supponenda," §§51–53.

12.   *Observationes*, vol. 1, *Observatio* 24, §37.

13.   Ibid.; see also Thomasius, *Historia contentionis inter imperium et sacer-dotium breviter delineata usque ad saeculum XVI* (Halle: Renger, 1722), preface (no pagination).

14.   "[A]morem fratrum, & fructus spiritus charitatem, gaudium, pacem, leni-tatem, benignitatem, bonitatem, fidem, mansuetudinem, temperantiam" (Thomasius, "Fundamenta Historica in Expositione Tituli Codicis de Summa Trinitate etc. Supponenda," §8).

15.   "[V]erbis certis ac determinatis, & ut ita dicam, terminis technicis, sed suf-ficere quibuscunque verbis exponere mysteria Dei, modo non abducerent a spiritu & fructibus ejus" (ibid.).

16.   Thomasius, *Historia contentionis*, chap. 2, §8, and chap. 3, §19; "Fundamenta Historica in Expositione Tituli Codicis de Summa Trinitate etc. Supponenda," §8.

17.   "Fundamenta Historica in Expositione Tituli Codicis de Summa Trinitate etc. Supponenda, §19.

18.   "[D]iversae Philosophiae Professores, Iudaei, Graeci, alii adsueti partim doctrinae systematicae & speculationibus subtilissimis de Deo, partim ceremoniis & ritibus externis" (ibid., §20). Thomasius seems to have been drawing on a common attribution of corruption in the early church to the influence of pagan philosophy and a supposed emphasis in Judaism on external ritual (see, for example, Friedrich Spanheim, *Summa historiae ecclesiasticae, A Christo nato ad seculum XVI. Inchoatum.* [Leiden: Johann Verbessel, 1689], 153).

19. "[R]elegationibus & poenis" (Thomasius, "Fundamenta Historica in Expositione Tituli Codicis de Summa Trinitate etc. Supponenda," §47).

20. Thomasius, "Fundamenta Historica in Expositione Tituli Codicis de Summa Trinitate etc. Supponenda," §67: as soon as the Arians found an emperor well-disposed toward them they "par pari retulerunt."

21. See Samuel Pufendorf, *Jus feciale divinum* (Lübeck, 1695), §9: controversies over dogmas could be resolved, for "ubi datur principium fallere nescium, quale in Theologicis controversiis est Sacra Scriptura, non potest non demum controversiarum eo spectantium exitus reperiri."

22. Samuel Pufendorf, *De habitu religionis Christianae ad vitam civilem* (Bremen: Schwerdfeger, 1687), §47.

23. "Ea causa, postquam universae civitates ipsis cum Principibus sacra Christianae sunt amplexae, hactenus expiravit, quod non amplius ista morum sanctimonia ad pudorem ethnicis incutiendum faceret, cum hisce exterminatis jam omnes cives ad parem morum puritatem contenderunt" (ibid.).

24. "[I]sta [sc. disciplina] facile in abusum trahi, & in genus aliquod imperii invalescere potest, non sine insigni summorum imperantium praejudicio" (ibid.).

25. Samuel Pufendorf, *Politische Betrachtung der Geistlichen Monarchie des Stuhls zu Rom mit Anmerckungen zum Gebrauch des Thomasischen Auditorii*, ed. C. Thomasius (Halle: Renger, 1714), 58.

26. Pufendorf, *Politische Betrachtung*, 60–61.

27. "Als aber der Heydnische Kayser mit seinen Heydnischen Sitten/ Gesetzen und Ordnungen in das Reich Christi kam/ da ward aus der Christenheit ein Babel" (quoted in Kruse, *Speners Kritik*, 159).

28. "Ich habe aber immer gemeinet, daß es bis dahin [that is, Constantine] gerade elend gegangen" (ibid.).

29. "Es ist der Kirche nie ärger gegangen, als da sie unter Konstantine Luft bekam" (ibid., 159–60).

30. Kruse, *Speners Kritik*, 172.

31. See also his praise for Christian Hoburg in his *Versuch von Wesen des Geistes*, chap. 6.

32. "[B]este und nuetzlichste Buch nach der Heiligen Schrift" (Christian Thomasius, *Auserlesene und in Deutsch noch nie gedruckte Schrifften. Theil II* (Frankfurt and Leipzig: Renger, 1714), 226; see also Thomasius, *Bedencken über die Frage: Wieweit ein Prediger gegen seinen Landes-Herrn/ Welcher zugleich Summus Episcopus mit ist/ sich des Binde-Schlüssels bedienen könne?* 3rd ed. (Wolfenbüttel: Freytag, 1707), 150, for more praise of Arnold. Gottfried Arnold was born in Annaberg and studied in Wittenberg, before going to Dresden as a private tutor, where he met Phillip Jakob Spener. Following the publication of his first history of the early church, the *Die erste Liebe der Gemeinen JESU Christi, d. i. wahre Abbildung der ersten Christen* (Frankfurt am Main: Friedeburg, 1696), he was offered a chair in history at the University of Gießen. He accepted, but then withdrew in the same year. In 1699, he published the work for which he is best known, the *Unpartheyische Kirchen- und Ketzer-Historie* (Frankfurt am Main: Fritsch, 1700). On Arnold, see also Jürgen Büchsel, *Gottfried Arnold. Sein Verständnis von Kirche und Wiedergeburt* (Witten: Luther-Verlag, 1970); Hermann Dörries, *Geist und Geschichte bei Gottfried Arnold* (Göttingen: Vandenhoeck & Ruprecht, 1963);

Dietrich Blaufuß and Friedrich Niewöhner, eds, *Gottfried Arnold (1666–1714)* (Wiesbaden: Harassowitz, 1995).

33. Gottfried Arnold, "Kurtze Nachricht Von dem Bruder- und Schwester-Namen in der ersten Kirchen," in *Historie der Weißheit und Thorheit*, ed. C. Thomasius (Halle: Salfeld, 1693), "Der neunte Monat"; Arnold, "Historia Christianorum ad Metalla damnatorum," in *Historia Sapientiae et Stultitiae*, vol. 3, ed. C. Thomasius (Halle: Salfeld, 1693), chap. 7.

34. Gottfried Arnold, *Gottfried Arnold in Auswahl*, ed. E. Seeberg (Munich: Langen Müller, 1934), 44.

35. "[A]uch dahero die gantze Bibel/ wie sie jetzo als unfehlbar angenommen wird/ nicht zur norm allerseits recipirt worden" (ibid., 48).

36. "[V]ernunfft/ heydnische Philosophie und eigne menschen-satzungen" (ibid., 42).

37. "[D]en bedrängten Zustand der ersten Kirchen nicht vor den rechten und von GOTT intentionirten . . . /weil ja insgemein das Menschliche Hertze dieses vor eine grosse Seeligkeit und höchste Art der Göttlichen Gnade hält/ wenn das Fleisch von allen/ oder doch von vielen Leyden frey seyn kan. Dahero preiset die Vernunfft ein solches Leben vor dem trübseligen Stand der wahren Christen" (in Arnold, *Gottfried Arnold in Auswahl*, 28).

38. "[D]ie Trübsalen der Gemeinen eben ihren Glauben geprüfet und die erste Liebe befestigt/ hingegen die sicherheit der folgenden beydes geschwächet und endlich verlöschet habe" (ibid., 32).

39. "[V]ermeinte Gückseligkeit bey dem Schutz/ Überfluß und Schein unter Constantino und den folgenden Kaysern" (ibid., 32).

40. "[G]lantz von der ersten Seeligkeit entfernet" (ibid., 32).

41. For Arnold's opinion on Cave, cf. Arnold's letter to Thomasius in Jürgen Büchsel and Dietrich Blaufuß, "Gottfried Arnolds Briefwechsel. Eine erste Bestandsaufnahme—Arnold an Christian Thomasius 1694," in *Pietismus, Herrnhutertum, Erweckungsbewegung. Festschrift für Erich Beyreuther*, ed. D. Meyer (Cologne: Rheinland-Verlag, 1982). 95. Arnold describes Cave as being "a supporter of the [ecclesiastical] hierarchy" ("Hierarchiae fautore").

42. Büchsel, *Gottfried Arnold*, 40.

43. Gretchen E. Minton, "Cave, William (1637–1713)," in the *Oxford Dictionary of National Biography*, ed. H. C. G. Matthew and Brian Harrison (Oxford: Oxford University Press, 2004).

44. See Mark Goldie, "The Theory of Religious Intolerance in Restoration England," in *From Persecution to Toleration*, ed. Ole Grell, Jonathan Israel, and Nicholas Tyacke (Oxford: Clarendon Press, 1991), 342.

45. William Cave, *Ecclesiastici: or, the History of the Lives, Arts, Death and Writings of the most Eminent Fathers of the Church, That Flourisht in the Fourth Century* (London: Richard Chiswel, 1683), "The Epistle Dedicatory."

46. See William Cave, *Apostolici or the Lives of the Primitive Fathers for the three first Ages of the Christian church* (London: Richard Chiswel, 1677), "Introduction," §§17, 19, 26, 28.

47. Ibid., "Introduction," §§17 and 29.

48. Ibid., "Introduction," §7.

49. Arnold, *Gottfried Arnold in Auswahl*, 31.

50. The frontispiece of Cave's *Ecclesiastici* shows Constantine at the Nicene Council.

51. See, for example, Cave, *Ecclesiastici,* "Introduction," section 1, §12, xiv–xv.

52. Cave, *Ecclesiastici,* "Preface to the Reader."

53. Cave, *Ecclesiastici,* "Introduction," ii.

54. Ibid., section 1, §12, xiv.

55. "Force may make Men Hypocrites, but not Religious" (ibid., section 4, §2, li).

56. This question has been discussed by Goldie, "The Theory of Religious Intolerance in Restoration England," 347.

57. Cave, *Apostolici,* "Introduction," §11, x.

58. Cave, *Ecclesiastici,* section 4, §16, xlv–xlvi.

59. Joachim Lange, *Auffrichtige Nachricht von der Unrichtigkeit der so genanten Unschuldigen Nachrichten . . . Erste Ordnung Auff das Jahr 1701* (Leipzig: Heinichen, 1707), 7.

60. Ibid., "Vorbericht."

61. Ibid., 18–21.

62. See, for example, Joachim Lange, *Historia Ecclesiastica a Mundo Condito* (Halle: Waisenhaus, 1718), 481–83.

63. For Lange's definition of heresy, see ibid., 386.

64. Ibid., 500–506 and 571–80.

65. Ibid., 512, 580, 655.

66. Ibid., 512.

CHAPTER FIVE

1. For a general survey of the use of the *Corpus Iuris* in this period, see Franz Wieacker, *Privatrechtsgeschichte der Neuzeit* (Göttingen: Vandenhoeck & Ruprecht, 1996), §§12–14.

2. Gulielmus Best, "De Aequitate iuris Romani illiusque studii iucunditate," in his *Ratio emendandi leges Pandectarum Florentinarum* (Leipzig: Schoenmark, 1745).

3. "Regna . . . Europea fere omnia idem pro Jure Communi, non ex necessitate legis, sed ex ductu aequissimarum rationum, quibus Jurisprudentia innititur, aestimant, & specialibus Regni juribus deficientibus, eo sponte recurrunt" (Samuel Stryk, *Specimen Usus Moderni Pandectarum ad Libros V. Priores* [Frankfurt and Wittenberg: Schrey & Meyer, 1690], 36). I am grateful to Dr. Heinz Mohnhaupt for his advice on stryk's work.

4. See Fritz Sturm, *Das römische Recht in der Sicht von Gottfried Wilhelm Leibniz* (Tübingen: Mohr, 1968), 17; Justinian, *The Digest of Justinian,* ed. by Theodor Mommsen with the aid of Paul Krueger, English translation ed. by Alan Watson (Philadelphia: University of Pennsylvania Press, 1985).

5. Roderich von Stintzing, *Geschichte der Deutschen Rechtswissenschaft,* Abt. III.1 (München: Oldenbourg, 1898), 82; Wolfgang Ebner, "Die Kritik des römischen Rechts bei Christian Thomasius" (Ph.D. thesis, Frankfurt am Main, 1971).

6. The *Codex,* like the *Digest,* was part of the total body of Roman law, the *Corpus Iuris Civilis.*

7.   Thomasius, "Fundamenta Historica in Expositione Tituli Codicis de Summa Trinitate etc. Supponenda," §2; see also his "Ad Legem I. C. de Summa Trinitate," and the "Ad Legem II. C. de Summa Trinitate," in vol. 3 of the *Observationes*.

8.   "[C]ertis symbolis confessionem inclusisse non constat" (Thomasius, "Fundamenta Historica in Expositione Tituli Codicis de Summa Trinitate etc. Supponenda," §25).

9.   "[A]d nullam formulam, & terminos technicos erat redactum, & Patres primitivae Ecclesiae phrasibus utebantur, quae post Constantinum non fuissent toleratae" (ibid., §26).

10.   He was born in 1632 and died 1705. An edition of the *Praxis* with a preface by Thomasius was published in 1713.

11.   An edition with notes by Thomasius was published in Thomasius's 1713 *Notae ad singulos Institutionum et Pandectarum titulos varias juris Romani antiquitates imprimis usum eorum hodiernum in foris Germaniae ostendentes* (Halle: Renger).

12.   Stryk, *Specimen*, 30.

13.   Wieacker, *Privatrechtsgeschichte*, 207.

14.   Douglas Osler, "Budeus and Roman Law," *Ius Commune* 13 (1985): 195–213; Douglas Osler revises Donald Kelley's interpretation of Budé in Kelley's *Foundations of Modern Historical Scholarship* (New York and London: Columbia University Press, 1970), chap. 3, 68. For the applicability of this statement to late seventeenth-century jurisprudence, see Govaert C. J. J. van den Bergh, *The Life and Work of Gerard de Noodt (1657–1725). Dutch Legal Scholarship between Humanism and the Enlightenment* (Oxford: Clarendon Press, 1988), 110.

15.   "[N]on ergo captanda Legum verba, aut ex his facienda applicatio, sed quid intenderit quondam Legislator, de publicis causis disponendo, attendendum. . . . Non quadrant quidem hodie omnia, quadrabunt tamen plurima" (Stryk, 33).

16.   "[A]c earundem sententiam mentemque exponere; hinc recurrendum est ad rationem legis tanquam eius animam, & si in ipsa lege expressa non reperiatur aliis adminiculis indagandam & ex ea iudicium postea de tota lege ferendum: maxime quod concernit leges Romanas" (Johann Samuel Stryk, *De Jure Liciti sed non Honesti* [Halle: Waisenhaus, 1702], 138–39).

17.   Justus Henning Boehmer, *Exercitationes ad Pandectas, in quibus praecipua Digestorum capita explicantur* (Hannover and Göttingen: Schmid, 1745), "Exercitatio III ad Libr. I. Pand. Tit. I. de interpretationis grammaticae fatis et usu vario in iure Romano."

18.   On the history of imperial public law, see especially Michael Stolleis, *Geschichte des öffentlichen Rechts in Deutschland*, vol. 1 (Munich: Beck, 1988).

19.   See Aristotle, *The Politics of Aristotle* trans. and ed. Ernest Barker (Oxford: Clarendon Press, 1948), 1282b: "The one clear fact is that laws must be constituted in accordance with constitutions; and if this is the case, it follows that laws which are in accordance with right constitutions must necessarily be just, and laws which are in accordance with wrong or perverted constitutions must be unjust."

20.   On Conring and the Lotharian legend, see especially Klaus Luig, "Conring, das deutsche Recht und die Rechtsgeschichte," in *Hermann Conring (1606–1681); Beiträge zu Leben und Werk*, ed. Michael Stolleis (Berlin: Duncker & Humblot, 1983), 355–95.

21. "Et quidem in comperto est, multa quae ad Statum Rei Romanae pristinum pertinent, a Justiniano in Corpore juris exhibere; Verum an his LL. utendum in dijudicandis controversiis ad Statum Imperii modernum pertinentibus, hoc Dd. quorundam (inter quos eminent Dn. *Tabor* & Dn. *Conringius*) Concertationibus huc usque ventilatum" (Stryk, *Specimen*, 32).

22. "Quod si ergo Reipubl. forma, vel modus administrandi Rempubl. aliter se habere incipiat, necessitas salutis publicae exigit, ut novis Juribus praesens Status muniatur, & quae olim constituta vel tollantur penitus, vel prudenti consilio ita circumscribantur, ne praesens Regimen impediant, sed potius conservent & promoveant" (ibid.).

23. "[N]on attenta diversitate principiorum, ac iuris ratione" (Johann Schilter, *Praxis Juris Romani in Foro Germanico*, 3rd ed., with a preface and annotations by Christian Thomasius [Frankfurt and Leipzig: Boetticher, 1713], Schilter's dedication to V. L. von Seckendorff, 3).

24. "[I]us & statum publicum" (ibid.).

25. Ibid., 4.

26. "[A]lterum est peccatum, invidia & suspicio Statuum adversus Impp. quasi forma Reip. immutanda foret, Libertas Germanica cum inaniis Senatus Romani commutanda, & Imperium plane Iustinianeum oriundum" (ibid., 3–4).

27. Ibid., 3.

28. See the introductory chapter in James O. Whitman, *The Legacy of Roman Law in the German Romantic Era* (Princeton, NJ: Princeton University Press, 1990).

29. Published by Thomasius in his *Notae ad singulos Institutionum et Pandectarum titulos varias juris Romani antiquitates imprimis usum eorum hodiernum in foris Germaniae ostendentes*.

30. "Vidimus post tempora adultiora ex legum a majoribus latarum, neglectione, insignem morbum esse contractum, vim & arma, quae illis successerunt, tandem proscripsimus, revocavimus iterum leges, sed tales, quae in se quidem & gentes ejus, cui ferebantur, intuitu, optimae, pro conditione vero nostri status minus utiles haberi debebant. Romani enim accommodati erant imperio plene monarchico, nobis libertas quaedam erat conservanda, quae nostris legibus praeclare contemperabatur, quarum loco cum aliena illa jura fuerant usurpata, non potuit aliter fieri, quam ut in applicatione ad casus occurrentes, disciplina ubique haereret, impedireturque a se ipsa. Initio ergo revocati quasi postliminio juris, misera de publicis controversiis judicia fuere lata, in detrimentum communis salutis, in bella civilia, in ipsum denique reipublicae interitum valitura" (Johannes Kulpis [writing as "Conradus Sincerus"], *De Germanicarum legum veterum, ac Romani juris in republica nostra origine, auctoritateque praesenti dissertatio epistolica*, in Thomasius, *Notae ad singulos Institutionum et Pandectarum titulos*, §104, 124–25).

31. Ibid., §105.

32. "[I]nforme chaos" (Thomasius, *Institutiones*, 1688, bk. 2, chap. 10, §66).

33. "[S]umma diligentia praeditis; sed omni literarum & historiae studio destitutis" (ibid., §65).

34. Thomasius's views on the *laesio enormis* are discussed in Thomas Ahnert, "Roman Law in Early Enlightenment Germany: The Case of Christian Thomasius' *De Aequitate Cerebrina Legis Secundae Codicis de Rescindenda Venditione* (1706)," *Ius Commune* 24, 1997: 52–170.

35. Reinhard Zimmermann, *The Law of Obligations: Roman Foundations of the Civilian Tradition* (Cape Town: Juta, 1990), 259–70; Alan Watson, "The Hidden Origins of Enorm Lesion," *Journal of Legal History* 2, 1981, 186–93.

36. Justinian, *Codex Justinianus*, ed. P. Krüger (Berlin: Weidmann, 1877), 4.44.2.

37. Wolfgang Ebner, "Die Kritik des römischen Rechts bei Christian Thomasius," Ph.D. thesis (Frankfurt am Main, 1971).

38. "Das als gemeines Recht im Reiche positiv geltende römische Recht hat also in diesem Punkte für Thomasius keine naturrechtliche Legitimation: es ist naturrechtswidrig" (Klaus Luig, "Der Gerechte Preis in der Rechtstheorie und Rechtspraxis von Christian Thomasius (1655–1728)," in *Diritto e potere nella storia europea: atti in onore di Bruno Paradisi*, 775–803 [Florence, 1982], 782).

39. "Differt haec aequitas cerebrina a vera aequitate, quod ipsa plane non sit aequitas, sed aequitatem mentiatur, aut sit aequitas irrationalis, differt ab iniquitate, quod non omnis iniquitas, sit aequitas cerebrina, sed saltem ea, quae speciem aequitatis habet" (Thomasius, *De Aequitate Cerebrina*, chap. I, §4).

40. See also Caspar Schott, "Aequitas cerebrina," in *Hans Thieme zum 70. Geburtstag zugeeignet von seinen Schülern*, ed. Bernhard Diestelkamp (Cologne and Vienna: Böhlau, 1977).

41. "[S]i originem pretii consideres, quocumque te vertas, deprehendes, id totum, quantum quantum est, dependere ab arbitrio mero hominum" (Thomasius, *De Aequitate Cerebrina*, chap. 2, §15); "Idque non in regulis quibusdam justitiae fundatum, sed merum ac liberum, nullum aliud fundamentum agnoscens quam voluntatem" (ibid., §16).

42. "Cupiditas hominum primus fons est pretii rerum, secundus raritas" (ibid., §16).

43. Nor is the just price that price which will preserve equality in exchange. Thomasius rejects the Aristotelian concept of commutative justice which required this equality. The just price, to him, is just because it is legally binding after both parties to the contract have agreed to it freely (*De Aequitate Cerebrina*, chap. 2, 64).

44. Ibid., §30.

45. Ibid., §33. Thomasius argued that the concept of the *pretium commune*, was the result of a misinterpretation of two further laws in the *Corpus*, other than the second and eighth law referred to above. For scholastic concepts of the just price, see Odd Langholm, *Price and Value in the Aristotelian Tradition. A Study in Scholastic Economic Sources* (Bergen and Oslo: Universitetsforlaget, 1979). See also James Gordley, *The Philosophical Origins of Modern Contract Doctrine* (Oxford: Clarendon Press, 1991), 95 and 101; contrary to Gordley's argument, it is clear that Thomasius did understand the scholastic concept of *pretium commune*.

46. See Udo Wolter, "Die Fortgeltung des kanonischen Rechts und die Haltung der protestantischen Juristen zum kanonischen Recht in Deutschland bis in die Mitte des 18. Jahrhunderts," in *Canon Law in Protestant Lands*, ed. R. Helmholz (Berlin: Duncker & Humblot, 1992), 30.

47. *De Aequitate Cerebrina*, chap. 2, 33. The passage Thomasius is referring to in particular is in the Decretals of Gregory IX, III, xvii, "De Emtione et Venditione," chapter 3 (see *Corpus Iuris Canonici*, 2 vols., ed. E. Friedberg [Graz: Akademische Verlagsanstalt, 1959]).

48. Christian Friedrich Jan, *Tractatus Iuridicus Theoretico-Practicus de Denuntiatione Evangelica, in quo, de Aequitate Juris Canonici ex professo agitur* (Wittenberg: Berger, 1673).

49. "J. Can. remedium suppletorium & subsidiarium, quod miseris & suppressis subveniat nova actione fori avocatoria" (ibid., 9).

50. Ibid., 18.

51. Jan, *Tractatus,* chap. 3, §11: nothing "magis aptae esse possunt ad imponendum denuo cervicibus nostris Pontificiae Tyrannidis jugum, quam illa ipsa Juris Pontificii observatio."

52. *De Aequitate Cerebrina,* chap. 2, 44–45.

53. "[I]nfelicitas seculi, in quo Justinianus & ejus ministri operam dederunt emendandae jurisprudentiae. Regnabat jam tum vera barbaries, hoc est ignorantia justi & aequi, & ubique clerus hanc doctrinam ad se rapuerat, non proponens eam secundum regulas rectae rationis, sed secundum principia ethicae monachicae, laqueos ponentis conscientiis laicorum, prout interesse autoritatis clericalis modo sic, modo aliter suaderet. Ne vero fraus sentiretur, si rationibus disceptatum fuisset, hoc artificio utebatur clerus, ut, cum Deus omnium gentium & hominum cordibus semina doctrinae justi & aequi, seu legis naturalis, inscripsisset, ipsis ante omnia persuaderet, rationem rectam ad doctrinam morum esse insufficientem, sed eam unice petendam esse ex scriptura sacra, potissimum ex legibus Mosaicis. Ita vero solus clerus regnabat in doctrina morum, cum ipse explicationem scripturae sibi soli vindicaret, & leges Mosaicas illas omnes pro legibus moralibus venditaret, quae facerent ad stabiliendam auctoritatem & imperium cleri in laicos. Quin & ubi deficerent leges Mosaicae, alia loca sacrarum literarum pro autoritate misere torquebantur, ut nulla sententia in doctrina justi & aequi tam absurda esset, quae non hoc modo defendi potuerit, non audentibus contra vel hiscere saltem laicis, qui jam per aliquot secula partim metu, partim dolosa persuasione coeca obedientiae eo perducti erant, ut putarent, credulitatem esse summam virtutum laicarum, & doctores ista inculcantes esse infallibiles" (*De Aequitate Cerebrina,* chap. 2, 42).

54. Thomasius lists several in ibid., chap. 1, §XVII.

55. See Thomasius, *Fundamenta Juris Naturae et Gentium* (4th ed., 1718, bk. 2, chap. 10, §§17–19. Thomasius there argued that the conquests of Louis XIV in the Holy Roman Empire were made under the pretext of *mala fides* of the previous occupants.

56. "[P]raecipuus acquirendi modus" (*Fundamenta* [4th ed., 1718], bk. 2, chap. 10, §12).

57. See also Christian Thomasius, *Disputatio de origine successionis testamentariae apud Romanos* (Halle: Zeitler, 1705).

58. Thomasius, *De desertione ordinis ecclesiastici* (Halle: Zeitler, 1707); see also his *Fundamenta* (4th ed., 1718), bk. 2, chap. 7, §7.

59. Thomasius, *De singulari aequitate legis unicae Codicis quando Imperator inter Pupillos etc. cognoscat etc., eiusque usu practico* (Halle: Johann Grunert, 1725).

60. "[A]equissimam humanissimamque Constantini Magni constitutionem" (Thomasius, *De singulari aequitate,* 5).

61. "[S]ed Imperatorem flagitiosum" (ibid., 4).

62. "[P]er ipsius imprudentiam & distinctionem inter potestatem Ecclesiae internam & externam coepisse Clerum (etiam orthodoxum) fundamenta iacere se

eximendi a potestate & imperio magistratus Politici, & pro lubitu potentia principum tanquam brachio seculari utendi & abutendi, ad quamcunque tyrannidem exercendam" (ibid., 41).

63. "[R]apinas, incendia, uno verbo, si innumera & ineffabilia damna, quae Protestantium respublicae inde per duo secula passae sunt, si non unice, saltem praecipue huic aequitati cerebrinae & in thesi ejus fructibus adscribam" (Thomasius, *De Aequitate Cerebrina*, chap. 1, 24, footnote gg).

64. "Pleraeque academiae Protestantium olim fuere pontificiae, neque reformationis tempore ab omni fermento pontificiae doctrinae fuere penitus purgatae. At notum est, vel minimam partem fermenti ificere massam reliquam" (Thomasius, *De Aequitate Cerebrina*, chap. I, §19).

65. "Principes & Laici reliqui persuaderentur de sanctitate & aequitate canonum Ecclesiasticorum & juris inde denominati" (Thomasius, *De Aequitate Cerebrina*, chap. 1, §18).

CHAPTER SIX

1.   On this, see Thomas Ahnert, "Pleasure, Pain and Punishment in the Early Enlightenment: German and Scottish Debates," *Jahrbuch für Recht und Ethik* 12, 2004, 173–87.

2.   Frank Grunert, "Das Recht der Natur als Recht des Gefühls. Zur Naturrechtslehre von Johann Jacob Schmauss," *Jahrbuch für Recht und Ethik* 12, 2004, 137–53.

3.   "J'y montre d'abord, qu'au lieu de la *Raison*, dont je prouve l'insuffisance, ce n'est que dans les PASSIONS ENTANT QU'ELLES SONT CONFORMES A LA NATURE, qu'on peut trouver les loix dont il s'agit; & que la Raison ne fert proprement qu'a les interpréter, & qu'à en deduire les Règles de nos Devoirs, dont je rapporte les plus importans. J'y observe ensuite que l'*Obligation* qui accompagne les Loix Naturelles ne peut *consister* que dans la force inséparable des Passions, laquelle nous porte naturellement a nous satisfaire" (Frédéric-Henri Strube de Piermont, *Ébauche des Loix Naturelles et du Droit Primitif* (Amsterdam, 1744), vii). On related debates in British moral philosophy of the eighteenth century, see Stephen Darwall, *The British Moralists and the Internal "Ought," 1640–1740* (Cambridge: Cambridge University Press, 1995).

4.   On this, see Gerhard Sauder, *Empfindsamkeit. Band 1: Voraussetzungen und Elemente* (Stuttgart: J. B. Metzler, 1984).

5.   For an analysis of the responses to Pufendorf's *De Jure Naturae et Gentium*, see Fiammetta Palladini, *Discussioni seicentesche su Samuel Pufendorf. Scritti Latini: 166–700* (Bologna: Il Mulino, 1978). On Pufendorf's natural law theory, see Horst Denzer, *Moralphilosophie und Naturrecht bei Samuel Pufendorf* (Munich: Beck, 1972); and Jerome B. Schneewind, *The Invention of Autonomy: A History of Modern Moral Philosophy* (Cambridge: Cambridge University Press, 1998), chap. 7.

6.   This was first published in Leipzig in 1678; the edition used here is that of 1696, which is identical to the first, general, part of the 1678 edition but includes

additional comments and exegetical appendices. The second part, on particular precepts of natural law, is present only in the 1678 edition (see Ernst-Dietrich Osterhorn, "Die Naturrechtslehre Valentin Albertis" [Ph.D. thesis, Freiburg im Breisgau, 1962], 30).

7. Osterhorn, "Die Naturrechtslehre Valentin Albertis"; Hans-Peter Schneider, *Justitia Universalis. Studien zur Geschichte des Naturrechts bei Leibniz* (Frankfurt am Main: Klostermann, 1967), 247–53.

8. Thomasius, *Institutiones*, 1688, bk. 3, chap. 3, §76; see also Thomasius, *De crimine bigamiae* of 1685.

9. See, for example, Johann Adam Osiander, *Observationes Maximam partem Theologicae, in Libros Tres de Jure Belli et Pacis Hugonis Grotii* (Tübingen: Cotta, 1671), 185.

10. Samuel Pufendorf, *De Jure Naturae et Gentium Libri Octo* (London and Oxford: Clarendon Press, 1934), bk. 1, chap. 1, §§3–4.

11. "[J]ussus imperantis obligans subjectos, ut secundum istum jussum actiones suas instituant" (Thomasius, *Institutiones*, 1688, bk. 1, chap. 1, §28).

12. "[E]xtensio manus ad rem etiam alienam" (ibid., bk. 1, chap. 2, §90).

13. Ibid., §72.

14. Ibid., bk. 1, chap. 3, §48.

15. Ibid., §§43–45.

16. Ibid., §52.

17. "*Ratio absque sermone non est, sermonis extra societatem nullus est usus, nec ratio citra societatem se exerit*" (ibid., bk. 1, chap. 4, §54).

18. Ibid., §66.

19. "[N]ecessario periret, si alii homines non obligati forent, ut ipsi succurrant" (ibid., bk. 1, chap. 3, §84). This is, of course, similar to Pufendorf's argument from *imbecillitas* in his *De Jure Naturae et Gentium*.

20. Ibid., §86.

21. See, for example, Pufendorf's *De Jure Naturae et Gentium*, bk. 1, chap. 4.

22. Thomasius, *Institutiones*, 1688, bk. 1, chap. 1, §38.

23. "Voluntas hominis multum de libertate sua amisit, ita ut in hoc statu fere tota ad malum inclinet, quoniam affectus frequentissime exorbitant, & hominem quasi extra se ponunt, certe perpetuo frenum mordent" (ibid., bk. 1, chap. 2, §39).

24. "[U]t minimum quod actus exteriores libertatem efficaciter retinendi retinuerit" (ibid., bk. 1, chap. 2, §42).

25. This is in contrast to his later theory of imputation in the *Foundations* of 1705, which is discussed in chapter 7.

26. "[F]rustra puniret homo hominem" (*Institutiones*, 1720 reprint, bk. 1, chap. 2, §42; footnote u; see also *Institutiones*, 1688, bk. 1, chap. 1, §54).

27. "[S]ibi proprias instituit" (*Institutiones*, 1688, bk. 1, chap. 1, §34).

28. "[I]psi cum bestiis & plantis communes sunt" (ibid.).

29. "[S]impliciter apprehendit objecta sensuum externorum, propositionem aliquam de illorum natura aut bonitate ex accidentibus eorum organa sensuum ferientibus, ac corpus delectantibus, formando, aut etiam de objectis jam antea sensu perceptis confuse ideas sibi format" (Thomasius, ibid., bk. 1, chap. 1, §44).

30. "[D]e veritate earum propositionum & de objecti bonitate, item de ideis ulterius per discursum meditando *ratiocinatur*" (ibid., bk. 1, chap. 1, §44).

31. Ibid., bk. 1, chap. 1, §53.

32. "[J]ussus imperantis obligans subjectos, ut secundum istum jussum actiones suas instituant" (Thomasius, ibid., bk. 1, chap. 1, §28).

33. "Itaque, cum Deus, quaecunque egit, secundum normam divinae suae sanctitatis, bonitatis, sapientiae ac justitiae egerit, & ita legem quasi aeternam ex libera voluntate sibi ipsi posuerit, necesse est, ut ad hanc archetypum lex quoque naturalis actiones hominum dirigens sit extructa, & adeo conveniens esse cum recta ratione, idem sit, ac conveniens esse cum sanctitate & justitia divina" (Thomasius, ibid., bk. 1, chap. 4, §21).

34. See, for example, ibid., bk. 1, chap. 3, §49.

35. "[V]el extra vel citra Deum" (Alberti, *Compendium*, 2nd ed., 1696, 213).

36. "[A]ntecedenter ad omnem liberum [Dei] voluntatis actum" (ibid.).

37. In Thomasius, *Institutiones Jurisprudentiae Divinae*, I, ii, §6, for example.

38. "[C]um summo jure exlex sit, sibi ipsi quasi lex est" (Alberti, *Compendium* 2nd ed., 1696, 197).

39. Alberti, ibid., bk. 1, chap. 3, §24.

40. "[C]onvenienter intellectui suo practico" (Alberti, ibid., 197).

41. "[L]egem, quam vocant, aeternam consistere communiter dicunt" (ibid.).

42. "Cum ergo lex aeterna sit ratio gubernationis in supremo gubernante, necesse est quod omnes rationes gubernationis quae sunt in inferioribus gubernantibus a lege aeterna deriventur" (Thomas Aquinas, *Summa Theologiae*, ed. T. Gilby (London: Blackfriars, 1964–), 1a2ae, *quaestio* 93, *articulus* 3).

43. "[O]mnia indifferenter a Deo praecipi & prohiberi posse statuunt" (Alberti, *Compendium*, 2nd ed., 1696, 212).

44. "Ita principia quoque moralia pro necessariis haberi debent, sed propter eandem convenientiam cum eadem lege" (ibid., 213–14).

45. "[S]impliciter necessarium" (ibid., 89).

46. "[R]ationalitas hominis dependet a Deo, non minus ac homo ipse" (ibid.).

47. "[E]ssentiae creatae . . . necessariae quidem sunt, sed propter convenientiam cum lege aeterna" (ibid., 213).

48. "[R]atione existentiae tanquam effectus a sua causa" (ibid., 219).

49. "[R]atione existentiae, seu prout conscripta est, ortum traxit a JCtis; sed ratione obligationis a Magistratu ipso" (ibid.).

50. Thomasius, *Institutiones*, 1688, bk. 1, chap. 3, §60: "Igitur non auderem titulum virtuosi & justi Divinae majestati tribuere, nisi viderem ipsius infinitam Sapientiam in verbo revelato non respuisse terminos istos. . . ."

51. Gottfried Wilhelm Leibniz, "Opinion on the Principles of Pufendorf (1706)," in *Leibniz. Political Writings*, trans. and ed. Patrick Riley (Cambridge: Cambridge University Press, 1992), 64–76.

52. Ibid., 70.

53. Ibid., 73–74.

54. Ibid., 71. On Leibniz's critique of Pufendorf's voluntarism, see Tim Hochstrasser, *Natural Law Theories in the Early Enlightenment* (Cambridge: Cambridge University Press, 2000), chap. 3.

55. "[I]imperanti pare" (Thomasius, *Institutiones*, 1688, bk. 1, chap. 3, §34).

56. "Imperans est, qui habet facultatem alterum obligandi" (ibid., §35).

57. "[J]ussus imperantis obligans subjectos" (ibid., §6).

58. Thomasius, *Fundamenta*, 4th ed., 1718, bk. 1, chap. 5, §41: "Imo etsi sapiens Deum sibi conciperet, ut hominem imperantem, tamen magis conciperet ut patrem, quam ut Dominum, quia magis convenit perfectioni bonitatis divinae quaerere bonum hominum, quam in legibus hominum cordi inscriptis quaerere utilitatem suam more despotico"; ibid., §43: "[M]ulti homines secundum connatum insipientiam Deum, ut despotam." Schneewind argues that the change in Thomasius's natural jurisprudence between the *Institutiones* of 1688 and the *Fundamenta* of 1705 is due to the theoretical problems of grounding natural law in God's free will (see Schneewind, *The Invention of Autonomy*, 159–66).

59. "Dominum, qui poenas externas arbitrarias velit inferre iis, qui contra praecepta juris naturae faciunt" (Thomasius, *Fundamenta*, 4th ed., 1718), bk. 1, chap. 5, §37).

60. "Porro omnis poena visibliter infertur, at mala, quae Deus ordinavit transgressoribus juris naturae, occulte veniunt, i. e. ut connexio mali cum peccato non sit visibilis, etsi forte ipsum malum visibile sit" (*Fundamenta*, bk. 1, chap. 5, §39).

61. *Fundamenta*, bk. 1, chap. 5, §50.

CHAPTER SEVEN

1. See Thomasius, *Institutiones*, 1688, bk. 1, chap. 3, §§88–92, where Thomasius considers the consequences of a world without God, or of a God who does not take an interest in human affairs. See especially §89: "[S]i Deus negotia hominum non curat, nullus dabitur imperans, nullus adeo erit, cui parendum sit."

2. Leibniz, "Opinion on the Principles of Pufendorf (1706)," 64–76; see also Riley, *Leibniz' Universal Jurisprudence*, 68–69.

3. See, for example, his lecture, "On the Greeks as Founders of Rational Theology," 1714, which is discussed in Riley, *Leibniz' Universal Jurisprudence*, 64–65.

4. See Seckendorff, *Christen-Stat*, chap. 8, §4.

5. Thomasius, *Institutiones*, 1688, bk. 1, chap. 3, §67: "de *angelis & anima separata* ne quidem quod sint, extra Verbum Dei aliquid scire (scire dico) possimus." In a footnote in the seventh edition, Thomasius adds: "Ratio enim animam separatam sibi concipere nequit."

6. "Diximus, cogitationes omnes fieri de rebus organa sensuum ferientibus, quare necesse est, ut Objectum ratiocinationis etiam sint *res, quae in sensus incurrunt*" (Thomasius, *Introductio ad philosophiam aulicam*, 1688, chap. 7, §1).

7. Seckendorff, *Christen-Stat*, chap. 8, §8.

8. Letter to Bierling (1713), quoted in Riley, *Leibniz' Universal Jurisprudence*, 68.

9. Fiammetta Palladini has argued that Pufendorf was secretly a Hobbesian (in her *Samuel Pufendorf, Discepolo di Hobbes* [Bologna: Il Mulino, 1990]) and used references to Stoicism only to disguise the Hobbesian character of his theory. Palladini bases her argument mainly on Pufendorf's use of self-preservation as first principle of his natural law theory, but to Pufendorf the pursuit of self-preservation in the state of nature and sociableness are not opposites, as they are to Hobbes. On Pufendorf's use of Stoic authors to refute Hobbes, see Hochstrasser, *Natural Law Theories in the Early Enlightenment*, 60–65.

10. *"Est ipsa utilitas justi prope mater & aequi; nec natura potest secernere iniquum.* Atqui hoc ipsum Carneades statuit, . . . recoxit maximam partem Epicureus Hobbesius"* (Thomasius, *Institutiones*, 1688, bk. 1, chap. 2, §95). The two hexameters are, of course, by Horace and famously referred to in the Prolegomena of Grotius's *De Jure Belli et Pacis.* Richard Tuck has discussed the responses to Carnedean skepticism in the natural law theory of the first half of the seventeenth century in his *Philosophy and Government 1572–1651* (Cambridge: Cambridge University Press, 1993).

11. In the "Dissertatio Prooemialis" to his *Institutiones*, 1688, Thomasius quotes a long passage from a piece by Seckendorff, the *Versuch von dem allgemeinen oder natuerlichen Recht*, in which Seckendorff rejects the idea that it is only necessity that impels humans to form societies (§53).

12. "Non omne quidem quod utile est, honestum est, omne tamen honestum est utile" (*Institutiones*, 1688, bk. 1, chap. 2, §96). Thomasius here is refuting the charge of Hobbism and Epicureanism.

13. Werner Schneiders, *Naturrecht und Liebesethik. Zur Geschichte der praktischen Philosophie im Hinblick auf Christian Thomasius* (Hildesheim and New York: Olms, 1971), 172.

14. Thomasius, *Von der Kunst . . . Einleitung zur Sitten Lehre* (Halle: Salfeld, 1692), "Unterthänigste Zuschrift."

15. Ibid.

16. Nannerl Keohane, *Philosophy and the State in France* (Princeton, NJ: Princeton University Press, 1980), 283; for examples of Thomasius's familiarity with the works of French authors, see Lieberwirth, "Die französischen Kultureinflüsse auf den deutschen Frühaufklärer Christian Thomasius," 63–73. Lieberwirth points out that of the 881 volumes of Thomasius's library, which were in a modern foreign language and were auctioned after his death, 723 were in French. In total, the auction catalogue contained 4,900 volumes (see *Bibliotheca Thomasiana, continens libros theologico-polemicos, medicos, autores classicos; accedunt disputationes, plerumque rariores, cuius auctio publica fiet Halae Die VI. Ju 1739* [Halle: Lehmann, 1739]).

17. See Thomasius, *Von der Kunst . . . Einleitung zur Sitten Lehre*, chap. 1, §§28–47.

18. Thomasius derived this triad of the three main vices opposed to rational love from a fusion of the first letter of the John the Evangelist, which lists "the lust of the flesh, and the lust of the eyes, and the pride of life" (1 John 2:16) as the three main sins, with Aristotle's *Nicomachean Ethics* (Oxford: Oxford University Press, 2002), 1095a, which depicts physical pleasure, honor, and glory as secondary goods (see Schneiders, *Naturrecht und Liebesethik*, 212).

19. "[S]ich mit andern Menschen zu vereinigen, die eine dergleichen Gemueths-Ruhe besitzen" (*Von der Kunst . . . Einleitung zur Sitten Lehre*, chap. 1, §65).

20. "[D]as Recht der Natur in der allgemeinen Glueckseeligkeit des Menschlichen Geschlechts gegruendet sey/ weshalben er destomehr fuer etwas gutes halten muß/ daß er sein Leben nach Gottes Willen einrichte/ weil unter der allgemeinen Glueckseeligkeit auch seine eigene mit begriffen wird" (ibid., §85).

21. The relationship of Thomasius to this tradition has been examined by Schneiders in his *Naturrecht und Liebesethik*.

22. See Keohane, *Philosophy and the State in France*, 311. The catalogue of Thomasius's books auctioned after his death included a 1692 edition of Abbadie's *L'Art* as item no. 506 in the section "Libri Gallici, Belgici, Anglicani &c." (*Bibliotheca Thomasiana*).

23. Christian Thomasius, *Von Der Artzeney Wider die unvernünfftige Liebe und der zuvorher nöthigen Erkäntnüß Sein Selbst. Oder: Ausübung der Sitten Lehre,* 1696, 4th ed. (Halle: Salfeld, 1708).

24. Quoted in Keohane, *Philosophy and the State in France*, 311–12.

25. Thomasius, *Von Der Artzeney . . . Ausübung der Sitten Lehre*, chap. 1, §§2–3.

26. Riley, *Leibniz' Universal Jurisprudence*, 77; see also Thomas Hobbes, *Leviathan*, ed. Richard Tuck (Cambridge: Cambridge University Press, 1991), part I, chap. 6. Or, as Thomasius observed in the *Fundamenta*, first published in 1705, "[i]psa tamen voluntas non est potentia voluntaria, alias enim daretur voluntas voluntatis . . . sed & ipsa in se naturalis potentia hominis est & necessaria, & non voluntaria" (*Fundamenta*, 4th ed., 1718, bk. 1, chap. 1, §56).

27. "[A]ußerordentliche Bewegung der Lebens-Geister im Geblüth" (Thomasius, *Von Der Artzeney . . . Ausübung der Sitten Lehre*, chap. 3, §43).

28. Thomasius, *Von Der Artzeney . . . Ausübung der Sitten Lehre*, chap. 3.

29. See Thomasius, *Fundamenta*, 4th ed., 1718, bk. 1, chap. 3, §1, note.

30. Pufendorf, *De Jure Naturae et Gentium*, bk. 1, chap. 4, §2.

31. After the Fall, the will, Thomasius wrote in the *Institutiones*, "inclinet quidem ad malum, sic tamen, ut minimum quod actus exteriores libertatem efficaciter retinendi retinuerit" (*Institutiones*, 1688, bk. 1, chap. 2, §42).

32. Ibid., 514. See also Christian Thomasius, "Natura Hominis. Libertas Voluntatis. Imputatio in Poenam," in *Observationes selectae ad rem litterariam spectantes*, vol. 2, *Observatio* 22 (Halle: Renger, 1701), §54, 287.

33. Thomasius refers to him in the fourth edition of the *Fundamenta,* 1718, 64: "non viderat [Buddeus] quomodo negata libertate voluntatis humanae doctrina de imputatione sustineri posset." Johannes Buddeus was professor of moral philosophy in Halle, where he edited the *Observationes Selectae ad Rem Literariam Spectantes* together with Thomasius and the professor of medicine, Georg Ernst Stahl, and later became professor of theology in Jena.

34. "Spontaneum duplex est, vel liberum (extrinsece) ubi voluntas impulit locomotivam absque extrinseca excitatione vel voluntatis primae, vel spei, & absque metu: vel coactum, ubi voluntas vel excitatione extrinseca spei vel metus fuit necessitata & coacta" (*Fundamenta*, 4th ed., 1718, bk. 1, chap. 2, §117).

35. See *Fundamenta*, 4th ed., 1718, bk. 1, chap. 2, §§102–3.

36. "[V]el excitatione extrinsece spei vel metus . . . necessitata & coacta" (ibid., bk. 1, chap. 2, §117).

37. "Cur enim actio ad quam voluntas hominis invisibiliter et metu coacta, pro voluntaria non deberet haberi, cum tamen pro voluntaria habeatur, ubi hominis voluntas vel prima vel spes ei connata excitatione extrinseca potentiae, v.g. amica persuasione, propositione praemii &c. fuit necessitata, cum tamen utrobique sit eadem ratio, id est coactio voluntatis" (ibid.).

38. "Ita pacta pacis bello exorta, ita actiones legis conformes, etsi ex (ulterioris belli vel) poenae metu processerint, sunt communi consensu voluntariae & imputantur etiam" (ibid., §118).

39. "[P]otestatem incutiendi [metum]" (ibid., bk. 1, chap. 7, §6).

40. Ibid., chap. 15, 521.

41. "Doctrina communis de libertate interna voluntatis est praecipuum fulcrum doctrinae Papisticae de acquirenda salute aeterna per bona opera. Contra negatio hujus libertatis magis cohaeret cum doctrina Protestantium de carentia virium voluntatis humanae in rebus spiritualibus" (ibid., bk. 1, chap. 3, §1, footnote).

42. Thomasius, *Von der Kunst . . . Einleitung zur Sitten Lehre*, "Vorrede."

43. The information on Prasch is based on Schneider, *Justitia Universalis*, 292ff.

44. "Sed sicut antehac monuimus saepe, non semper ex omni parte licitum est quod juri stricto sumto congruit, saepe enim proximi caritas non permittetut summo jure utamur" (Hugo Grotius, *De Jure Belli ac Pacis Libri Tres* [Washington, DC: Carnegie Institution of Washington, 1913], I, iv, 2).

45. On the relationship between the principle of self-interest and Grotius's theory of natural law, see Tuck, *Philosophy and Government*, chap. 5.

46. Schneider, *Justitia Universalis*, 297.

47. Johann Ludwig Prasch, *Kurtze Gegen-Antwort auf Herrn Christian Thomas Einwürffe wider seine Schrifft Vom Gesetz der Liebe* (Regensburg and Leipzig, 1689).

48. "Die groeste Glueckseeligkeit bestehet in der Liebe GOttes und des Nechsten. Und ob schon die vernuenfftige Liebe nicht so vollkommen ist als die Christliche Liebe/ so ist doch die vernuenfftige Liebe so zu sagen ein Staffel/ dadurch man zu der Christlichen Liebe gelangen kan/ und wie derjenige GOTT ohnmoeglich lieben kan/ der nicht einmahl seinen Bruder liebet; Also kan derjenige ohnmoeglich andere Menschen Christlicher Weise lieben/ der nicht einmahl dieselbigen vernuenfftig liebet" (Thomasius, *Von der Kunst . . . Einleitung zur Sitten Lehre*, "Unterthänigste Zuschrift").

49. See chapter 2, above.

50. Schneiders, *Naturrecht und Liebesethik*, 245.

51. "Non poterit vero applicare, quamdiu ob actionibus propriis judicium est corruptum, ita ut non agnoscat, se aegrotare. Inde pleraeque causae dissidiorum, quod quilibet velit emendare alios, se ipsum vero non putet opus habere emendatione" (*Fundamenta*, 4th ed., 1718, bk. 1, chap. 1, §95, footnote).

52. Cf. Ibid., bk. 1, chap. 2, §63, footnote, where Thomasius observes that one must not think the *emendatio moralis* of humans to be impossible.

53. Ibid., bk. 1, chap. 1, §§92–93: "intellectus hic rectitudinem suam retinere potest."

54. "Cum tamen quidam affectus ita subtiliter movent sanguinem in corde, ut vix ab eo, qui maxime attentus est, motus affectuum horum sentiri possit, difficulter etiam saepe cognoscitur discrimen rationis rectae a corrupta. Etsi enim omnes affectus habeant sua intervalla, adeoque nullum sit dubium, quin tempore intervalli ratio libera recte judicare possit de bono & malo, tamdiu tamen ratio hominis non poterit tuto sibimet ipsi fidere, quamdiu non certa est de illo intervallo" (ibid., §91).

55. Ibid., bk. 1, chap. 3, §5.

56. "[S]e putent esse praestantissimos & sapientissimos inter omnes creaturas visibiles" (ibid., 8).

57. "[P]raestantiam hominis prae reliquis creaturis quaerant in intellectu" (ibid., §9).

58. "[G]ratia . . . universalis naturae non opposita, quo Deus actiones omnium hominum, etiam infidelium, ad felicitatem hujus vitae dirigit, secundum ductum luminis naturae, uti etiam providentia sua cuncta gubernat" (*Cautelae*, chap. 2, §23, note p).

59. "Etsi enim sapientia tanquam habitus virtutis divinae, & subtilissimus Spiritus, penetrans omnia etiam Spiritus subtiles, (*Sap*. c. 7 v. 23) necessario prope sit omnibus hominibus, nemini tamen se obtrudit, neminemque cogit, sed attrahitur quasi magnete orationis, & conservatur, simul vero stultitia in nobis suffocatur & ligatur" (ibid., note a).

60. *Fundamenta*, "Caput Prooemiale," §7: "Pufendorffius . . . in multis adhuc nimis opponit moralia naturalibus, & in definiendis entibus moralibus nimium impositioni tribuit, cum res ipsa ostendat, intimam esse moralium & naturalium connexionem, & imo moralia omnia demonstrari posse ex naturalibus."

61. "[P]otentias corporum coelestium" (ibid., bk. 1, chap. 1, §29).

62. "[C]orporum terrenorum tam potentiarum unitarum, quam separatorum" (ibid.).

63. "[H]at es einmal in der Natur also gesetzt/ daß sich alles Gute selbst belohnet/ und alles Boese selbst bestraffet. Unterdem bono & malo poenae physico und ethico ist eigentlich zu reden kein Unterscheid e.g. Wenn du seuffst oder hurest/ so kriegstu die Wassersucht oder die Franzosen" (footnote a by Thomasius in Anon. and Christian Thomasius, "Vertheidigung des Regiments der Kirchen Jesu Christi aus dem Latein uebersetzt/ und durch stete Anmerckungen beantwortet," in *Dreyfache Rettung des Rechts Evangelischer Fuersten in Kirchen-Sachen/ etc. Beyde letztere aus des Herrn Thomasii Lectionibus publicis mit Fleiß zusammen getragen von Johann Gottfried Zeidlern*, ed. J. G. Zeidler [Frankfurt am Main: J. G. Zeidler, 1701], 80).

64. "Porro omnis poena visibiliter infertur, at mala, quae Deus ordinavit transgressoribus juris naturae, occulte veniunt, i. e. ut connexio mali cum peccato non sit visibilis, etsi forte ipsum malum visibile sit" (Thomasius, *Fundamenta*, 4th ed., 1718, bk. 1, chap. 5, §39).

CHAPTER EIGHT

1. Thomasius, *Versuch vom Wesen des Geistes*, chap. 6, §20. There Thomasius argues that both *experimenta mechanicohydraulica* and Aristotelian *distinctiones, resolutiones*, and *problemata* neglect the need to pray in order to achieve wisdom.

2. Wilhelm Schmidt-Biggemann, "Pietismus, Platonismus und Aufklärung: Christian Thomasius's *Versuch von Wesen des Geistes*," in *Aufklärung als praktische Philosophie. Werner Schneiders zum 65. Geburtstag*, ed. Frank Grunert and Friedrich Vollhardt (Tübingen, Niemeyer, 1998), 84. Schmidt-Biggemann concludes that Cartesianism was not the true object of Thomasius's critique in the *Versuch*, but Thomasius believed he was criticizing a form of Cartesian physics. See also Thomas Ahnert, "De Sympathia et Antipathia Rerum. Natural Law, Religion and the Rejection of Mechanistic Science in the Works of Christian Thomasius," in *Early Modern Natural Law Theories: Strategies and Contexts in the Early Enlightenment*, ed. Tim Hochstrasser and Peter Schröder (Dordrecht: Kluwer, 2003).

3.   Thomas Hankins, *Science and the Enlightenment* (Cambridge: Cambridge University Press, 1988), 120–24.

4.   Daniel Garber, *Descartes' Metaphysical Physics* (Chicago: University of Chicago Press, 1992), 62. Garber gives the examples of Henricus Regius's *Fundamenta Physica*, 1646, and Jacques Rohault's *Traité de physique*, 1671.

5.   See, for example, the *Versuch vom Wesen des Geistes*, "Vorrede," §17.

6.   Herbert Jaumann, "Frühe Aufklärung als historische Kritik. Pierre Bayle und Christian Thomasius," in *Frühaufklärung*, ed. Sebastian Neumeister (Munich: Fink, 1994), 149–170.

7.   Albrecht, Michael. "Thomasius—kein Eklektiker?" In *Christian Thomasius (1655–1728)*, ed. Werner Schneiders (Hamburg: Meiner, 1989), 91. In an article in the same volume, Hans-Joachim Engfer ("Christian Thomasius. Erste Proklamation und erste Krise der Aufklärung in Deutschland," 21–36) has argued that the *Versuch* and its preoccupation with human sinfulness reflects the "Christian or Lutheran" nature of the Enlightenment in Germany (ibid., 31). It is, not, however, sufficient to refer to a Lutheran element in Thomasius's thought to explain the *Versuch*. It is Thomasius's notion of *fides cordis* and its opposition to the orthodox Lutherans' emphasis on doctrine that constitutes the religious context to the *Versuch*.

8.   In the *Versuch*, Thomasius wrote, he had disproved the idea that "homines aeque esse ejusdem naturae, uti alias species infimas corporum naturalium," which had been central to his earlier theory of natural law in the *Institutiones* (*Fundamenta*, 4th ed., 1718, "Caput Prooemiale," §6).

9.   A "media inter praejudicia Cartesianorum, & ineptias Peripateticorum . . . via" (Thomasius, *Introductio ad philosophiam aulicam*, title page).

10.   Gerhard Wiesenfeldt, *Leerer Raum in Minervas Haus: experimentelle Naturlehre an der Universität Leiden* (Berlin: Verlag für Geschichte der Naturwissenschaften und der Technik, 2002), 41–64.

11.   Garber, *Descartes' Metaphysical Physics*, 80–85.

12.   Ibid., chap. 3.

13.   Thomasius, *Introductio ad philosophiam aulicam*, 1688, chap. 1, §75, and chap. 6, §§16–17; see also Thomasius, *Einleitung zu der Vernunft-Lehre* (Halle: Salfeld, 1699), "Vorrede an die studirende Jugend," 33.

14.   Thomasius, *Introductio ad philosophiam aulicam*, 1688, chap. 3, §13.

15.   "Quod corpus Substantiam *extensam* vocet, tolerari posset, modo non dixisset *extensionem* esse ipsam *Substantiam* corporis" (ibid.).

16.   Garber, *Descartes' Metaphysical Physics*, 68. The exposition of Descartes' ideas in this section is strongly indebted to Garber's analysis, especially in chap. 3.

17.   "[U]nio plurium accidentium" (Thomasius, *Introductio ad philosophiam aulicam*, 1688, chap. 7, §19).

18.   "Et sentio quidem, esse *aliquid*, quod unionem illam faciat, nescio vero, *quia* sit" (ibid., §19).

19.   "[C]ognitio nostra de existentia rei omnis ab Accidentibus incipit. . . . Neque ab his *abstrahi* potest Substantia, quia abstractio vera convenire debet cum rebus sensui praesentatis. Unde abstractiones ab Accidentibus semper erunt *abstractiones Accidentium*" (Thomasius, ibid., §20).

20.   "*Homo nullum habet distinctum & clarum conceptum ullius Substantiae creatae*" (ibid., §19).

21. "[P]rimo quasi intuitu, naturas, virtutes ac formas rerum creatarum, quae hodie vel nos latent vel laboriosissima meditatione vix ac ne vix quidem percipiuntur, cognovisset" (Thomasius, *Institutiones,* 1688, I, ii, §24).

22. "[V]ivere, nutriri & crescere" (Thomasius, *Introductio ad philosophiam aulicam,* 1688, chap. 7, §36).

23. "[I]ntra se deprehenderit aliquid, quod in reliquis corporibus non apparet, facultatem nempe imagines & schemata corporum externorum per motum eorundem cerebro impressorum, apprehendendi, easque conferendi inter se, & dijudicandi, uno verbo *cogitandi*" (ibid., chap. 3, §17).

24. "[S]ubstantia externa principio vitali operationes suas partim per motum intrinsecum, partim extrinsecum exercente praeditum" (ibid., §9).

25. "Ens quod cogitare potest" (ibid., §20).

26. "[*H*]*ominem* aliter perspicue definire non possum, quam quod sit Substantia corporea locomotiva & facultate cogitandi praedita" (ibid., §21).

27. On the *cogito* in Descartes' philosophy, see Peter Markie, "The Cogito and its Importance," in *The Cambridge Companion to Descartes,* ed. John Cottingham (Cambridge: Cambridge University Press, 1992), 140–73.

28. On Descartes' argument that it was possible to know of the immortality of the soul on the basis of natural reason, see John Cottingham, "Cartesian Dualism: Theology, Metaphysics, and Science," in *The Cambridge Companion to Descartes,* ed. John Cottingham (Cambridge: Cambridge University Press, 1992).

29. "*Cogitatio est actus mentis, quo homo vel mens in cerebro de schematibus a motu corporum externorum per organa sensuum cerebro impressis aliquid per modum discursus & orationis verbis constantis vel affirmat vel negat vel quaerit*" (Thomasius, *Introductio ad philosophiam aulicam,* 1688, chap. 3, §82).

30. "[N]ecesse est quam diu mentem per modum cogitandi concipimus ut de eo non habeamus Conceptum distinctum citra reflexionem ad corpus" (ibid., §38).

31. Ibid., §41. The question of natural knowledge of the immortality of the soul was of considerable importance to the problem of punishments in natural law (see chapter 7, above).

32. See chapter 7 on the development of Thomasius's natural law theory.

33. Thomasius, *Versuch vom Wesen des Geistes,* chap. 4, §1.

34. "[*O*]*mne* corpus constet ex materia & spiritus [my italics]" (*Cautelae,* chap. 12, 176, footnote k).

35. This dissertation was the *Theoremata physica convellentia fundamenta novae hypotheseos: omnia corpora naturalia constare ex materia at spiritu* (*Physical Theorems Refuting the Foundations of the New Hypothesis That All Natural Bodies onsist of Matter and Spirit*); see Gierl, *Pietismus und Aufklärung,* 451.

36. Thomasius, *Versuch von Wesen des Geistes,* chap. 3, §18.

37. Ibid., chap. 5, §19.

38. Man has "seine Unwissenheit oder Irrthümer zu bemänteln zu denen qualitatibus occultis seine Zuflucht genommen" (ibid., chap. 7, §69).

39. On Robert Boyle and the debate over air pressure, see Simon Schaffer and Steven Shapin, *Leviathan and the Air-Pump* (Princeton, NJ: Princeton University Press, 1985), passim.

40. "Daß man also durch unterschiedene Herumdrehung des Haehngens das Quecksilber in dem cylindrischen Glase gleichsam tantzend machen kan" (*Versuch vom Wesen des Geistes*, "Vorrede," §20).

41. For Thomasius's description of this experiment, see the *Versuch vom Wesen des Geistes*, "Vorrede," §21.

42. Thomasius, *Versuch vom Wesen des Geistes*, chap. 3, §2.

43. Catherine Wilson, "De Ipsa Natura. Sources of Leibniz' Doctrines of Force, Activity and Natural Law," *Studia Leibnitiana* 19, no. 2, 1987: 148–72.

44. On Henry More's "Spirit of Nature," see John Henry, "Henry More versus Robert Boyle: The Spirit of Nature and the Nature of Providence," in *Henry More 1614–1687. Tercentenary Studies*, ed. Sarah Hutton (Dordrecht: Kluwer, 1990), 55–76.

45. "So koente auch keine Bewegung seyn/ wenn alles voll materie und kein Geist waere/ der und in welchem die materie beweget wuerde; Denn es ist wieder alle richtige Sinnlikeit/ daß ich viele einander beruehrende Coerper durch Bewegung des einen/ oder eines theils bewegen koenne/ wenn alle spatia vollgestopft seynd" (*Versuch vom Wesen des Geistes*, chap. 3, §11).

46. "Denn entweder waeren diese Klumpen rund und rundlicht/ oder eckigt gewesen. In dem ersten Fall waeren zwischen ihnen Zwickel blieben/ wie an Fenster-Scheiben/ die nothwendig mit nichts/ oder mit diesem edlern Wesen/ oder mit andern Klumpen materie angefuellet gewesen waeren. Das erste wuerde einen absurden Raum geben/ da nichts drinnen waere/ das andere wuerde unseren Geist beweisen/ das dritte aber wuerde alle Bewegung und Abschleiffung auffheben" (ibid., §9).

47. Ibid., §7; see also *Dissertatio ad Petri Poireti libros*, §26: "spiritus est ens activum, uniens materia ab intra."

48. Thomasius, *Versuch vom Wesen des Geistes*, chap. 3, §6.

49. Thomasius, *Cautelae*, chap. 12, §75, footnote on page 190: reason "sibi relicta" knows nothing about the existence of spirit separate from the human body and so has no cause to deny "ea, quae scriptura de anima separata tradit."

50. Leibniz, "Discourse on Metaphysics [1686]," in *G. W. Leibniz. Philosophical Texts*, trans. and ed. R. S. Woolhouse and Richard Francks (Oxford: Oxford University Press, 1998), especially 71–72.

51. Thomasius, *Cautelae*, chap. 13, §42: "Experimenta monstrant effectus causarum ignotarum, quae per effectus inveniri nequeunt, ideo, quia unius rei plures possunt esse causae."

52. Thomasius, *Versuch vom Wesen des Geistes*, chap. 1, §14.

53. Ibid., §44, note q.

54. "[I]s experientia non cadit in totum genus humanum, tantum abest, ut in unum hominem cadere posit" (ibid., §46, note s).

55. Thomasius, *Introductio ad philosophiam aulicam,* 1688, chap. 7, §35.

56. Robert Fludd, *Philosophia Moysaica: in qua Sapientia & scientia creationis & creaturarum sacra vereque Christiana . . . ad amussim . . . explicatur* (Gouda: Rammazenius, 1638).

57. Johannes Amos Comenius, *Physicae ad Lumen Divinum Reformatae Synopsis* (Leipzig: Grossius, 1633), especially 8–9, where Comenius derives three *principia mundi* from the first verses of Genesis: earth, spirit, and light.

58. King James version.

59. *Versuch vom Wesen des Geistes*, chap. 7, §191.

60. "[C]ontra Cartesianos recte quidem defendit [Poiretus] de attractu. Nam Cartesiani ideo attractum negare coguntur, quia materia tantum patitur. Si ergo motus tantum a materia est, non poterit alius esse nisi pulsio" (Thomasius, "Dissertatio ad Petri Poireti libros," §26).

61. "Die Pflantzen und Baeume empfinden ihren Lebens-Safft, saugen denselben in sich, breiten sich aus, bringen dadurch Frucht und Saamen hervor; ihre Liebe und Haß oder Begierden werden durch so viel tausend Exempel dargethan derer, die *de sympathia & antipathia rerum* geschrieben haben. Denn die sympathie ist nichts anderes als die Liebe des Geistes der Pflantzen, mineralien und Thiere, und die antipathie ihr Haß" (Thomasius, *Versuch vom Wesen des Geistes*, chap. 7, §68).

62. "[J]a daß die Thiere von einer Art einerley Begierden und zwar die gantze Zeit ihres Lebens haben, hingegen bey den Menschen so viel unterschiedene Begierden als Menschen seyn und ein Mensch in einer kleinen viertelstunde von unterschiedenen mit sich selbst streitenden Begierden hingerissen und unruhig gemacht wird" (ibid., §178).

63. "[H]omo regenitus et irregenitus specie different" (Thomasius, "Natura Hominis. Libertas Voluntatis, Imputatio in Poenam," 1701, §24, 283).

64. Thomasius, *Versuch vom Wesen des Geistes*, chap. 7, §179 and §161.

65. "Die Krafft des Hertzen bestehet darinnen, daß da die Thiere von Natur keine Feindschaft zusammen tragen, der Mensch von Natur einen anderen Menschen nicht liebet, wohl aber viele hasset, und da die Begierden der Thiere in ihren Unterhalt und Dauerung gerichtet seyn, der Geist des menschlichen Hertzens zwar eine Dauerung verlanget, aber alle Begierden des Menschen denselbigen ruinieren" (ibid., §178).

66. See ibid., chap. 7, §186.

67. "Der Geist der Metalle, Pflantzen und Thiere kan keine Chimaeren und syllogismos machen. . . . Aber er macht hingegen Demanten, Rubinen, Zedern, Elephanten, und dein Verstand kannicht eine Lauß machen: Er macht lauter conclusiones die seinen Coerper und dessen Daurung unterhalten, und dein Verstand rechnet Dinge aus, da das facit offt an Galgen koemmt, und macht kuenstliche syllogismos, in deren conclusion der Tod ist. Mein welcher Geist ist nun weiser?" (ibid., §81).

68. Roth, "Synopsis Errorum Thomasianorum in Theologia, Christologia et Anthropologia," 1699, 28.

69. Ibid., 63–64.

70. Roth describes Thomasius as an enthusiast in the preface to his *Thomasius portentosus*.

71. Johanna Geyer-Kordesch, "Die Medizin im Spannungsfeld zwischen Aufklärung und Pietismus: Das unbequeme Werk Georg Ernst Stahls und dessen kulturelle Bedeutung," in *Halle. Aufklärung und Pietismus*, ed. Norbert Hinske (Heidelberg: Schneider, 1989), 255–74; Johanna Geyer-Kordesch's chapter also offers an excellent account of the religious context of medical theory in Halle; for a fuller discussion, see her book, *Pietismus, Medizin und Aufklärung in Preußen im 18. Jahrhundert. Das Leben und Werk Georg Ernst Stahls* (Tübingen: Niemeyer, 2000); on Stahl, see also Hankins, *Science and the Enlightenment*, 120–24; Jürgen

Helm, "Hallesche Medizin zwischen Pietismus und Frühaufklärung," in *Universitäten und Aufklärung*, ed. Notker Hammerstein (Göttingen: Wallstein, 1995), 63–96; and Axel Bauer, "Georg Ernst Stahl (1659–1734)," in *Klassiker der Medizin. Erster Band: Von Hippokrates bis Christoph Wilhelm Hufeland*, ed. Friedrich von Engelhardt and Fritz Hartmann (Munich: Beck, 1991), 190–201. On Hofmann's general medical theory, see Ingo Wilhelm Müller, *Iatromechanische Theorie und ärztliche Praxis im Vergleich zur galenistischen Medizin (Friedrich Hoffmann—Pieter van Forest, Jan van Heurne)* (Stuttgart: Stainer, 1991). On Hoffman's theory of interaction between soul and body, see Karl E. Rothschuh, "Studien zu Friedrich Hoffmann (1660–1742). Erster Teil: Hoffmann und die Medizingeschichte. Das Hoffmannsche System und das Aetherprinzip," *Sudhoffs Archiv* 60, 1976: 163–93.

72. Michael Alberti, "De Usu et Abusu Mechanismi in Corporibus Animantibus," in *Additamentum ad Observationum Selectarium ad Rem Litterariam Spectantium Tomos Decem* (Halle: Renger, 1705), 56.

73. Robert Boyle, *A Free Inquiry into the Vulgarly Receiv'd Notion of Nature* (London: John Taylor, 1686), 330.

74. Georg Ernst Stahl, *Über den mannigfaltigen Einfluß von Gemütsbewegungen auf den menschlichen Körper*, trans. and ed. Bernward Josef Gottlieb (Leipzig: Barth, 1961), §12. This was Stahl's inaugural disputation, published in Halle in 1695 as *Disputatio inauguralis de passionibus animi corpus humanum varie alterantibus*.

75. Ibid., §14.

76. Ibid., §15.

77. Ibid., §27; the effects of a pregnant woman's imagination on her as yet unborn child were a common subject in neo-Platonic, hermetic literature; see, for example, Alfred Rupert Hall, *Henry More: Magic, Religion and Experiment* (Oxford: Blackwell, 1990), 25.

CONCLUSION

1. See in particular the important article by Hans-Erich Bödeker, "Die Religiösität der Gelehrten," in *Religionskritik und Religiösität in der deutschen Aufklärung*, ed. Karlfried Gründer and Karl Heinrich Rengstorf (Heidelberg: Schneider, 1989), 145–95.

2. Gay, *The Enlightenment: An interpretation. Vol. 1: The Rise of Modern Paganism*.

3. Sorkin, *The Berlin Haskalah*, 17.

4. On the "apologetic" rather than "critical" use of reason in relation to religion, see Wilhelm Schmidt-Biggemann, *Theodizee und Tatsachen* (Frankfurt am Main: Suhrkamp, 1988), 61.

5. See Samuel Pufendorf, *Ius Feciale Divinum* (Lübeck, 1695), §17.

6. Ibid., §43.

7. Ibid., §44.

8. Ibid., §46.

9. On Pierre Bayle's ideas on the relationship of faith to reason, see especially W. H. Barker, "Pierre Bayle: Faith and Reason," in *The French Mind. Studies in Honour of Gustave Rudler*, ed. Will Moore, Rhoda Sutherland, and Enid Starkie (Oxford: Clarendon Press, 1952), 124.

10. Gottfried Wilhelm Leibniz, *Theodicy. Essays on the Goodness of God and the Freedom of Man and the Origin of Evil*, ed. Austin Farrer, trans. E. M. Huggard (London: Routledge and Kegan, 1951). For a lucid summary of Leibniz's argument, see Riley, *Leibniz' Universal Jurisprudence*, chap. 3.

11. But see also Leibniz, "Von der wahren Theologia mystica" (ca. 1695–1700): "Among the external teachings there are two that best awaken the inner light: Sacred Scripture and the experience of nature" ("Unter den äußerlichen Lehren sind zwei die das innerliche Licht am besten wecken: das Buch der Heiligen Schrift und die Erfahrung der Natur"; quoted in Schneider, *Justitia Universalis*, 465).

12. Leibniz, "Opinion on the Principles of Pufendorf (1706)," 72.

13. Riley, *Leibniz' Universal Jurisprudence*, 106.

14. See the 1714 Vienna lectures on the Greeks, which are discussed in ibid., 107.

15. See Leibniz, "Discourse on Metaphysics [1686]," 89: "Ancient philosophers had very little knowledge of these important truths. Only Jesus Christ has expressed them divinely well, and in a manner so clear and so accessible that even the dullest minds could understand them"; see also Schneider, *Justitia Universalis*, 460.

16. Riley, *Leibniz' Universal Jurisprudence*, 107.

17. On the Wertheim Bible, see Jonathan Israel, *Radical Enlightenment: Philosophy and the Making of Modernity 1650–1750* (Oxford: Oxford University Press, 2001), 552–58.

18. Israel, Radical Enlightenment, 554.

19. On this, see Henry E. Allison, *Lessing and the Enlightenment. His Philosophy of Religion and Its Relation to Eighteenth-Century Thought* (Ann Arbor: University of Michigan Press, 1966), chap. 3.

20. On this, see especially Friedrich Vollhardt, *Selbstliebe und Geselligkeit. Untersuchungen zum Verhältnis von naturrechtlichem Denken und moraldidaktischer Literatur im 17. und 18. Jahrhundert* (Tübingen: Niemeyer, 2001).

21. For a summary and criticism of this view of *Empfindsamkeit* as "secularized Pietism," see Sauder, *Empfindsamkeit*, 58.

22. On this, see especially Vollhardt, *Selbstliebe*.

23. For a summary of the debate over Newton's alchemical interests, see Margaret Osler, "The Canonical Imperative: Rethinking the Scientific Revolution," in *Rethinking the Scientific Revolution*, ed. Margaret Osler (Cambridge: Cambridge University Press, 2000), 15–16.

BIBLIOGRAPHY

I. WRITINGS BY CHRISTIAN THOMASIUS

The works are arranged in order of the first date of publication. Dissertations for which Thomasius was *praeses* are listed under his name.

De iniusto Pontii Pilati iudicio. Leipzig: Georg, 1675.
De crimine bigamiae. Leipzig: Johann Georg, 1685.
Institutiones Jurisprudentiae Divinae. Frankfurt and Leipzig: M. G. Weidmann, 1688.
Institutiones Jurisprudentiae Divinae. Aalen: Scientia Verlag, 1994. Reprint of 7th ed., Halle, 1720.
Introductio ad philosophiam aulicam. Hildesheim: Olms, 1993. Reprint of 1688 Leipzig ed.
Introductio ad philosophiam aulicam. 2nd ed. Halle: Renger, 1702.
Rechtmäßige Erörterung der Ehe-und Gewissensfrage, ob zwey Fürstliche Personen in Römischen reich, deren eine der lutherischen, die andere der Reformirten Religion zugethan ist, einander mit gutem Gewissen heyrathen können? Halle: Salfeld, 1689.
De felicitate subditorum Brandenburgicorum. 1690. Halle: Grunert, 1749.
Von der Kunst, Vernünfftig und Tugendhafft zu lieben. Als dem eintzigen Mittel zu einen glückseligen, galanten und vergnügten Leben zu gelangen oder Einleitung zur Sitten Lehre. Halle: Salfeld, 1692.
"Rechtliches Bedencken über die Leipzigsche Universitätsakta." In *Gerichtliches Leipziger Protocoll in Sachen die so genannten Pietisten betreffend.* Ed. C. Thomasius, Leipzig, 1692.
"Partes hominis tres." In *Historia Sapientiae et Stultitiae.* Edited by Christian Thomasius. Halle: Salfeld, 1693.
"Dissertatio ad Petri Poireti libros de Eruditione solida, superficiaria et falsa." 1694. In *Programmata Thomasiana.* Halle and Leipzig: Krebs, 1724.
De Jure Principis circa Adiaphora. Halle: Christoph Salfeld, 1695.
"Das Recht evangelischer Fürsten in theologischen Streitigkeiten." 1696. In *Dreyfache Rettung des Rechts evangelischer Fürsten in*

Kirchen-Sachen. Edited by Johann Gottfried Zeidler. Frankfurt am Main: Zeidler, 1701.

Von Der Artzeney Wider die unvernünfftige Liebe und der zuvorher nöthigen Erkäntnüß Sein Selbst. Oder: Ausübung der Sitten Lehre. 1696. 4th ed. Halle: Salfeld, 1708.

De Jure Principis circa Haereticos. Halle: Salfeld, 1697.

Problema Juridicum An Haeresis sit Crimen? Halle: Salfeld, 1697.

Bericht von Einrichtung des Paedagogii zu Glaucha in Halle/Nebst der von einem gelehrten Manne verlangten Erinnerung ueber diese Einrichtung. Ed. C. Thomasius, Frankfurt and Leipzig, 1699.

Einleitung zu der Vernunft-Lehre. Halle: Salfeld, 1699.

Versuch vom Wesen des Geistes. 1699. 2nd ed. Halle: Renger, 1709.

"Fides Scriptorum Vitae Constantini Magni." In *Observationes selectae ad rem litterariam spectantes,* vol. 1, *Observatio* 22. Halle: Renger, 1700.

"Fabulae de Parentibus Constantini Magni." In *Observationes selectae ad rem litterariam spectantes,* vol. 1, *Observatio* 23. Halle: Renger, 1700.

"Fabulae de Constantino Magno et Potissimum de Eius Christianismo." In *Observationes selectae ad rem litterariam spectantes,* vol. 1, *Observatio* 24. Halle: Renger, 1700.

"Fundamenta Historica in Expositione Tituli Codicis de Summa Trinitate etc. Supponenda." In *Observationes selectae ad rem litterariam spectantes,* vol. 2, *Observatio* 8. Halle: Renger, 1701.

"Natura Hominis. Libertas Voluntatis. Imputatio in Poenam." In *Observationes selectae ad rem litterariam spectantes,* vol. 2, *Observatio* 22. Halle: Renger, 1701.

"Ad Legem I. C. de Summa Trinitate." In *Observationes selectae ad rem litterariam spectantes,* vol. 3, *Observatio* 18. Halle: Renger, 1701.

"Ad Legem II. C. de Summa Trinitate." In *Observationes selectae ad rem litterariam spectantes,* vol. 3, *Observatio* 19. Halle: Renger, 1701.

Anon., and Christian Thomasius. "Vertheidigung des Regiments der Kirchen Jesu Christi aus dem Latein uebersetzt/ und durch stete Anmerckungen beantwortet." In *Dreyfache Rettung des Rechts Evangelischer Fuersten in Kirchen-Sachen/ etc. Beyde letztere aus des Herrn Thomasii Lectionibus publicis mit Fleiß zusammen getragen von Johann Gottfried Zeidlern,* edited by J. G. Zeidler. Frankfurt am Main, 1701.

Disputatio de origine successionis testamentariae apud Romanos. Halle: Zeitler, 1705.

Fundamenta Juris Naturae et Gentium. Halle and Leipzig: Salfeld and Groß, 1705.

Fundamenta Juris Naturae et Gentium, 4th ed. Halle and Leipzig: Salfeld, 1718.

Dissertatio Iuridica Inauguralis de Aequitate Cerebrina l. II. C. de Rescind. Vendit. et ejus usu practico. Halle: Salfeld, 1706.

Bedencken über die Frage: Wieweit ein Prediger gegen seinen Landes-Herrn/ Welcher zugleich Summus Episcopus mit ist/ sich des Binde-Schlüssels bedienen könne? 3rd ed. Wolfenbüttel: Freytag, 1707.

De desertione ordinis ecclesiastici. Halle: Zeitler, 1707.

"Dissertatio nova ad Petri Poireti libros de eruditione triplici solida, superficiaria et falsa." 1708. In *Programmata Thomasiana.* Halle: Renger, 1724.

Cautelae circa Praecognita Jurisprudentiae. Halle: Renger, 1710.

Notae ad singulos Institutionum et Pandectarum titulos varias juris Romani antiquitates imprimis usum eorum hodiernum in foris Germaniae ostendentes. Halle: Renger, 1713.

Auserlesene und in Deutsch noch nie gedruckte Schrifften. Theil II. Frankfurt and Leipzig: Renger, 1714.

Historia contentionis inter imperium et sacerdotium breviter delineata usque ad saeculum XVI. Halle: Renger, 1722.

"Kurtze Lehr-Sätze vom Recht eines Christlichen Fürsten in Religions-Sachen." In *Vernünfftige und Christliche aber nicht Scheinheilige Thomasische Gedancken und Erinnerungen über allerhand Philosophische und Juristische Händel. Andrer Theil.* Halle: Renger, 1724.

"Meine zu Leipzig Anno 1689 gehaltenen Lectiones de praciudiciis." In *Vernünfftige und Christliche aber nicht Scheinheilige Thomasische Gedancken und Erinnerungen über allerhand Gemischte Philosophische und Juristische Händel. III. Theil.* Halle: Renger, 1725.

De singulari aequitate legis unicae Codicis quando Imperator inter Pupillos etc. cognoscat etc., eiusque usu practico. Halle: Johann Grunert, 1725.

Vollstaendige Erlaeuterung der Kirchenrechts-Gelahrtheit oder Gruendliche Abhandlung vom Verhaeltniß der Religion gegen den Staat. Aalen: Scientia-Verlag, 1981. Reprint of 2nd ed., Frankfurt and Leipzig, 1740.

II. Primary Sources by Other Authors

Abbadie, Jacques. *L'art de se connoitre soi-même, ou La Recherche de sources de la Morale.* Rotterdam, 1692.

Alberti, Michael. "De Usu et Abusu Mechanismi in Corporibus Animantibus." In *Additamentum ad Observationum Selectarum ad Rem Litterariam Spectantium Tomos Decem.* Halle: Renger, 1705.

Alberti, Valentin. *Compendium Juris Naturae Orthodoxae Theologiae Conformatum.* Leipzig: Frommann, 1678.

———. *Compendium Juris Naturae Orthodoxae Theologiae Conformatum.* 2nd ed. Leipzig: Jacob Fritsch, 1696.

———. *Eros Lipsicus quo Eris Scandica Samuelis Pufendorfii cum convitiis & erroribus suis mascule, modeste tamen refutetur.* Leipzig: Weidmann, 1687.

Anon. (= Gustav Phillip Mörl). *Repetitio Doctrinae Orthodoxae ad Amicos quosdam scripta, de Fundamento Fidei occasione cujusdam Disputationis halensis de Quaestione: An Haeresis sit Crimen?* Leipzig: Brandenburger, 1697.

Anon., and Christian Thomasius. "Vertheidigung des Regiments der Kirchen Jesu Christi aus dem Latein uebersetzt/ und durch stete Anmerckungen beantwortet." In *Dreyfache Rettung des Rechts Evangelischer Fuersten in Kirchen-Sachen/ etc. Beyde letztere aus des Herrn Thomasii Lectionibus publicis mit Fleiß zusammen getragen von Johann*

Gottfried Zeidlern, edited by J. G. Zeidler. Frankfurt am Main: J. G. Zeidler, 1701.

Anton, Paul. *Disputatio Hallensis prima de harmonia fidei quae justificat, & fidei, quatenus justificare dicitur*. Halle: Henckel, 1702.

Aquinas, Thomas. *Summa Theologiae*. Edited by T. Gilby. London: Blackfriars, 1964–.

Aristotle. *Nicomachean Ethics*. Oxford: Oxford University Press, 2002.

———. *The Politics of Aristotle*. Translated and edited by Ernest Barker. Oxford: Clarendon Press, 1948.

Arnold, Gottfried, *Die erste Liebe der Gemeinen JESU Christi, d. i. wahre Abbildung der ersten Christen*. Frankfurt am Main: Friedeburg, 1696.

———. *Gottfried Arnold in Auswahl*. Edited by E. Seeberg. Munich: Langen Müller, 1934.

———. "Historia Christianorum ad Metalla damnatorum." In *Historia Sapientiae et Stultitiae*, edited by C. Thomasius, vol. 3. Halle: Salfeld, 1693.

———. "Kurtze Nachricht Von den Bruder- und Schwesternamen in der ersten Kirchen." In *Historie der Weißheit und Thorheit*, edited by C. Thomasius, vol. 3. Halle: Salfeld, 1693.

———. *Unpartheyische Kirchen-und Ketzer-Historie*. Frankfurt am Main: Fritsch, 1700.

Augustine. *The City of God*. Cambridge: Cambridge University Press, 1998.

Best, Gulielmus. *Ratio emendandi leges Pandectarum Florentinarum*. Leipzig: Schoenmark, 1745.

Bibliotheca Thomasiana, continens libros theologico-polemicos, medicos, autores classicos; accedunt disputationes, plerumque rariores, cuius auctio publica fiet Halae Die VI. Ju 1739. Halle: Lehmann, 1739.

Boehmer, Justus Henning. *Exercitationes ad Pandectas, in quibus praecipua Digestorum capita explicantur*. Hannover and Göttingen: Schmid, 1745.

Boyle, Robert. *A Free Enquiry into the Vulgarly Receiv'd Notion of Nature*. London: John Taylor, 1686.

Breithaupt, Justus Joachim. *Observationes Theologicae de Haeresi juxta S. Scripturae Sensum*. Halle: Zeitler, 1697.

Bücher, Christian Friedrich. *Plato mysticus in Pietista redivivus*. Danzig: Reiniger, 1699.

Carpzov, Benedict. *Opus Definitionum Ecclesiasticarum seu Consistorialium*. Leipzig: Ritzsch, 1665.

Carpzov, Johann Benedict. *De Jure decidendi controversias theologicas*. Leipzig: Tietze, 1695.

Carpzov, Johann Benedict, and Christian Thomasius. *Disputatio Theologi Lipsiensis De Jure Decidendi Controversias Theologicas, Cum Scholiis Jurisconsulti Hallensis*. Halle: Salfeld, 1701.

Cave, William. *Apostolici or the Lives of the Primitive Fathers for the three first Ages of the Christian church*. London: Richard Chiswel, 1677.

———. *Ecclesiastici: or, the History of the Lives, Arts, Death and Writings of the most Eminent Fathers of the Church, That Flourisht in the Fourth Century*. London: Richard Chiswel, 1683.

Cave, William. *Primitive Christianity, or, The religion of the ancient Christians in the first ages of the gospel: in three parts*. London: Richard Chiswel, 1673.

Cicero, Marcus Tullius. *De Officiis*. Oxford: Clarendon Press, 1994.

―――. *De Republica. De Legibus*. London: Heinemann, 1928.

Comenius, Johannes Amos. *Physicae ad Lumen Divinum Reformatae Synopsis*. Leipzig: Grossius, 1633.

Conring, Hermann. *De Origine Juris Germanici Liber Unus*. 1643. 4th ed. Helmstedt: Hamm, 1695.

Corpus Iuris Canonici. Edited by. E. Friedberg. 2 vols. Graz: Akademische Verlagsanstalt, 1959.

Fecht, Joachim. *Scrutinium profligatae ex Ecclesia Haeretificationis, Godofredo Arnoldo oppositum*. Rostock and Leipzig: Russworm, 1714.

Flacius, Matthias, Johann Wigand, Matthaeus Richter, Basilius Faber, et al. *Historia Ecclesiastica, integram Ecclesiae Christianae conditionem, inde a Christo ex Virgine nato, juxta seculorum seriem exponens*. Basel: Ludovicus Rex, 1624.

Fludd, Robert. *Philosophia Moysaica: in qua Sapientia & scientia creationis & creaturarum sacra vereque Christian . . . ad amussim . . . explicatur*. Gouda: Rammazenius, 1638.

Francke, August Hermann. *Apologia oder Defensions—Schrifft an Ihre Chur—Fürstliche Durchlaucht zu Sachsen*. 1689.

―――. *Auffrichtige und gruendliche Beantwortung eines an ihn abgelassenen und hiebey abgedruckten Send-Schreibens eines Christlichen Theologi der Professorum Theologiae zu Halle und seine eigene Orthodoxie in der Lehre I. Von der Rechtfertigung II. Von der wahren und realen Gottseligkeit Und III. Wie deren Grund allein in Christo zu legen sey betreffend*. Halle: Waisenhaus, 1706.

―――. *Bericht von Einrichtung des Paedagogii zu Glaucha Nebst der von einem gelehrten Manne verlangten Erinnerung ueber eine solche Einrichtung*. Ed. C. Thomasius, Frankfurt am Main and Leipzig, 1699.

―――. "H. M. August Hermann Franckens . . . Lebenslauff." 1690/91. In *August Hermann Francke. Werke in Auswahl*, edited by E. Peschke, 4–29. Berlin: Evangelische Verlagsanstalt, 1969.

Friedlibius, Eric (= Johann Friedrich Ludovici). *Untersuchung des Indifferentismi Religionum*. Glück-Stadt: Treumund, 1700.

Gigas, Ernst, ed. *Briefe Samuel Pufendorfs an Christian Thomasius*. Munich and Leipzig: R. Oldenbourg, 1897.

Grotius, Hugo. *De Iure Belli ac Pacis Libri Tres*. Washington, DC: Carnegie Institution of Washington, 1913.

Hobbes, Thomas. *Leviathan*. Edited by. Richard Tuck. Cambridge: Cambridge University Press, 1991.

Hume, David. *Treatise of Human Nature*. Oxford: Clarendon Press, 1978.

Jan, Christian Friedrich. *Tractatus Iuridicus Theoretico-Practicus de Denuntiatione Evangelica, in quo, de Aequitate Juris Canonici ex professo agitur*. Wittenberg: Berger, 1673.

Justinian. *Codex Justinianus*. Edited by P. Krüger. Berlin: Weidmann, 1877.

Justinian. *The Digest of Justinian.* Edited by Theodor Mommsen with the aid of Paul Krueger, English translation edited by Alan Watson. Philadelphia: University of Pennsylvania Press, 1985.

Kulpis, Johannes (writing as "Conradus Sincerus"). *De Germanicarum legum veterum, ac Romani juris in republica nostra origine, auctoritateque praesenti dissertatio epistolica.* In Christian Thomasius, *Notae ad singulos Institutionum et Pandectarum titulos.*

Lange, Joachim. *Auffrichtige Nachricht von der Unrichtigkeit der so genanten Unschuldigen Nachrichten . . . Erste Ordnung Auff das Jahr* 1701. Leipzig: Heinichen, 1707.

Lange, Joachim. *Historia Ecclesiastica a Mundo Condito.* Halle: Waisenhaus, 1718.

Leibniz, Gottfried Wilhelm. "Discourse on Metaphysics [1686]." In *G. W. Leibniz. Philosophical Texts,* translated and edited by R. S. Woolhouse and Richard Francks, 54–93. Oxford: Oxford University Press, 1998.

———. *Leibniz. Textes inédits.* Edited by Gaston Grua. 2 vols. New York: Garland, 1985.

———. "Opinion on the Principles of Pufendorf (1706)." In *Leibniz. Political Writings,* translated and edited by Patrick Riley, 64–76. Cambridge: Cambridge University Press, 1992.

———. *Theodicy. Essays on the Goodness of God and the Freedom of Man and the Origin of Evil.* Edited by Austin Farrer. Translated by E. M. Huggard. London: Routledge and Kegan, 1951.

Locke, John. *Essay Concerning Human Understanding,* 5th ed. London: Awnsham and John Churchill, 1706.

Löscher, Valentin (*praeses*), and Georg Habbius (*respondens*). *Deismus Fanaticorum.* Wittenberg: Gerdesius, 1708.

———, ed. *Unschuldige Nachrichten von alten und neuen theologischen Sachen.* Leipzig: Grosse, 1702–19.

Ludewig, Johann Peter von, ed. *Consilia Hallensium Jureconsultorum,* vol. 1. Halle: Renger, 1733.

Masius, Hector Gottfried. *Interesse principum circa religionem evangelicam.* Copenhagen: Bockenhoffer, 1687.

Mayer, Johann Friedrich. *Eines Schwedischen Theologi Kurtzer Bericht von Pietisten samt denen Königlichen Schwedischen EDICTEN wider dieselben.* Leipzig: Gross, 1706.

Osiander, Johann Adam. *Observationes Maximam partem Theologicae, in Libros Tres de Jure Belli et Pacis Hugonis* Grotii. Tübingen: Cotta, 1671.

Piermont, Frédéric-Henri Strube de. *Ébauche des Loix Naturelles et du Droit Primitif.* Amsterdam, 1744.

Prasch, Johann Ludwig. *De lege caritatis commentario ad Hug. Grotii opus de jure bellis pacis.* Regensburg: Hoffman, 1688.

———. *Kurtze Gegen-Antwort auf Herrn Christian Thomas Einwürffe wider seine Schrifft Vom Gesetz der Liebe.* Regensburg and Leipzig, 1689.

Pufendorf, Samuel. *Briefe Samuel Pufendorfs an Christian Thomasius.* Edited by Ernst Gigas. Munich and Leipzig: R. Oldenbourg, 1897.

———. *De habitu religionis Christianae ad vitam civilem.* Bremen: Schwerdfeger, 1687.

Pufendorf, Samuel. *De Jure Naturae et Gentium Libri Octo.* 1688. London and Oxford: Clarendon Press, 1934.

————. *De Jure Naturae et Gentium Libri Octo.* Lund: Junghans, 1672.

————. *The Divine Feudal Law.* 1703. Edited by Simone Zurbuchen. Translated by Theophilus Dorrington. Indianapolis: Liberty Fund, 2002.

————. *Eris Scandica und andere polemische Schriften über das Naturrecht.* Edited by Fiammetta Palladini. Berlin: Akademie-Verlag, 2002.

————. *Ius feciale divinum.* Lübeck, 1695.

————. *Politische Betrachtung der Geistlichen Monarchie des Stuhls zu Rom mit Anmerckungen zum Gebrauch des Thomasischen Auditorii.* Edited by C. Thomasius. Halle: Renger, 1714.

————. *Samuel Pufendorf. Briefwechsel.* Edited by Detlef Döring. Berlin: Akademie-Verlag, 1996.

Reinking, Theodor. *Conclusiones CCXC. de brachio seculari et ecclesiastico seu potestate utraque.* Giessen: Hampel, 1616.

————. *Tractatus de Regimine Seculari et Ecclesiastico.* Basel: Genath, 1622.

Roth, Albrecht Christian. *Thomasius portentosus ωσ εν συνοψει & suis ipsius scriptis de portentis illis convictus.* Leipzig: Albrecht Christian Roth, 1700.

Rumpaeus, Justus Wesselus (*praeses*), and Daniel Harder (*respondens*). *Ex Loco de Imagine Dei Quaestionum Recentiorum imprimis Pietisticarum Pentadem.* Greifswald: Adolphus, 1705.

Schiller, Friedrich, and Johann Wolfgang von Goethe. *Der Briefwechsel zurischen Schiller und Goethe.* Edited by Siegfred Seidel. Munich: Beck, 1985.

Schilter, Johann. *Praxis Juris Romani in Foro Germanico.* 1684. 3rd ed., with a preface and annotations by Christian Thomasius. Frankfurt and Leipzig: Boetticher, 1713.

Seckendorff, Veit Ludwig von. *Christen-Stat.* Leipzig: Gleditsch, 1685.

Spanheim, Friedrich. *Summa historiae ecclesiasticae. A Christo nato ad seculum XVI. Inchoatum.* Leiden: Johann Verbessel, 1689.

Spener, Philipp Jakob. "Pia desideria." 1675. In *Philipp Jakob Spener. Schriften,* edited by Ernst Beyreuther and Dietrich Blaufuß, vol. 1. Hildesheim and New York: Olms, 1979.

Stahl, Georg Ernst. *Über den mannigfaltigen Einfluß von Gemütsbewegungen auf den menschlichen Körper.* Translated and edited by Bernward Josef Gottlieb. Leipzig: Barth, 1961.

Stryk, Johann Samuel. *De Jure Liciti sed non Honesti.* Halle: Waisenhaus, 1702.

————. *De Jure Sabbathi.* 1702. 5th ed. Halle: Waisenhaus, 1715.

Stryk, Samuel. *Specimen Usus Moderni Pandectarum ad Libros V Priores.* Frankfurt and Wittenberg: Schrey & Meyer, 1690.

Der Theologischen Facultät auf der Universität zu Halle Verantwortung gegen Hn.D. Joh. Fried. Mayers/Professoris Theologi auf der Universität Greiffswald/unter dem Namen eines Schwedischen Theologi heraus- gegebenen so genannten kurtzen Bericht von Pietisten. Halle: Waisenhaus, 1707.

Walch, Johann Georg. *Historische und Theologische Einleitung in die Religions-Streitigkeiten der Evangelisch-Lutherischen Kirche.* 5 vols. Stuttgart-Bad Cannstatt: Frommann, 1972–85.

Wernsdorfer, Georg (*praeses*), and Johann Harpff (*respondens*). *De Indifferentismo Religionum in Genere.* Wittenberg: Gerdes, 1707.

Wernsdorfer, Georg (*praeses*), and Johann Ambrosius Hillig, (*respondens*). *De Verbo Dei Scripto, sive Scriptura Sacra.* Wittenberg: Gerdes, 1708.

Zedler, Johann Heinrich *Grosses vollständiges Universal-Lexikon.* 64 vols. Halle and Leipzig: Zedler, 1733–54.

III. SECONDARY WORKS

Ahnert, Thomas. "De Sympathia et Antipathia Rerum. Natural Law, Religion and the Rejection of Mechanistic Science in the Works of Christian Thomasius." In *Early Modern Natural Law Theories: Strategies and Contexts in the Early Enlightenment,* edited by Tim Hochstrasser and Peter Schröder, 257–77. Dordrecht: Kluwer, 2003.

———. "Enthusiasm and Enlightenment: Faith and Philosophy in the Thought of Christian Thomasius." Modern Intelluctual History 2, 2 (2005): 153–77.

———. "Pleasure, Pain and Punishment in the Early Enlightenment: German and Scottish Debates." *Jahrbuch für Recht und Ethik* 12 (2004): 173–87.

———. "The Relationship between Prince and Church in the Thought of Christian Thomasius." In *Natural Law and Civil Sovereignty. Moral Right and State Authority in Early Modern Political Thought.* Ed. Ian Hunter and David Saunders, 91–105. Basingstoke, UK: Palgrave, 2002.

———. "Roman Law in early Enlightenment Germany: The Case of Christian Thomasius' *De Aequitate Cerebrina Legis Secundae Codicis de Rescindenda Venditione* (1706)." *Ius Commune* 24 (1997): 152–70.

Albrecht, Michael. "Thomasius—kein Eklektiker?" In *Christian Thomasius (1655–1728),* edited by Werner Schneiders, 73–94. Hamburg: Meiner, 1989.

Allison, Henry E. *Lessing and the Enlightenment. His Philosophy of Religion and Its Relation to Eighteenth-Century Thought.* Ann Arbor: University of Michigan Press, 1966.

Aretin, Karl Otmar von. *Das Reich. Friedensgarantie und europäisches Gleichgewicht (1648–1806).* Stuttgart: Klett-Cotta, 1986.

Barker, W. H. "Pierre Bayle: Faith and Reason." In *The French Mind. Studies in Honour of Gustave Rudler,* edited by Will Moore, Rhoda Sutherland, and Enid Starkie, 109–25. Oxford: Clarendon Press, 1952.

Barnard, Frederick. "The Practical Philosophy of Christian Thomasius," *Journal of the History of Ideas* 32 (1971): 221–46.

Bauer, Axel. "Georg Ernst Stahl (1659–1734)." In *Klassiker der Medizin. Erster Band: Von Hippokrates bis Christoph Wilhelm Hufeland,* edited by Friedrich von Engelhardt and Fritz Hartmann, 190–201. Munich: Beck, 1991.

Bergh, Govaert C. J. J. van den. *The Life and Work of Gerard de Noodt (1657–1725). Dutch Legal Scholarship between Humanism and the Enlightenment.* Oxford: Clarendon Press, 1988.

Bianco, Bruno. "Freiheit gegen Fatalismus: Zu Joachim Langes Kritik an Wolff." In *Zentren der Aufklärung*, vol. 1, *Halle. Aufklärung und Pietismus*, edited by Norbert Hinske, 111–55. Heidelberg: Schneider, 1989.

Bienert, Walther. *Der Anbruch der christlichen deutschen Neuzeit dargestellt an Wissenschaft und Glauben des Christian Thomasius.* Halle: Akademischer Verlag, 1934.

Blaufuß, Dietrich, and Friedrich Niewöhner, eds. *Gottfried Arnold (1666–1714).* Wiesbaden: Harassowitz, 1995.

Bloch, Ernst. *Naturrecht und menschliche Würde.* Frankfurt am Main: Suhrkamp, 1985.

Bödeker, Hans-Erich. "Aufklärung als Kommunikationsprozess." *Aufklärung* 2, no. 2 (1988): 86–111.

———. "Die Religiösität der Gelehrten." In *Religionskritik und Religiösität in der deutschen Aufklärung*, edited by Karlfried Gründer and Karl Heinrich Rengstorf, 145–95. Heidelberg: Schneider, 1989.

Boor, Friedrich de. "Die ersten Vorschläge des Christian Thomasius 'wegen auffrichtung einer Neuen Academie zu Halle' aus dem Jahre 1690." In *Europa in der frühen Neuzeit. Festschrift für Günther Mühlpfordt*, edited by E. Donnert, vol. 4, 57–84. Weimar: Böhlau, 1997.

Brecht, Martin. "Philipp Jakob Spener, sein Programm und dessen Auswirkungen." In *Der Pietismus vom siebzehnten bis zum frühen achtzehnten Jahrhundert*, edited by Martin Brecht, 281–390. Göttingen: Vandenhoeck & Ruprecht, 1993.

———, ed. *Der Pietismus vom siebzehnten bis zum frühen achtzehnten Jahrhundert.* Göttingen: Vandenhoeck & Ruprecht, 1993.

Buchholz, Stefan. "Historia Contentionis inter Imperium et Sacerdotium. Kirchengeschichte in der Sicht von Christian Thomasius und Gottfried Arnold." In *Christian Thomasius (1655–1728). Neue Forschungen im Kontext der Frühaufklärung*, edited by F. Vollhardt, 165–78. Tübingen: Niemeyer, 1997.

Büchsel, Jürgen. *Gottfried Arnold. Sein Verständnis von Kirche und Wiedergeburt.* Witten: Luther-Verlag, 1970.

Büchsel, Jürgen, and Dietrich Blaufuß. "Gottfried Arnolds Briefwechsel. Eine erste Bestandsaufnahme- Arnold an Christian Thomasius 1694." In *Pietismus, Herrnhutertum, Erweckungsbewegung. Festschrift für Erich Beyreuther*, edited by D. Meyer, 71–106. Cologne: Rheinland-Verlag, 1982.

Buisson, Ludwig. *Potestas und Caritas. Die Päpstliche Gewalt im Spätmittelalter.* Cologne and Graz: Böhlau Verlag, 1958.

Champion, Justin. *The Pillars of Priestcraft Shaken.* Cambridge: Cambridge University Press, 1992.

Cottingham, John. "Cartesian Dualism: Theology, Metaphysics, and Science." In *The Cambridge Companion to Descartes*, edited by. John Cottingham, 236–57. Cambridge: Cambridge University Press, 1992.

Darwall, Stephen. *British Moralists and the Internal "Ought," 1640–1740*. Cambridge: Cambridge University Press, 1995.

Denzer, Horst. *Moralphilosophie und Naturrecht bei Samuel Pufendorf*. Munich: Beck, 1972.

Deppermann, Klaus. *Der hallesche Pietismus und der preußische Staat unter Friedrich III. (I.)*. Göttingen: Vandenhoeck & Ruprecht, 1961.

Dickmann, Fritz. *Der Westfälische Frieden*. 2nd ed. Münster: Aschendorff, 1965.

Doody, Margaret. "The Mystics' Enlightenment." The Saintsbury Lecture, University of Edinburgh, 1 November 2002.

Döring, Detlef. *Pufendorf-Studien. Beiträge zur Biographie Samuel von Pufendorfs und zu seiner Entwicklung als Historiker und theologischer Schriftsteller*. Berlin: Duncker & Humblot, 1992.

Dörries, Hermann. *Geist und Geschichte bei Gottfried* Arnold. Göttingen: Vandenhoeck & Ruprecht, 1963.

Dreitzel, Horst. "Christliche Aufklärung durch fürstlichen Absolutismus: Thomasius und die Destruktion des frühneuzeitlichen Konfessionsstaates." In *Christian Thomasius (1655–1728). Neue Forschungen im Kontext der Frühaufklärung*, edited by Friedrich Vollhardt, 17–50. Tübingen: Niemeyer, 1997.

Ebner, Wolfgang. "Die Kritik des römischen Rechts bei Christian Thomasius." Ph.D. thesis, Frankfurt am Main, 1971.

Engfer, Hans-Joachim. "Christian Thomasius. Erste Proklamation und erste Krise der Aufklärung in Deutschland." In *Christian Thomasius (1655–1728)*, edited by Werner Schneiders, 21–36. Hamburg: Meiner, 1989.

Evans, R. J. W. "German Universities after the Thirty Years' War." *History of the Universities* 1 (1981): 169–89.

Fleischmann, Max. "Christian Thomasius." In *Christian Thomasius. Leben und Lebenswerk*, edited by M. Fleischmann, 1–48. Halle: M. Niemeyer, 1931.

Forster, Georg. "Charlateneria eruditorum." In *Respublica litteraria. Die Institutionen der Gelehrsamkeit in der frühen Neuzeit*, edited by S. Neumeister and C. Wiedemann (Wiesbaden: Harrassowitz, 1987).

Fulbrook, Mary. *Piety and Politics. Religion and the Rise of Absolutism in England, Württemberg and Prussia*. Cambridge: Cambridge University Press, 1983.

Garber, Daniel. *Descartes' Metaphysical Physics*. Chicago: University of Chicago Press, 1992.

Gay, Peter. *The Enlightenment: An Interpretation*, vol. 1, *The Rise of Modern Paganism*. New York: Knopf, 1966.

Geyer-Kordesch, Johanna. "Die Medizin im Spannungsfeld zwischen Aufklärung und Pietismus: Das unbequeme Werk Georg Ernst Stahls und dessen kulturelle Bedeutung." In *Halle. Aufklärung und Pietismus*, edited by Norbert Hinske, 255–74. Heidelberg: Schneider, 1989.

———. *Pietismus, Medizin und Aufklärung in Preußen im 18. Jahrhundert. Das Leben und Werk Georg Ernst Stahls*. Tübingen: Niemeyer, 2000.

Gierl, Martin. *Pietismus und Aufklärung. Theologische Polemik und die Kommunikationsreform der Wissenschaft am Ende des 17. Jahrhunderts*. Göttingen: Vandenhoeck & Ruprecht, 1997.

Goldie, Mark. "The Civil Religion of James Harrington." In *The Languages of Political Theory in Early Modern* Europe, edited by A. Pagden, 197–224. Cambridge: Cambridge University Press, 1987.

Goldie, Mark. "Priestcraft and the Birth of Whiggism." In *Political Discourse in Early Modern Britain*, edited by Nicholas Phillipson and Quentin Skinner, 209–31. Cambridge: Cambridge University Press, 1993.

———. "The Theory of Religious Intolerance in Restoration England." In *From Persecution to Toleration*, edited by Ole Grell, Jonathan Israel, and Nicholas Tyacke, 331–68. Oxford: Clarendon Press, 1991.

Gordley, James. *The Philosophical Origins of Modern Contract Doctrine*. Oxford: Clarendon Press, 1991.

Grunert, Frank. "Antiklerikalismus und christlicher Anspruch im Werk von Christian Thomasius." In *Der Kampf der Aufklärung. Kirchenkritik und Religionskritik zur Aufklärungszeit*, edited by Jean Mondot, 39–56. Berlin: Berliner Wissenschafts-Verlag, 2004.

———. *Normbegründung und politische Legitimität. Zur Rechts- und Staatsphilosophie der deutschen Aufklärung*. Tübingen: Niemeyer Verlag, 2000.

———. "Das Recht der Natur als Recht des Gefühls. Zur Naturrechtslehre von Johann Jacob Schmauss." *Jahrbuch für Recht und Ethik* 12 (2004): 137–53.

———. "Zur aufgeklärten Kritik am theokratischen Absolutismus." In *Christian Thomasius (1655–1728)*, edited by Friedrich Vollhardt, 51–77. Tübingen: Niemeyer Verlag, 1997.

Haakonssen, Knud. *Natural Law and Moral Philosophy*. Cambridge: Cambridge University Press, 1996.

———, ed. *Enlightenment and Religion: Rational Dissent in Eighteenth-Century Britain*. Cambridge: Cambridge University Press, 1996.

Habermas, Jürgen. *The Structural Transformation of the Public Sphere*. Cambridge: Polity Press, 1992.

Hall, Alfred Rupert. *Henry More: Magic, Religion and Experiment*. Oxford: Blackwell, 1990.

Hammerstein, Notker. *Ius und Historie. Ein Beitrag zur Geschichte des historischen Denkens an deutschen Universitäten im späten 17. und im 18. Jahrhundert*. Göttingen: Vandenhoeck und Ruprecht, 1972.

Hankins, Thomas. *Science and the Enlightenment*. Cambridge: Cambridge University Press, 1988.

Heckel, Martin. *Staat und Kirche nach den Lehren der evangelischen Juristen in der ersten Hälfte des 17. Jahrhunderts*. Munich: Claudius, 1968.

Helm, Jürgen. "Hallesche Medizin zwischen Pietismus und Frühaufklärung." In *Universitäten und Aufklärung*, edited by Notker Hammerstein, 63–96. Göttingen: Wallstein, 1995.

Henry, John. "Henry More versus Robert Boyle: The Spirit of Nature and the Nature of Providence." In *Henry More (1614–87). Tercentenary Studies*, edited by Sarah Hutton, 55–76. Dordrecht: Kluwer, 1990.

Hinrichs, Carl. *Preußentum und Pietismus: Der Pietismus in Brandenburg-Preußen als religiös-soziale Reformbewegung*. Göttingen: Vandenhoeck & Ruprecht, 1971.

Hintze, Otto. "Die Epochen des evangelischen Kirchenregiments in Preußen." In *Regierung und Verwaltung. Gesammelte Abhandlungen zur Staats-, Rechts- und Sozialgeschichte Preußens*, vol. 3, 56–96. Göttingen: Vandenhoeck & Ruprecht, 1967.

Hochstrasser, Tim. *Natural Law Theories in the Early Enlightenment.* Cambridge: Cambridge University Press, 2000.

Hoffmann, Barbara. *Radikalpietismus um 1700.* Frankfurt am Main: Campus-Verlag, 1996.

Hunter, Ian. *Rival Enlightenments: Civil and Metaphysical Philosophy in Early Modern Germany.* Cambridge: Cambridge University Press, 2001.

Israel, Jonathan. *Radical Enlightenment: Philosophy and the Making of Modernity (1650–1750).* Oxford: Oxford University Press, 2001.

James, Susan. *Passion and Action. The Emotions in Seventeenth-Century Philosophy.* Oxford: Clarendon Press, 1997.

Jaumann, Herbert. "Frühe Aufklärung als historische Kritik. Pierre Bayle und Christian Thomasius." In *Frühaufklärung*, edited by Sebastian Neumeister, 149–70. Munich: Fink, 1994.

Kelley, Donald. *Foundations of Modern Historical Scholarship.* New York and London: Columbia University Press, 1970.

Keohane, Nannerl. *Philosophy and the State in France.* Princeton, NJ: Princeton University Press, 1980.

Kervorkian, T. "Piety Confronts Politics: Spener in Dresden, 1686–91." *German History* 16, no. 2 (1998): 145–64.

Kruse, Martin. *Speners Kritik am landesherrlichen Kirchenregiment und ihre Vorgeschichte.* Witten: Luther-Verlag, 1971.

Kusukawa, Sachiko. *The Transformation of Natural Philosophy: The Case of Philip Melanchthon.* Cambridge: Cambridge University Press, 1995.

Langholm, Odd. *Price and Value in the Aristotelian Tradition. A Study in Scholastic Economic Sources.* Bergen and Oslo: Universitetsforlaget, 1979.

Leube, Heinrich. *Orthodoxie und Pietismus. Gesammelte Schriften.* Bielefeld: Luther-Verlag, 1975.

Lieberwirth, Rolf. "Christian Thomasius (1655–1728)." In *Aufklärung und Erneuerung*, edited by G. Jerouschek and A. Sames, 29–45. Hanau: Dausien, 1994.

———. "Die französischen Kultureinflüsse auf den deutschen Frühaufklärer Christian Thomasius." In *Wissenschaftliche Zeitschrift der Universität Halle (Gesellschafts- und Sprachwissenschaftliche Reihe)* 33 (1984): 63–73.

Link, Christoph. *Herrschaftsordnung und bürgerliche Freiheit.* Vienna: Böhlau, 1979.

Luden, Heinrich. *Christian Thomasius nach seinen Schicksalen und Schriften.* Berlin: Unger, 1805.

Luig, Klaus. "Conring, das deutsche Recht und die Rechtsgeschichte." In *Hermann Conring (1606–81). Beiträge zu Leben und Werk*, edited by Michael Stolleis, 355–95. Berlin: Duncker & Humblot, 1983.

Luig, Klaus. "Der Gerechte Preis in der Rechtstheorie und Rechtspraxis von Christian Thomasius (1655–1728)." In *Diritto e potere nella storia europea: atti in onore di Bruno Paradisi*, 775–803. Florence, 1982.

Markie, Peter. "The Cogito and Its Importance." In *The Cambridge Companion to Descartes*, edited by John Cottingham, 140–73. Cambridge: Cambridge University Press, 1992.

Melton, James van Horn. "Pietism, Politics, and the Public Sphere in Germany." In *Religion and Politics in Enlightenment Europe*, edited by James E. Bradley and Dale K. Van Kley, 294–333. Notre Dame, IN: University of Notre Dame Press, 2001.

———. *The Rise of the Public in Enlightenment Europe*. Cambridge: Cambridge University Press, 2001.

Minton, Gretchen E. "Cave, William (1637–1713)." In *Oxford Dictionary of National Biography*. Ed. H. C. G. Matthew Brown and Brian Harrison. Oxford: Oxford University Press, 2004.

Müller, Ingo Wilhelm. *Iatromechanische Theorie und ärztliche Praxis im Vergleich zur galenistischen Medizin (Friedrich Hoffmann—Pieter van Forest, Jan van Heurne)*. Stuttgart: Steiner, 1991.

Nischan, Bodo. *Prince, People and Confession*. Philadelphia: University of Pennsylvania Press, 1994.

Obst, Helmut. *Der Berliner Beichtstuhlstreit. Die Kritik des Pietismus an der Beichtpraxis der Lutherischen Orthodoxie*. Witten: Luther-Verlag, 1972.

Osler, Douglas. "Budeus and Roman Law." *Ius Commune* 13 (1985): 195–213.

Osler, Margaret. "The Canonical Imperative: Rethinking the Scientific Revolution." In *Rethinking the Scientific Revolution*, edited by Margaret Osler, 3–22. Cambridge: Cambridge University Press, 2000.

Osterhorn, Ernst-Dietrich. "Die Naturrechtslehre Valentin Albertis." Ph.D. thesis, Freiburg im Breisgau, 1962.

Palladini, Fiammetta. *Discussioni seicentesche su Samuel Pufendorf. Scritti Latini: 1663–1700*. Bologna: Il Muline, 1978.

———. *Samuel Pufendorf, Discepolo di Hobbes*. Bologna: Il Mulino, 1990.

Pocock, J. G. A. "Enthusiasm: The Antiself of Enlightenment." In *Enthusiasm and Enlightenment in Europe, 1650–1850*, edited by A. J. La Vopa and L. Klein, 7–28. San Marino, CA: Huntington Library, 1998.

Pott, Martin. "Christian Thomasius und Gottfried Arnold." In *Gottfried Arnold (1666–1714)*, edited by D. Blaufuß and F. Niewöhner, 247–65. Wiesbaden: Harrassowitz, 1995.

Press, Volker. *Kriege und Krisen*. Munich: C. H. Beck, 1991.

Ranke, Leopold von. *Preussische Geschichte*. Wiesbaden: Vollmer, 1957.

Riley, Patrick. *Leibniz' Universal Jurisprudence*. London: Harvard University Press, 1996.

Rotermund, Heinrich. *Orthodoxie und Pietismus*. Berlin: Evangelische Verlagsanstalt, 1959.

Rothschuh, Karl E. "Studien zu Friedrich Hoffmann (1660–1742). Erster Teil: Hoffmann und die Medizingeschichte. Das Hoffmannsche System und das Aetherprinzip." *Sudhoffs Archiv* 60 (1976): 163–93.

Sauder, Gerhard. *Empfindsamkeit. Band 1: Voraussetzungen und* Elemente. Stuttgart: J. B. Metzler, 1984.

Schaffer, Simon, and Steven Shapin. *Leviathan and the Air-Pump. Hobbes, Boyle, and the Experimental* Life. Princeton, NJ: Princeton University Press, 1985.

Schlaich, Klaus. "Der rationale Territorialismus. Die Kirche unter dem staatsrechtlichen Absolutismus um die Wende vom 17. zum 18. Jahrhundert." *Zeitschrift der Savigny-Stiftung für Rechtsgeschichte, Kanonistische Abteilung* 85 (1968): 269–340.

Schmidt, Martin. *Der Pietismus als theologische Erscheinung.* Göttingen: Vandenhoeck & Ruprecht, 1984.

Schmidt-Biggemann, Wilhelm."Pietismus, Platonismus und Aufklärung: Christian Thomasius' *Versuch vom Wesen des Geistes.*" In *Aufklärung als praktische Philosophie. Werner Schneiders zum 65. Geburtstag,* edited by Frank Grunert and Friedrich Vollhardt, 83–98. Tübingen: Niemeyer, 1998.

———. *Theodizee und Tatsachen.* Frankfurt am Main: Suhrkamp, 1988.

Schneewind, Jerome B. *The Invention of Autonomy: A History of Modern Moral Philosophy.* Cambridge: Cambridge University Press, 1998.

Schneider, Hans. "Der radikale Pietismus im 17. Jahrhundert." In *Der Pietismus vom siebzehnten bis zum frühen achtzehnten Jahrhundert,* edited by Martin Brecht, 391–439. Göttingen: Vandenhoeck & Ruprecht, 1993.

Schneider, Hans-Peter. *Justitia Universalis. Studien zur Geschichte des Naturrechts bei Leibniz.* Frankfurt am Main: Klostermann, 1967.

Schneiders, Werner. *Naturrecht und Liebesethik. Zur Geschichte der praktischen Philosophie im Hinblick auf Christian Thomasius.* Hildesheim and New York: Olms, 1971.

Schott, Caspar. "Aequitas cerebrina." In *Hans Thieme zum 70. Geburtstag zugeeignet von seinen Schülern,* edited by Bernhard Diestelkamp, 132–60. Cologne and Vienna: Böhlau, 1977.

Schrader, Wilhelm. *Geschichte der Friedrichs-Universität.* 2 vols. Berlin: Dümmler, 1894.

Schröder, Peter. *Christian Thomasius zur Einführung.* Hamburg: Junius, 1999.

———. *Naturrecht und absolutistisches Staatsrecht. Eine vergleichende Studie zu Thomas Hobbes und Christian Thomasius.* Berlin: Duncker & Humblot, 2001.

———. "Thomas Hobbes, Christian Thomasius and the Seventeenth-Century Debate on the Church and State." *History of European Ideas* 23 (1997): 59–79.

Schubart-Fikentscher, Gertrud. "Christian Thomasius. Seine Bedeutung als Hochschullehrer am Beginn der deutschen Aufklärung." *Sitzungsberichte der Sächsischen Akademie der Wissenschaften zu Leipzig, Philologisch-historische Klasse* 119, no. 4 (1977).

Seidel, Siegfried, ed., *Briefe des Jahre (1798–1805),* vol. 2 of *Der Briefwechsel zwischen Schiller und Goethe.* Munich: Beck, 1985.

Skinner, Q. R. D. *The Foundations of Modern Political Thought.* 2 vols. Cambridge: Cambridge University Press, 1978.

Sorkin, David. *The Berlin Haskalah and German Religious Thought.* London: Vallentine Mitchell, 2000.

Sparn, Walter. *Wiederkehr der Metaphysik.* Stuttgart: Calwer Verlag, 1976.

Stintzing, Roderich von. *Geschichte der Deutschen Rechtswissenschaft,* Abt. III.1. Munich: Oldenbourg, 1898.

Stoeffler, F. Ernest. *The Rise of Evangelical Pietism.* Leiden: Brill, 1965.

Stolleis, Michael. *Geschichte des öffentlichen Rechts in Deutschland,* vol. 1. Munich: Beck, 1988.

———. "Veit Ludwig von Seckendorff." In *Staatsdenker in der frühen Neuzeit,* edited by Michael Stolleis, 14–1 (Munich: Beck, 1995),

Sträter, Udo. "Aufklärung und Pietismus—Das Beispiel Halle." In *Universitäten und Aufklärung,* edited by Notker Hammerstein, 49–61. Göttingen: Wallstein, 1995.

———. *Sonthom, Bayly, Dyke und Hall. Studien zur Rezeption der englischen Erbauungsliteratur in Deutschland im siebzehnten Jahrhundert.* Tübingen: Mohr, 1987.

Sturm, Fritz. *Das römische Recht in der Sicht von Gottfried Wilhelm Leibniz.* Tübingen: Mohr, 1968.

Thadden, Rudolf von. *Die brandenburgisch-preußischen Hofprediger im 17. und 18. Jahrhundert.* Berlin: de Gruyter, 1959.

Tuck, Richard. *Philosophy and Government (1572–1651).* Cambridge: Cambridge University Press, 1993.

Vollhardt, Friedrich. *Selbstliebe und Geselligkeit. Untersuchungen zum Verhältnis von naturrechtlichem Denken und moraldidaktischer Literatur im 17. und 18. Jahrhundert.* Tübingen: Niemeyer, 2001.

———, ed., *Christian Thomasius (1655–1728). Neue Forschungen im Kontext der Frühaufklärung.* Tübingen: Niemeyer Verlag, 1997.

Walch, Johann Georg. *Historische und Theologische Einleitung in die Religions-Streitigkeiten der Evangelisch-Lutherischen Kirche,* vol. 1. Stuttgart-Bad Cannstatt: Frommann, 1972.

Wallmann, Johannes. "Labadismus und Pietismus. Die Einflüsse des niederländischen Pietismus auf die Entstehung des Pietismus in Deutschland." In *Pietismus und Reveil,* edited by J. van den Berg and J. P. van Dooren, 141–68. Leiden: Brill, 1978.

———. *Philipp Jakob Spener und die Anfänge des Pietismus.* 2nd ed. Tübingen: Mohr, 1986.

Ward, William R. *The Protestant Evangelical Awakening.* Cambridge: Cambridge University Press, 1992.

Watson, Alan. "The Hidden Origins of Enorm Lesion." *Journal of Legal History* 2 (1981): 186–93.

Whaley, Joachim. *Religious Toleration and Social Change in Hamburg (1529–1819).* Cambridge: Cambridge University Press, 1982.

———. "A Tolerant Society? Religious Toleration and the Holy Roman Empire, 1648–1806." In *Toleration in Enlightenment Europe,* edited by O. P. Grell and R. Porter, 175–95. Cambridge: Cambridge University Press, 2000.

Whitman, James O. *The Legacy of Roman Law in the German Romantic Era.* Princeton, NJ: Princeton University Press, 1990.

Wieacker, Franz. *Privatrechtsgeschichte der Neuzeit.* Göttingen: Vandenhoeck & Ruprecht, 1996.

Wiesenfeldt, Gerhard. *Leerer Raum in Minervas Haus. Experimentelle Naturlehre and der Universität Leiden, 1675–1715.* Berlin: Verlag für Geschichte der Naturwissenschaften und der Technik, 2002.

Wilson, Catherine. "De Ipsa Natura. Sources of Leibniz' Doctrines of Force, Activity and Natural Law." *Studia Leibnitiana* 19, no. 2 (1987): 148–72.

Wolf, Erik. *Grosse Rechtsdenker der deutschen Geistesgeschichte.* Tübingen: Mohr, 1963.

Wolter, Udo. "Die Fortgeltung des kanonischen Rechts und die Haltung der protestantischen Juristen zum kanonischen Recht in Deutschland bis in die Mitte des 18. Jahrhunderts." In *Canon Law in Protestant Lands,* edited by R. Helmholz, 13–48. Berlin: Duncker & Humblot, 1992.

Wundt, Max. *Die deutsche Schulmetaphysik des 17. Jahrhunderts.* Tübingen: Mohr, 1939.

Young, Brian. *Religion and Enlightenment in Eighteenth-Century England. Theological Debate in England, from Locke to Burke.* Oxford: Clarendon Press, 1998.

Zimmermann, Reinhard. *The Law of Obligations: Roman Foundations of the Civilian Tradition.* Cape Town: Juta, 1990.

Zurbuchen, Simone. "Gewissensfreiheit und Toleranz: Zur Pufendorf-Rezeption bei Christian Thomasius." In *Samuel Pufendorf und die europäische Frühaufklärung,* edited by Fiammetta Palladini, 169–80. Berlin: Akademie-Verlag, 1996.

———. *Naturrecht und natürliche Religion: Zur Geschichte des Toleranzproblems von Samuel Pufendorf bis Jean-Jacques Rousseau.* Würzburg: Königshausen & Neumann, 1991.

INDEX

Abbadie, Jacques, 97
adiaphora, 48–51, 142n23
Alberti, Michael, 118
Alberti, Valentin, 10, 11, 13, 14, 29,
   84–85, 88–91, 102
Alciatus, Andreas, 71
Altona, 125
amor rationalis. See reasonable love
Anabaptism, 26, 46
Andreae, Johann Valentin, 21
anima, 31, 38, 39, 116. *See also* soul
antipathy (*antipathia*), 107, 116, 118,
   121
Anton, Paul, 12, 13, 14, 24, 37
Aquinas, Thomas, 90
Arianism, Arians, 60, 61, 65, 67, 79
Aristotelian philosophy, 71, 108–9
Arndt, Johann, 21
Arnold, Gottfried, 31, 40, 63–66, 67
Augsburg, Peace of, 18, 44
Augustine, bishop of Hippo, 30
Augustinianism, 30

Basel, 20, 21
Bayle, Pierre, 123–24
Bayly, Lewis, 20, 22
Becmann, Johann Christoph, 11
Berlin, 12, 15, 16, 19, 25, 48; *Berliner
   Religionsgespräche* ("Berlin religious
   debates") 19
Best, Wilhelm, 69

Betkius, Joachim, 21, 63
Boehmer, Justus Henning, 71
Boerhaave, Hermann, 107
Böhme, Jakob, 21, 115
Borelli, Giovanni, 107
Bourignon, Antoinette, 40
Boyle, Robert, 108, 112, 115, 118
Brandenburg, 3, 10, 12, 19, 25, 48, 53,
   54; Electors of Brandenburg, 3, 12,
   15, 16, 19, 43, 47–48, 53, 54, 121
Brant, Sebastian, 41
Breithaupt, Justus Joachim, 37, 67
Brenneysen, Enno, 37
Bücher, Christian Friedrich, 26
Buddeus, Johann Franz, 100
Budé, Guillaume, 70

Caesaro-Papism, 46
Calvinism, Calvinists, 3, 9, 10, 11, 12,
   15, 16, 18, 19, 20, 21, 27, 43, 44, 47,
   48, 49, 53, 56, 60, 121
Canisius, Henricus, 75
Carneades, 95
Carpzov, Benedict, 49
Carpzov, Johann Benedict, 10, 14, 16,
   35, 46, 60, 67
Cartesianism, 107–11, 112–14, 116–17,
   119. *See also* Descartes
Catholicism, 3, 10, 18, 19, 20, 27, 42,
   44, 49, 62, 101
Cave, William, 63–66

charity, 20, 28, 29, 31, 40, 43, 45, 49, 52, 61, 69, 102, 124
Charles William of Mecklenburg-Güstrow, 12
Collegia, 12–13, 14, 22–23, 24
Comenius, Jan Amos, 115
Conring, Hermann, 69, 70, 71, 73
Constantine the Great (Roman emperor), 59, 60, 61, 62, 63, 64, 65, 66, 70, 79
Copenhagen, 11
Corpus Iuris Civilis, 4, 68, 69–80. *See also* law

Dannhauer, Johann Conrad, 22
Descartes, 87, 107–11, 113, 114
Diocletian, 65, 74, 76, 77, 78
Dippel, Conrad, 40
doctrine, 3, 15, 17, 23, 25, 32, 33, 34, 37, 39, 41, 42, 43, 45, 46, 47, 48, 50, 55, 60, 61, 62, 67, 69, 118, 121, 123, 124
Domitian, 65
Dreiständelehre, 45–48
Dresden, electoral court of, 11, 12, 14, 15, 22
Duisburg, University of, 12
Dyke, David, 21

ecclesiastical discipline, 25, 45
ecclesia invisibilis, 34
ecclesia visibilis, 25, 34–35
enthusiasm, 2, 3, 17, 25, 26, 27–28, 29–35, 36–37, 38, 39, 40, 46, 67, 103, 118, 125
Epicureanism, 95
Epicurus, 95
Erasmus, Desiderius, 71
Erfurt, 12
excommunication, 23, 45. *See also* ecclesiastical discipline

faith. *See* religious belief
fall from grace. *See* original sin
fanaticism. *See* enthusiasm
Fecht, Joachim, 16, 34, 35
Feller, Joachim, 24–25
fides cerebrina, 68, 101

Fludd, Robert, 115
Francke, August Hermann, 12–15, 16–17, 25, 29, 36–37, 67
Frankfurt am Main, 22, 25
Frankfurt an der Oder, University of, 9, 10, 12
Frederick III (I), elector of Brandenburg and king of Prussia, 12, 15
Frederick William, elector of Brandenburg ("the Great Elector"), 19
Frederick William I, elector of Brandenburg and king of Prussia, 30
Fuchs, Paul von, 16, 144n52

Gay, Peter, 122, 128n9
Gedike, Friedrich, 1
Geneva, 21
Gierl, Martin, 5, 135n9
Glaucha, 15, 25
Gothofredus, Jacobus, 79
grace, 13, 31, 37, 38, 39, 64, 104
Greifswald, 32, 137n45
Grotius, Hugo, 10, 102, 126
Grunert, Frank, 2
Gustav II Adolf, king of Sweden, 21

Hall, Joseph, 20
Halle, 12, 15, 16, 26, 37, 66–67, 110; University of, 9, 12, 15, 16, 17, 24, 30, 35, 36–37, 54, 66–67, 69, 70, 71, 78, 95, 107, 110, 118
Hamburg, 26
Hanau, 21
Herborn, 21
heresy, 2, 3, 14, 15, 27, 28, 36, 37, 40, 43, 45, 60, 61, 63, 64, 65, 67, 121. *See also* enthusiasm; orthodoxy; sects, sectarianism
heterodoxy. *See* heresy
Heyland, Anna Christina, 10
Hobbes, Thomas, 30, 91, 95, 96, 99
Hoburg, Christian, 21, 31, 63
Hoffmann, Friedrich, 107, 112, 118
Holy Roman Empire, 4, 17, 27, 44, 68, 71–73

Hume, David, 30
Hunter, Ian, 2

indifferent matters in religion.
  See adiaphora
indifferentism: moral, 90; religious, 35,
  37, 142n23
intellect, 3, 4, 27, 29, 30, 32–33, 34, 36,
  37, 38, 41, 61, 83, 87–88, 89, 92, 97,
  98–99, 101, 103, 104, 105, 107, 112,
  117, 118, 119, 121, 124, 126
ius emigrandi, 18
ius reformandi, 18, 19, 44

Jablonski, Daniel, 16
Jan, Christian Friedrich, 75
Johann Sigismund, elector of
  Brandenburg, 19, 48
John George III (Saxon elector), 11
Julian, "the Apostate," Roman emperor,
  66
justification, 34, 36–37, 41
Jansenism, 20, 30, 96
Justinian (Roman emperor), 4, 68, 69,
  70, 71, 76, 78

Kant, Immanuel, 1
Kulpis, Johann, 70, 72

Labadists, 23
laesio enormis, 73–78
Lange, Joachim, 66–67
Lange, Johann Christian, 13
law: divine positive, 50, 53, 85, 86,
  129n10; eternal, 85, 88–90; natural, 4,
  10, 24, 53, 69, 74, 75, 83–106, 108,
  121, 126; Roman, 4, 69–80, 121
Leibniz, Gottfried Wilhelm, 9, 12, 30,
  69, 91–93, 94, 95, 96, 113, 114,
  123–25
Leiden, 107, 108
Leipzig, 3, 9, 10, 11, 12, 13, 14, 15, 16,
  24, 26, 28, 29, 34, 35, 37, 46, 84, 110,
  118
Lessing, Gotthold Ephraim, 125
Locke, John, 1, 38
Löscher, Valentin, 25–26, 32, 39

Lothair III (Holy Roman Emperor), 71
Low Countries. *See* United Provinces
love, 26, 30–31, 32, 33, 34, 35, 39, 41,
  45, 50, 61, 96, 97, 98, 99, 100, 101,
  103, 116, 117, 118. *See also* charity;
  passion; reasonable love; will
Lübeck, 12
Ludovici, Jacob Friedrich, 37
Luig, Klaus, 74
Lüneburg, 13, 21, 22
Luther, Martin, 22, 27, 46, 59
Lutheranism, Lutherans, 3, 4, 5, 10, 11,
  12, 15, 16, 17, 18, 19, 20, 21, 22, 23,
  25, 26, 27, 28, 29, 32, 33–35, 36–37,
  41, 42, 43, 44, 45–48, 49, 53, 55, 59,
  60, 62, 65, 66, 67, 70, 79, 84, 88–89,
  101, 107, 110, 119, 121, 122
Lützen, battle of (1632), 21

magistrate, 15, 45, 46, 47, 49, 52, 53,
  55, 62. *See also* prince
maiestas, 11–12, 54, 130n20
Masius, Hector Gottfried, 11–12, 14
Maurice of Sachsen-Naumburg Zeitz, 24
Maurice-William of Sachsen-Zeitz, 12,
  15, 60
Maxentius (Roman emperor), 65
Maximilian I (Holy Roman Emperor),
  72
Mayer, Johann Friedrich, 36–37
metaphysics, 27, 107, 114
Moliere, 11
monarchomachs, 11
More, Henry, 113, 114, 115
Mörl, Gustav, 16, 33–34
mysticism, mystics, 1, 4, 27, 30, 31, 40,
  62, 107, 115, 126

Nantes, Edict of, revocation of, 11, 97
natural law. *See* law
natural philosophy, 4, 107–19, 121, 122
natural reason. *See* reason
natural religion, 52, 53, 124
Nero, 65
Nestorians, 67
Neubauer, Georg, 16
Newton, Isaac, 108, 126

Nördlingen, battle of (1634), 21
Normaljahr, 18

Olearius, Johann, 14
Oppenheim, 21
original sin, 17, 22–23, 24, 29, 31, 34,
    84, 85, 88, 89, 109, 117
orthodoxy, 3, 4, 5, 11, 12, 14, 16, 17,
    23, 25, 26, 28, 29, 32, 33, 34, 35, 36,
    37, 38, 40, 41, 42, 43, 44–45, 46, 47,
    49, 55, 59, 60, 61, 62, 67, 83, 118,
    121. *See also* doctrine
Osler, Douglas, 70

Paedagogium (orphanage in Glaucha
    near Halle), 16, 17, 37
papalism, 3–4, 42, 43, 44, 46, 48, 50,
    51, 54, 55, 59–61, 62, 67, 70, 73–80,
    101, 121
Papo-Caesarism. *See* papalism
Paracelsus, 108
Pascal, Blaise, 31
passion(s), 3, 4, 30, 31, 39, 41, 52, 53,
    63, 83, 84, 87, 96, 99, 100, 103, 104,
    105, 117, 118, 119, 121, 126
pedantry, 1, 5, 11, 41, 121
Perkins, William, 20
Philadelphic societies, 33
Photinians, 67
Pietism, Pietists, 3, 5, 12, 14–15, 16, 17,
    20, 21, 23–26, 29, 35–37, 46, 66–67,
    126
Poiret, Pierre, 31, 38, 116
Prague, peace of (1635), 21
Prasch, Johann Ludwig, 102–3
prince, 3, 4, 11, 18, 19, 43–56, 59, 60,
    62, 65, 66, 79
public sphere, 5
Pufendorf, Samuel von, 9, 10, 11,
    12, 15, 24, 30, 52–53, 61–62, 67,
    83, 84, 85, 87, 90, 91–93, 94, 95,
    99, 105, 111, 122, 123, 124, 125,
    126
Puritanism, 20

Quakers, 33
Quietism, 20

rational love. *See* reasonable love
reason, 1, 2, 27, 28, 29, 30, 31, 38, 39,
    40, 52, 64, 78, 85, 86, 88, 89, 90, 94,
    95, 96, 98, 101, 102, 103, 104, 110,
    111, 114, 115, 117, 122–26. *See also*
    intellect; reasonable love
reasonable love, 31, 39, 96–105, 116,
    117, 118
regeneration, 25–26, 29, 31–34, 36, 38,
    39, 60, 103, 104, 105
Reichskammergericht, 72
Reimarus, Hermann Samuel, 125
Reinking, Theodor, 46, 47
religious belief, 1–5, 10, 16, 20, 22, 23,
    24, 25, 26, 27, 28, 29, 30, 31, 32,
    33–40, 41, 42, 43, 44, 45, 46, 47, 49,
    50, 51, 52, 54, 55, 56, 59, 60, 61, 62,
    63, 64, 66, 67, 68, 69, 70, 79–80, 83,
    88, 96, 99, 101, 102, 103, 104, 105,
    107, 111, 118, 119, 121–26. *See also*
    doctrine; *fides cerebrina*; orthodoxy;
    reasonable love
Religious Enlightenment, 2, 38, 122
Reuchlin, Johannes, 71
revelation, 2, 28, 29, 32, 33, 38, 40, 43,
    50, 53, 67, 84–85, 86, 88, 91, 95, 102,
    115, 122, 123, 124, 125, 129n10
Rhetius, Friedrich, 9, 12
ritual, religious, 25, 44, 45, 46, 48–56,
    61, 66, 124. *See also adiaphora*
Roman Law. *See Corpus Iuris Civilis*; law
Rostock, 16, 35
Roth, Albrecht Christian, 16, 26, 34, 39,
    118
Rumpaeus, Justus Wesselus, 32, 39

scandal (*scandalum*), 49
Schade, Johann Caspar, 15, 25
Schelwig, Samuel, 67
Schiller, Friedrich, 1
Schilter, Johann, 70, 71–72, 73
Schmauss, Johann Jacob, 83
Schmidt, Johann, 22
Schmidt, Johann Lorenz, 125
Schmidt, Martin, 23
Schneewind, Jerome, 92
Schneiders, Werner, 1

scholasticism, scholastics, 1, 5, 11, 27, 28, 32, 40, 41, 43, 71, 72, 73, 75, 83, 88, 93, 95, 99, 101, 110, 112, 114, 117, 119, 121
scripture, 2, 12, 13, 14, 17, 28, 29, 32, 33, 34, 36, 37, 39, 43, 45, 46, 50, 55, 61, 63, 78, 85, 88, 89, 123, 124, 125. *See also* revelation
Scudéry, Madeleine de, 96
Seckendorff, Veit Ludwig von, 24, 95
sects, sectarianism, 2, 3, 10, 17, 18, 19, 25, 27, 29, 33, 40, 44, 45, 46, 48, 55, 61, 62, 63, 67. *See also* heresy
Socrates, 124
Sonthom, Emmanuel, 21, 22
Sorkin, David, 2, 38, 122
soul, 31, 38, 39, 95–95, 103, 107, 111, 114, 116, 118, 124
Spener, Phillip Jakob, 13, 15, 21–25, 29, 36, 41, 54, 63
Spinoza, Spinozism, 32
spirit (*spiritus*), 31, 32, 38, 39. *See also* *anima*; soul
spiritual being in nature, 110–18
Stahl, Georg Ernst, 118–19
Stoltzen, Johann, 16
Strasbourg, 22
Stryk, Johann Samuel, 37, 54–55, 71
Stryk, Samuel, 9, 17, 54, 69, 70, 71
sympathy, 107, 116, 118, 121

Theodosius the Great (Roman emperor), 59, 60
Thieme, Clemens, 14

Thirty Years' War, 1, 17, 19, 21, 63, 73
Thomasius, Christian: appointed professor in Halle, 15; controversy with Hector Gottfried Masius, 11–12; death, 17; dispute with August Hermann Francke, 16–17; dispute with Unversity of Leipzig, 10–15; leaves Saxony, 15; university education of, 9–10
Thomasius, Jacob, 9
Thomasius, Maria, 9
Tribonian, 78

United Provinces, 10, 20, 97, 108, 125

volition. *See* will
voluntarism, 28, 30, 88, 91, 93, 121

Wallmann, Johannes, 23
Weber, Jeremias, 9
Weigel, Valentin, 115
Wernsdorfer, Georg, 32, 35
Westphalia, peace treaties of, 18, 19, 43, 44
will: divine, 28, 40, 85, 86, 88–93, 97; human, 30, 32–33, 36, 37, 38, 39, 40–41, 61, 83, 87–88, 93, 96, 97, 98, 99, 100, 101, 103, 104, 105, 107, 110, 111, 116, 117, 119, 121, 122, 125, 126. *See also* passion; reasonable love
wisdom (*sapientia*), 5, 38, 39, 40, 104, 107, 117–18, 121, 125
Wittenberg, 32, 35, 75
Wolff, Christian, 30, 125